Collins

AQA GCSE 9-1
Spanish
Revision Guide

Helen Farrar and Amy Bates

About this Revision & Practice book

Revise

These pages provide a recap of everything you need to know for each topic.

HT Higher Tier content is highlighted with this icon.

You should read through all the information before taking the Quick Test at the end. This will test whether you can recall the key facts.

> **Quick Test**
>
> 1. Translate into Spanish: My parents are separated.
> 2. Translate into English: **Quiero a mi marido.**
> 3. What is the Spanish for 'marriage'?
> 4. Choose the correct forms:
>   **Mi madre es / está simpática. Mis padres son / están casados.**

Practise

These topic-based questions appear shortly after the revision pages for each topic and will test whether you have understood the topic. If you get any of the questions wrong, make sure you read the correct answer carefully.

Review

These topic-based questions appear later in the book, allowing you to revisit the topic and test how well you have remembered the information. If you get any of the questions wrong, make sure you read the correct answer carefully.

Mix it Up

These pages feature a mix of questions from the different topics. They will make sure you can recall the relevant information to answer a question without being told which topic it relates to.

Workbook & Audio

This section features even more topic-based questions as well as practice exam papers, providing two further practice opportunities for each topic to guarantee the best results.

Visit our website at **www.collins.co.uk/collinsGCSErevision** to download listening tracks to accompany the listening exam paper. You will also find lots more information about the advantages of spaced practice and how to plan for it.

ebook

To access the ebook revision guide visit
collins.co.uk/ebooks
and follow the step-by-step instructions.

QR Codes

Found throughout the book, the QR codes can be scanned on your smartphone for extra practice and explanations.

A QR code in the Revise section links to a Quick Recall Quiz and/or the Key Sounds on that topic.

A QR code in the Practise and Review sections links to audio content to be used with a question indicated by the ● icon.

A QR code in the Workbook section links to one or both of the following:
- a video working through the solution to one of the questions on that topic, indicated by the ● icon
- audio content to be used with a question, indicated by the ● icon.

Acknowledgements

The authors and publisher are grateful to the copyright holders for permission to use quoted materials and images.

All images © Shutterstock.com

Every effort has been made to trace copyright holders and obtain their permission for the use of copyright material. The authors and publisher will gladly receive information enabling them to rectify any error or omission in subsequent editions. All facts are correct at time of going to press.

Published by Collins
An imprint of HarperCollinsPublishers Ltd
1 London Bridge Street
London SE1 9GF

HarperCollinsPublishers
Macken House, 39/40 Mayor Street Upper,
Dublin 1, D01 C9W8, Ireland

© HarperCollinsPublishers Limited 2024

ISBN 9780008664213

10 9 8 7 6 5 4 3 2 1

British Library Cataloguing in Publication Data.

A CIP record of this book is available from the British Library.

Authors: Helen Farrar, Amy Bates, Libby Mitchell and Sherrie A. Spinks
Publishers: Sara Bennett and Clare Souza
Project editor: Chantal Addy
Cover Design: Sarah Duxbury and Kevin Robbins
Inside Concept Design: Sarah Duxbury and Paul Oates
Text Design and Layout: Jouve India Private Limited
Production: Bethany Brohm
Printed in India by Multivista Global Pvt.Ltd

This book contains FSC™ certified paper and other controlled sources to ensure responsible forest management.

For more information visit: www.harpercollins.co.uk/green

Contents

	Revise	Practise	Review

Key Concepts

1 Draw lines to match the bingo balls with the correct numbers.

(8)		treinta y siete
(10)		veinticinco
(13)		ochenta y seis
(15)		cuarenta y dos
(25)		sesenta y uno
(37)		noventa
(42)		setenta y cuatro
(53)		quince
(61)		trece
(74)		cincuenta y tres
(86)		diez
(90)		ocho

[12 marks]

2 Write the dates in English.

a) lunes, once de julio de 2013 ....

b) jueves, treinta y uno de mayo de 2008 ....

c) sábado, cinco de junio de 2011 ....

d) viernes, diecisiete de enero de 2015 ....

e) domingo, ocho de octubre de 2012 ....

f) miércoles, veintinueve de noviembre de 2017 ....

g) martes, trece de junio de 2009 ....

[7 marks]

3 Draw lines between the boxes to match the times on the left with the digital times on the right.

Son las ocho y media.	12:45
Es la una y veinte.	1:20
Son las nueve menos veinte.	2:25
Es la una menos cuarto.	3:00
Son las dos y veinticinco.	7:05
Son las diez y diez.	8:30
Es el mediodía en punto.	8:40
Son las siete y cinco.	10:10
Son las once y cuarto.	11:15
Son las tres.	12:00

[10 marks]

4 Write the correct letters A–J to match the weather descriptions with the pictures.

A  B  C  D   E

F  G  H   I   J

a) Hoy en el norte hace mucho sol. _____

b) ¡Qué calor hace! _____

c) Ayer hizo mucho viento. _____

d) Está nublado. _____

e) Creo que está nevando. _____

f) Está lloviendo a cántaros. _____

g) ¡Cuidado! Hay tormenta. _____

h) Hace mucho frío en otoño. _____

i) El tiempo es variable. _____

j) Está despejado. _____

[10 marks]

My Family and Me

You must be able to:

- Talk and write about yourself
- Describe your family members
- Make adjectives agree correctly.

Quick Recall Quiz

Key Sounds

Family Members

mi padre	my father	**mi madre**	my mother
mi papá	my dad	**mi mamá**	my mum
mi padrastro	my stepfather	**mi madrastra**	my stepmother
mi hermano	my brother	**mi hermana**	my sister
mi hijo	my son	**mi hija**	my daughter
mi abuelo	my grandfather	**mi abuela**	my grandmother
mi tío	my uncle	**mi tía**	my aunt
mi primo	my (boy) cousin	**mi prima**	my (girl) cousin
mi amigo	my friend (boy)	**mi amiga**	my friend (girl)
el bebé	baby	**el familiar**	relative / family member
los niños	children		
el niño	(boy) child	**la niña**	(girl) child

Key Sound

h is silent at the beginning of words in Spanish, e.g. **hay** (there is), **hermana** (sister), **hijo** (son).

Introducing and Describing People

¡Descríbete a ti mismo/a!	Describe yourself!
Me presento…	Let me introduce myself…
¿Cómo te llamas?	What's your name?
Me llamo…	I'm called / My name is…
Mi nombre es…	My name is…
Mi apellido es…	My surname is…
¿Cómo se escribe tu nombre?	How do you spell your name?
Ana se escribe ah-enneh-ah.	Ana is spelled A-N-A.
¿Cuántos años tienes?	How old are you?
Tengo quince años.	I'm 15 years old.
Pronto voy a cumplir dieciséis años.	Soon, I'm going to be 16 years old.
¿Cuándo es tu cumpleaños?	When's your birthday?
Mi cumpleaños es el cinco de julio.	My birthday is on the 5th of July.
¿Cuándo naciste?	When were you born?
Nací en dos mil nueve.	I was born in 2009.
¿Cuántos años tiene tu hermano?	How old is your brother?
Mi hermano tiene nueve años.	My brother is 9 years old.
¿Cuántos años tienen tus hermanas?	How old are your sisters?
Mis hermanas tienen dieciséis y catorce años.	
My sisters are 16 and 14 years old.	
HT **¡Describe a tu familia!**	Describe your family!
¿Cómo eres de carácter?	What sort of person are you?
Soy…	I am…

Key Sound

ll is a 'y' sound in Spanish:

Me llamo…	My name is…
Me llevo…	I get along with…
Se llama…	They are called…

Key Point

Remember that when forming a question you need to use a ¿ at the beginning of a question and ? at the end. The same applies when using exclamation marks:

¿Cómo se llama? What is your name?

¡Qué guay! That's cool!

Adjectives

- Adjectives **must** agree with the noun they describe. The exceptions – some adjectives **never** change their spelling, e.g. **rosa** (pink), **naranja** (orange), **cada** (every).

	Masculine	Feminine	Masculine plural	Feminine plural
pleasant	**agradable**	**agradable**	**agradables**	**agradables**
artistic	**artístico**	**artística**	**artísticos**	**artísticas**
thin	**delgado**	**delgada**	**delgados**	**delgadas**
ugly	**feo**	**fea**	**feos**	**feas**
fat	**gordo**	**gorda**	**gordos**	**gordas**
funny	**gracioso**	**graciosa**	**graciosos**	**graciosas**
good-looking	**guapo**	**guapa**	**guapos**	**guapas**
talkative	**hablador**	**habladora**	**habladores**	**habladoras**
young	**joven**	**joven**	**jóvenes**	**jóvenes**
lazy	**perezoso**	**perezosa**	**perezosos**	**perezosas**
sensitive	**sensible**	**sensible**	**sensibles**	**sensibles**
kind	**simpático**	**simpática**	**simpáticos**	**simpáticas**
shy	**tímido**	**tímida**	**tímidos**	**tímidas**
tolerant	**tolerante**	**tolerante**	**tolerantes**	**tolerantes**
HT ambitious	**ambicioso**	**ambiciosa**	**ambiciosos**	**ambiciosas**
HT lazy	**vago**	**vaga**	**vagos**	**vagas**
HT loyal / brave	**fiel**	**fiel**	**fieles**	**fieles**
HT understanding	**comprensivo**	**comprensiva**	**comprensivos**	**comprensivas**

En mi familia hay cinco personas. In my family there are five people.
Somos cuatro en mi familia. There are four of us in my family.

> HT **En mi opinión soy deportista pero a veces puedo ser vago.**
> In my opinion, I am sporty but sometimes I can be lazy.
> HT **Mi madre es sensible y muy comprensiva a mi modo de ver.**
> My mum is sensitive and very understanding in my opinion.

Possessive Adjectives

- Possessive adjectives come **before** the noun and **must** agree with the noun.

mi hijo	my son	**nuestra abuela**	our grandmother
mis padres	my parents	**vuestros padres**	your parents
tu hija	your daughter	**vuestras hermanas**	your sisters
sus primos	his / her cousins	**sus abuelos**	their grandparents

> **Quick Test**
>
> 1. Say your name, spell it and say how old you are.
> 2. Ask someone their name and how old they are.
> 3. Translate into English: **Me llamo Sara y tengo dieciséis años. Normalmente soy tímida pero mi madre dice que soy agradable. A veces puedo ser perezosa. Mi mejor amigo se llama Juan y tiene quince años. Es muy hablador. Me llevo bien con él porque es gracioso.**

> ## Key Point
>
> An adjective is a word that describes a noun. In Spanish, adjectives sometimes have different endings depending on whether the word they are describing is masculine, feminine, singular or plural. In general, adjectives are placed after the noun they are describing in Spanish.

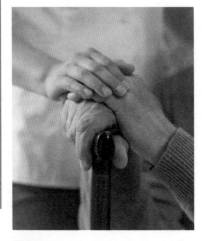

> ## Key Point
>
> Possessive adjectives show who something or someone belongs to.

> ## Key Point
>
> Possessive adjectives agree with the noun that is possessed and not the person who owns (possesses) them.

My Friends and Me

You must be able to:

- Describe a friend's appearance and personality
- Explain why you are friends
- Describe your relationships with others.

Describing Appearance

Tengo el pelo...	I have… hair.	**Tiene los ojos...**	He / She has… eyes.
rubio	blonde	**verdes**	green
pelirrojo	ginger / red	**azules**	blue
marrón	dark brown	**castaños**	hazel
castaño	chestnut brown	**marrones**	brown
negro	black		
gris	grey		
moreno	dark hair		

Mi hermano tiene el pelo marrón, corto y rizado.
My brother has brown, short, curly hair.

Mis abuelos tienen el pelo gris y los ojos azules.
My grandparents have grey hair and blue eyes.

Mi tía es morena con los ojos verdes.
My aunt is dark haired with green eyes.

Soy...	I am	**Es...**	He / She is…

	Masculine	Feminine
happy	**alegre**	**alegre**
tall	**alto**	**alta**
short	**bajo**	**baja**
pretty	**bonito**	**bonita**
thin	**delgado**	**delgada**
ugly	**feo**	**fea**
fat	**gordo**	**gorda**
good-looking / handsome	**guapo**	**guapa**
beautiful	**hermoso**	**hermosa**
independent	**independiente**	**independiente**
HT proud	**orgulloso**	**orgullosa**
HT romantic	**romántico**	**romántica**

de estatura mediana   of medium height

Soy bastante alto y delgado. Mis amigos dicen que soy guapo.
I am quite tall and thin. My friends say that I am good-looking.

Mi hermano lleva gafas y tiene una barba y un bigote.
My brother wears glasses and has a beard and a moustache.

> HT **Mi novio es muy romántico y también está orgulloso de mí.**
> My boyfriend is very romantic and also very proud of me.

Key Verbs

tengo	I have
tienes	you (sing.) have
tiene	he / she has
tenemos	we have
tenéis	you (pl.) have
tienen	they have

Key Sound

Double **r** has a slightly longer roll:

marrón	dark brown
pelirrojo	ginger / red

Verbs

aguantar	to put up with / stand
charlar	to chat
conocer a	to know (a person)
cuidar	to look after
detestar	to hate / detest
discutir	to argue / discuss
enfadarse con	to get annoyed with
entenderse bien / mal con	to get on well / badly with
jubilarse	to retire
jugar	to play
llevarse bien / mal con	to get on well / badly with
molestar	to annoy / bother
odiar	to hate
parecerse a	to look like
sonreír	to smile
HT **comprender**	to understand
HT **confiar**	to trust / confide
HT **engañar**	to trick / deceive
HT **reírse**	to laugh
HT **relacionarse con**	to get along with

Key Point

Use quantifiers to make your adjectives more interesting:

muy	very
bastante	quite
demasiado	too
un poco	a little
tan	so

Relationships with Others

Siempre es…	He / She is always…	**Nunca es…**	He / She is never…
A veces es…	He / She is sometimes…	**A menudo es…**	He / She is often…
Puede ser…		He / She can be…	

¿Te llevas bien con tu familia? — Do you get on well with your family?

Pues, me llevo bastante bien con mi padre porque charlamos mucho, pero no me llevo bien con mi madre porque discutimos siempre.
Well, I get on quite well with my dad because we chat a lot, but I don't get on well with my mum because we always argue.

¿Y qué tal con tus hermanos? ¿Te llevas bien con ellos?
And what about your siblings? Do you get on well with them?

Pues, me llevo bastante bien con mi hermana, pero a veces me enfada; sin embargo me llevo muy bien con mi hermano ya que jugamos al fútbol juntos.
Well, I get on quite well with my sister, but sometimes she annoys me, however I get on really well with my brother because we play football together.

¿Cómo son tus amigos? — What are your friends like?

Me entiendo bastante bien con mis amigos, pero de vez en cuando me molestan.
I get on quite well with my friends, but now and then they annoy me.

HT **No me relaciono bien ni con mi hermano ni con mi hermana porque me engañan.**
I don't get on well with my brother or my sister because they deceive me.

 Key Sound

j as in the Scottish lo**ch**:
jugar	to play
jubilarse	to retire

 Key Point

Use conjunctions to make your speaking and writing flow better:

y	and
pero	but
sin embargo	however
porque	because
dado que	given that
por eso	therefore
HT **ni… ni…**	neither… nor…
HT **sino**	but (rather) / except

Quick Test

1. Translate into Spanish: I am quite short but very thin. I have long, brown straight hair and green eyes.
2. Choose the correct forms: **Mi madre es bastante alto / alta y tengo / tiene los ojos marrón / marrones.**

Relationships

Quick Recall Quiz

Key Sounds

You must be able to:

- Describe people's marital status
- Give your opinions on marriage and future relationships
- Use the verbs **ser** and **estar**.

Talking about Marital Status

Estoy…	I am…
Está…	He / She is…
casado	married
separado	separated
divorciado	divorced
viudo	widowed
soltero	single

Estoy casado pero mi hermana no está casada, está soltera.
I am married but my sister is not married, she is single.

Mis tíos están divorciados. My aunt and uncle are divorced.

Mi prima estaba casada pero ahora está separada de su marido.
My cousin was married but now she is separated from her husband.

Marriage and Relationships

casarse	to get married
compartir	to share
confiar en	to trust
enamorarse de	to fall in love with
llorar	to cry
molestar	to bother / annoy
pelearse	to fight / argue
perdonar	to forgive
preocuparse por	to worry about
relacionarse con	to get on with (people)
querer	to want / love
separarse	to separate
el amigo	(male) friend
la amiga	(female) friend
el amor	love
el hombre	man
el matrimonio	marriage
el marido	husband
la mujer	woman / wife
el novio	boyfriend / groom
la novia	girlfriend / bride
HT **abrazar**	to hug
HT **atraer**	to attract
HT **el cariño**	affection
HT **el familiar**	relative / family member

Key Sounds

For words ending in 'n', 's' or a vowel, the penultimate syllable is stressed:

recepcionista	receptionist
patatas	potatoes
cena	dinner

For words ending in a consonant other than 'n' or 's', the last syllable is stressed:

beber	to drink
caminar	to walk
universidad	university

When the above rules do not apply, an acute accent appears over the stressed syllable:

inglés	English
marrón	brown
recepción	reception

¿Te gustaría casarte en el futuro?
Would you like to get married in the future?

Espero casarme en el futuro. I hope to get married in the future.

Mis abuelos se enamoraron con veinte años.
My grandparents fell in love at the age of twenty.

Mi novia y yo nunca nos peleamos y confío en ella totalmente.
My girlfriend and I never fight, and I trust her completely.

HT **Mis abuelos me hablan con cariño.** My grandparents speak to me with affection.

HT **Me encanta abrazar a mi perro.** I love to hug my dog.

Using the Verb ser

- The verb **ser** is used to talk about the following: dates, occupation, characteristics, time, origin (country) and relationships.

soy…	I am…
eres…	you (sing.) are…
es…	he / she is…
somos…	we are…
sois…	you (pl.) are…
son…	they are…
Eres muy hablador.	You are very chatty.

HT **¿Cuál es el nombre de tu familiar con el pelo pelirrojo?**
What is the name of your relative with the red hair?

Using the Verb estar

- The verb **estar** is used to talk about the following: positions, locations, actions, conditions, emotions and states.

Estamos casados. We are married.

Key Point

Use the verb **estar** to talk about temporary states and marital status. Use the verb **ser** to talk about permanent states and personal characteristics.

Quick Test

1. Translate into Spanish: My parents are separated.
2. Translate into English: **Quiero a mi marido.**
3. What is the Spanish for 'marriage'?
4. Choose the correct forms:
   Mi madre es / está simpática. Mis padres son / están casados.

Identity and Relationships with Others

1 Choose the correct form of the adjective to complete these sentences.

a) Mi madre es bonito / bonita / bonitos / bonitas.

b) Tengo dos perros blanco / blanca / blancos / blancas.

c) Mis primas son hablador / habladora / habladores / habladoras.

d) Mi hermano es bajo y gordo / bajo y delgada / baja y delgado / baja y delgada.

e) Mis tíos están divorciado / divorciada / divorciados / divorciadas.

f) Mi prima es muy guapo / guapa / guapos / guapas.

g) Mi hermano y yo somos simpático / simpática / simpáticos / simpáticas.

h) Tus abuelos están casado / casada / casados / casadas.

i) Confío en mi hermana ya que es responsable / reponsabla / responsables / responsablos.

j) Tengo los ojos azul / azule / azulas / azules.   [10 marks]

2 Fill in the gaps using the words from the box.

es	tiene	somos	se llama	eres
se llaman	tengo	son	tienen	está
están	tenemos	me llaman	me llamo	

a) Mi padre .... Juan.

b) Mi madre y yo .... altos.

c) Mis amigos .... Marisa, pero de verdad, ... María Luisa.

d) Mis abuelos .... casados.

e) Mi hermana y yo .... el pelo marrón, corto y rizado.

f) Mi marido .... Andrés.

g) ¿............................... hablador?

h) Mis padres .... delgados y altos.

i) Mi prima .... separada de su marido.   [10 marks]

3 Unscramble the sentences.

a) tiene   pelo   el   primo   liso   castaño   mi   corto   y

(My cousin has chestnut brown, straight, short hair.)

b) bajo   y   bastante   los   verdes   ojos   soy   tengo

(I am quite short and I have green eyes.)

c) estatura   mediana   es   mi   de   hermano

(My brother is of medium height.)

d) casados   está   separada   están   mis   mi   su   hermana   pero   tíos

marido   de

(My aunt and uncle are married but my sister is separated from her husband.)   [4 marks]

4 Fill in the gaps in the verb tables.

Subject Pronouns / Infinitives	tener	ser	estar
yo	....	soy	estoy
tú	....	....	estás
él / ella / usted	tiene	....	....
nosotros / nosotras	tenemos	somos	....
vosotros / vosotras	tenéis	....	estáis
ellos / ellas / ustedes	....	son	....

[9 marks]

5 Read the sentences. Write **P** for a positive opinion, **N** for a negative opinion or **P+N** for a positive and negative opinion.

a) Mi marido, Carlos, es muy responsable y le quiero mucho.   ....

b) Mi novia, Marta, es muy comprensiva, pero yo diría que es demasiado optimista.   ....

c) Mis padres se pelean mucho, y me molesta cuando los oigo.   ....

[3 marks]

6 Correct the mistakes in the following sentences.

a) Mis padres está casados.   d) Mi madre es bajo.

b) Mi hermano es separado de su mujer.   e) Mi abuelos tienen el pelo gris.

c) Mi primo y mi prima tiene los ojos azules.   f) Mis amigas se llama Sara y Ana.   [6 marks]

Food and Healthy Eating

Quick Recall Quiz

Key Sounds

You must be able to:

- Discuss food and drink, including likes and preferences
- Talk and write about mealtimes and eating out
- Use past tenses to talk about what you have eaten or drunk.

Health and a Healthy Lifestyle

el régimen	diet
la dieta equilibrada	balanced diet
la comida basura	junk food
la grasa	fat / grease
la bebida	drink
vegano	vegan
vegetariano	vegetarian
saludable	healthy
estar en forma	to be fit
cocinar	to cook
el hambre	hunger
la sed	thirst
HT el alimento	food / nourishment

Soy vegano. No como carne, ni bebo leche.
I am vegan. I don't eat meat or drink milk.

Soy vegetariana. No como pescado pero tomo leche.
I am vegetarian. I don't eat fish but I drink milk.

Key Verbs

Tengo hambre y tengo sed.
I am (have) hungry and I am (have) thirsty.

Key Sounds

g followed by **i** or **e** is a soft 'ch' sound as in 'loch'.
g followed by **a** or **o** is a hard g sound.
v sounds like **b**, e.g., **vegano**, **vegetariano**

In the Restaurant

la mesa	table
la carta	menu
el vaso	(drinking) glass
el plato	plate / dish
la botella	bottle
la copa	cup / glass
el desayuno	breakfast
la comida	food / meal / lunch
dulce	sweet
el camarero	waiter
la camarera	waitress
reservar	to book / reserve
desayunar	to have breakfast
beber	to drink
tomar	to have / take / drink
comer	to eat
cenar	to have your evening meal
la cena	dinner / evening meal
¿Tienes una mesa para dos, por favor?	Do you have a table for two, please?
¡La carta, por favor!	The menu, please!
Quiero una botella de vino.	I want a bottle of wine.

Quiero un vaso de vino rosado. — I want a glass of rosé wine.
Para mí una hamburguesa con patatas fritas.
I'll have a burger and chips.
¿Qué hay de postre? — What is there for dessert?
¡La cuenta! — The bill!

Food and Drink

la carne	meat	**la naranja**	orange
el agua	water	**la manzana**	apple
el café	coffee	**el pescado**	fish
el pan	bread	**el pollo**	chicken
el vino	wine	**la hamburguesa**	burger
la leche	milk	**la sal**	salt
la fruta	fruit	**la paella**	paella (rice dish)
el huevo	egg	**las patatas fritas**	chips
el azúcar	sugar	**las tapas**	tapas / bar snacks
HT **el arroz**	rice		
HT **el aceite**	oil		
HT **el alcohol**	alcohol		

¿Qué sueles desayunar?
What do you usually have for breakfast?
Tomo café y suelo desayunar pan tostado.
I have a coffee and I usually have toast for breakfast.
¿Qué comes a mediodía? — What do you have at lunchtime?
Como un bocadillo y bebo agua. — I eat a sandwich and I drink water.
¿Cenas en casa o en un restaurante?
Do you have dinner at home or in a restaurant?
**Ceno en casa con mi familia. Comemos paella de mariscos,
y bebemos vino.**
I have supper at home with my family. We eat seafood paella, and we drink wine.
**Anoche fuimos a un restaurante donde comí carne con verduras,
y bebí café.**
Last night we went to a restaurant where I ate meat and vegetables, and
I drank coffee.

Key Verbs

The verbs **comer**, **beber**,
desayunar, **cenar** and
tomar are all regular in the
present and past tenses.
Present tense:
bebo (I drink), **bebes** (you
drink), **bebe** (he / she
drinks) **ceno** (I have dinner),
cenas (you have dinner),
cena (he / she has dinner)
Preterite tense:
bebí (I drank), **bebiste** (you
drank), **bebió** (he / she
drank) **cené** (I had dinner),
cenaste (you had dinner),
cenó (he / she had dinner)

Quick Test

1. You are at a restaurant. Ask for a table for four people in Spanish.
2. You are at a restaurant. Ask for the menu in Spanish.
3. Translate into English: **Soy vegano y desayuno fruta.**
4. Fill in the gaps with the correct verbs in the present tense:
   a) _____ **hamburguesas.**
   b) _____ **agua.**
   c) _____ **hambre.**
   d) _____ **sed.**
   e) **No** _____ **vino pero** _____ **cerveza.**
5. Fill in the gaps with the correct verbs in the preterite tense:
   a) **Ayer** _____ **café pero mi madre** _____ **té.**
   b) **Anoche** _____ **pollo con patatas fritas y tú,
      ¿qué** _____ **?**

Daily Routine

Quick Recall Quiz

Key Sound

You must be able to:

- Talk and write about your daily routine and weekend activities
- Use reflexive verbs with confidence
- Use the verb **haber** to form compound tenses.

Daily Routine

Useful Verbs

llegar	to arrive	**ver**	to watch
salir	to go out	**andar**	to walk
comenzar	to start	**viajar**	to travel
terminar	to finish	**ir**	to go
hacer	to do	**volver**	to come back / return
estudiar	to study		

Reflexive Verbs

despertarse	to wake (oneself) up
levantarse	to get (oneself) up
lavarse	to wash (oneself)
ponerse	to put on (oneself)
vestirse	to get (oneself) dressed
cambiarse	to get (oneself) changed
quitarse	to take (clothes) off (oneself)
dormirse	to fall asleep (oneself)
HT **arreglarse**	to get (oneself) ready
HT **pintarse**	to put make up on (oneself)
HT **acostarse**	to go to bed

Key Verbs

In Spanish, reflexive verbs are commonly used to talk about motion, your body, your clothing, your state of mind and your routines. The reflexive pronouns are: **me** (I), **te** (you sing.), **se** (he / she), **nos** (we), **os** (you pl.), **se** (they).

Los fines de semana, me levanto a las nueve, me ducho y me visto.
At weekends, I get up at nine o'clock, I have a shower and I get dressed.

Salgo de la casa a las ocho y media después de desayunar y llego al colegio a las nueve menos cuarto.
I leave the house at eight thirty after having breakfast and I arrive at school at quarter to nine.

Ando al colegio.   I walk to school.

Las clases comienzan a las nueve en punto y terminan a las tres y diez.
Classes start at nine o'clock on the dot and finish at ten past three.

Me duermo a las diez y cuarto.   I go to sleep at quarter past ten.

¿A qué hora te despiertas?   What time do you wake up?

HT **Me despierto a las siete y me levanto enseguida.**
I wake up at seven o'clock and I get up straight away.

HT **Me arreglo, me pinto y los días de colegio me pongo mi uniforme.**
I get ready, I put my make up on and on school days I put my uniform on.

HT **Me lavo la cara, y me lavo los dientes también.**
I wash my face and I brush my teeth also.

The Verb haber

- The verb **haber** is the Spanish verb meaning 'to have'. It is a very unique verb as it can be used as an auxiliary verb to form compound tenses.
- It comes before the main verb in the sentence. The verb **haber** is: **he** (I have), **has** (you have sing.), **ha** (he / she has) **hay** (there is / are), **hemos** (we have), **habéis** (you have pl.), **han** (they have).
- The verb **haber** must always be followed by a past participle, e.g. **comido** (eaten), **bebido** (drunk), **llegado** (arrived), **puesto** (put), **visto** (seen).

Esta mañana [me he… + past participle]	This morning [I have… + past participle]
me he despertado	I woke up / I have woken up
me he levantado	I got up / I have got up
me he lavado	I washed / I have got washed
me he puesto	I put on / I have put on
me he vestido	I got dressed / I have got dressed
me he cambiado	I got changed / I have got changed
me he quitado	I took off / I have taken off
me he dormido	I fell asleep / I have fallen asleep
HT me he arreglado	I got ready / I have got ready
HT me he pintado	I put make up on / I have put make up on
HT me he acostado	I went to bed / I have gone to bed

Esta mañana me he despertado a las siete, pero mi hermano se ha despertado más tarde a las siete y media.
This morning I woke up at seven o'clock, but my brother woke up later at half past seven.

Anoche mis padres se han acostado temprano a las nueve, pero yo me he acostado a medianoche.
Last night my parents went to bed early at nine o'clock, but I went to bed at midnight.

¿Os habéis levantado temprano, hoy?   Did you (all) get up early today?
¿Te has dormido tarde anoche?   Did you fall asleep late last night?

Key Sound

The letter 'h' is always silent at the beginning of a word in Spanish. Try pronouncing the following words and phrases: **hora**, **hay mucho que hacer**, **no me he acostado temprano**, **haber**

Quick Test

1. Translate the following into English: **Cada día me despierto a las ocho menos cuarto y me levanto enseguida.**
2. Translate the following into Spanish:
   Every night I go to bed at ten o'clock and I go to sleep immediately.
3. Fill in the spaces with the correct form of the verb **haber**.
   a) Me _____ levantado.
   b) Él se _____ acostado.
   c) ¿Te _____ pintado?
   d) Nos _____ lavado.
   e) Mis padres se _____ dormido.
4. Describe **three** actions in your own daily routine with times in both the present and the perfect (recent) past tense. Write them down and say them out loud.
5. Write **three** questions asking your friend what they do in their daily routine. Say them out loud.

Keeping Healthy

You must be able to:

- Discuss elements of a healthy lifestyle
- Talk and write about health and illness
- Describe pains in parts of the body.

Quick Recall Quiz

Key Sound

Your Health

para estar en forma	(in order) to be fit
dar un paseo	to go for a walk
hacer ejercicio	to do exercise
buenas / malas costumbres	good / bad habits
tomar drogas	to take drugs
para tener más energía	(in order) to have more energy
sufrir de una enfermedad	to suffer from an illness
contener grasa	to contain fat
ser grasiento	to be greasy
ser bueno / malo para la salud	to be good / bad for your health
hacer deporte	to do sports
evitar el estrés	to avoid stress
entender los peligros	to understand the dangers
conocer los riesgos	to know the risks
beber vino	to drink wine
HT **tener una vida (mal)sana**	to have a (un)healthy life
HT **beber mucho alcohol**	to drink a lot of alcohol
HT **comer alimentos saludables**	to eat healthy food
HT **sufrir de cáncer**	to suffer from cancer
HT **fumar cigarrillos**	to smoke cigarettes
HT **bajar el consumo de…**	to lower the consumption of…
HT **sufrir de sobrepeso**	to suffer from obesity

Bad Habits

Mi madre fuma diez cigarrillos cada día.
My mum smokes ten cigarettes a day.

Mi amigo toma drogas, pero yo no tomo nunca drogas porque son malas para la salud.
My friend takes drugs, but I never take drugs because they are bad for your health.

Para tener más energía hay que hacer ejercicio frecuentemente y seguir un régimen sano. Es importante dormir bien, al menos ocho horas cada noche y en vez de beber mucho alcohol, es necesario beber mucha agua.
To have more energy you have to exercise frequently and follow a healthy diet. It is important to sleep well, at least eight hours every night and instead of drinking alcohol, it is necessary to drink lots of water.

No como muchos caramelos, ya que son malos para la salud, dado que son altos en azúcar, y no quiero tener dolor de dientes.
I don't eat many sweets since they are bad for your health, given that they are high in sugar, and I don't want toothache.

Key Sound

Que is a blended sound. The first part is like 'k' in 'key' and the second sound is a short 'e' as in 'bet'. The combined sound is **que** (ke). Try pronouncing these words: **queso** (cheese), **que** (what), **qué** (what), **querer** (to want)

Creo que estoy en forma porque intento comer una dieta equilibrada,
o sea muchas verduras, mucha fruta y carne solamente dos o tres veces
a la semana.
I believe that I am fit because I try to eat a balanced diet, that is to say, lots of
vegetables, a lot of fruit and meat only two or three times a week.

**Las malas costumbres como fumar cigarrillos, beber alcohol y comer
alimentos altos en grasa son malos para la salud y pueden causar muchas
enfermedades.**
Bad habits such as smoking cigarettes, drinking alcohol and eating high-fat
foods are bad for your health and can cause lots of illnesses / diseases.

En el futuro tengo la intención de comer bien.
In the future I intend to eat well.

Valdría la pena no tomar drogas ni fumar cigarrillos.
It would be worthwhile to not take drugs nor smoke cigarettes.

The Body

la cabeza	the head	HT **la boca**	the mouth
el corazón	the heart	HT **la mente**	the mind
la piel	the skin	HT **la pierna**	the leg
la mano	the hand	HT **la sangre**	the blood
el ojo	the eye	HT **el brazo**	the arm
el pie	the foot	HT **el cerebro**	the brain

ir al médico	to go to the doctor
dar un consejo	to give advice
tomar medicina	to take medicine
tener un accidente	to have an accident
HT **doler los dientes**	to have toothache
HT **tener dolor de…**	to have pain in…
HT **sufrir una herida**	to suffer an injury

Una cita con el médico A doctor's appointment

¿Qué le pasa? What's wrong? **¿Algo más?** Anything else?

Me duele la cabeza desde hace dos días.
I've had a headache for two days.

Tengo dolor de pie, y me duelen los dientes.
I have a pain in my foot, and I have toothache.

¿Me puede dar un consejo, por favor? Can you give me some advice, please?

Tiene que tomar unas aspirinas y descansar en casa. Hay que ir al dentista.
You have to take some aspirin and rest at home. You have to go to the dentist.

Tiene que tomar dos aspirinas tres veces al día por dos días.
You have to take two aspirins three times a day for two days.

Pienso que me he roto la pierna. I think I have broken my leg.

Tiene que ir al hospital. You have to go to the hospital.

Quick Test

1. Say the following in Spanish:
   a) I have a headache.
   b) I have a pain in my arm.
   c) I have toothache.
   d) I have a sore leg.
   e) My foot hurts.
2. Translate into English:
   Me duelen las manos porque he jugado mucho al voleibol.
3. Translate into Spanish: I am fit because I eat a balanced diet, that is to say
   I eat fish and vegetables every day and drink lots of water.
4. Say in Spanish if you are fit or not and why.

Practice Questions

Healthy Living and Lifestyle

1 Translate the food items into English.

a) **Dos copas de vino** ....

b) **Cuatro botellas de agua** ....

c) **Una hamburguesa con patatas fritas** ....

d) **Mucha carne** ....

e) **Un vaso de leche** ....

f) **Un plato de arroz con pollo y verduras** ....

g) **Un kilo de manzanas** ....

h) **Medio kilo de naranjas** ....

i) **Tres piñas** ....

j) **Un pescado con huevos duros** ....

2 Match the Spanish with the English translation.   [10 marks]

a) **¿Tienes una mesa para dos, por favor?**   i)   I'll have a fish and chips.

b) **¡La carta, por favor!**   ii)   The bill!

c) **Quiero una botella de vino.**   iii)   I want a bottle of wine.

d) **Quiero un vaso de vino rosado.**   iv)   What is there for dessert?

e) **Para mí, pescado con patatas fritas.**   v)   Do you have a table for two, please?

f) **¿Qué hay de postre?**   vi)   I want a glass of rosé wine.

g) **¡La cuenta!**   vii)   The menu, please!   [7 marks]

3 Read the food list in **1.** aloud.   [10 marks]

4 Translate the following questions into English.

a) ¿Qué sueles comer para el desayuno?

b) ¿Qué comes a mediodía?

c) ¿Dónde y qué cenas?

d) ¿Qué bebes normalmente?

e) ¿Prefieres el pescado o las hamburguesas?

f) ¿Estás en forma?　　　　　　[6 marks]

5 Fill in the gaps with an appropriate word from the box below.

estaba	me gustaría	tengo	hay	estar
hago	estoy	me acosté	me levanto	prefieres

a) Anoche _____ temprano porque _____ cansado.

b) Cada día _____ tarde.

c) _____ una mesa para cuatro personas, por favor.

d) ¿Qué _____ de postre?

e) ¿_____ la leche o el café?

f) _____ en forma.

g) _____ una dieta equilibrada.

h) _____ deporte cada día para _____ en forma.　　　　[10 marks]

6 Rearrange the words into the correct order to give advice on living a healthy life.

a) dieta　hay　evitar　que　malsana　una

b) acostarte　temprano　debes

c) que　dormir　al　tienes　menos　horas　ocho　noche　cada

d) practicar　veces　tres　a　semana　la　debes　deporte

e) se　debe　no　fumar　ni　drogas　tomar

f) que　tratar　hay　evitar　de　estrés　el

g) relajarte　música　para　debes　escuchar　　　　　　[7 marks]

Review Questions

Identity and Relationships with Others

1 Choose the correct form of the verbs from the box below to complete the sentences.

soy	eres	se llama	es	somos
son	tengo	tienes	se llaman	tienen

a) Mi padre .... Juan.

b) Y tú, ¿cómo ....?

c) .... cuatro en mi familia.

d) Mis padres .... los ojos marrones.

e) Tus primas .... muy guapas.

f) Mis abuelos .... Ana y Luis.

g) ¿.......................... hermanos o hermanas?

h) Yo .... muy alta y bastante gorda.

i) Mi madre .... bastante comprensiva y siempre me escucha.

j) Yo .... el pelo rubio, largo y rizado.   [10 marks]

2 Rearrange the words into the correct order to form sentences.

a) pelo Tiene el marrón, los corto ojos y liso verdes y
   (He has brown, short, straight hair and green eyes.)

b) Soy y bastante comprensivo alto, amable y muy también delgado soy y
   (I am quite tall and very thin and I am also friendly and understanding.)

c) padre Mi de estatura mediana es
   (My dad is of medium height.)

d) son Mis menores hermanos muy deportistas
   (My little brothers are very sporty.)   [4 marks]

3 Read the sentences. Write **P** for a positive opinion, **N** for a negative opinion or **P+N** for a positive and negative opinion.

a) Mi mujer es muy comprensiva y sensible, la quiero mucho. ....

b) Mi marido es bastante impaciente, sin embargo, es muy amable y cariñoso. ....

c) Mis padres discuten mucho y me molestan mucho. .... [3 marks]

4 Say the following sentences aloud.

a) Me llamo Juan.

b) Vivo en Málaga en España.

c) Tengo quince años.

d) Mi abuela tiene el pelo gris y los ojos marrones.

e) Mi tía es muy comprensiva y bastante inteligente.

f) Me llevo bien con mis padres, pero mi hermana me molesta a veces. [6 marks]

5 Translate the following sentences into Spanish.

a) There are four people in my family, my mum, my stepdad, my younger brother and me.

....

b) I am quite sporty, but I can be very lazy at times.

....

[2 marks]

6 Read the following text aloud.

Me llamo Carlos y vivo en Málaga. Mis padres se llaman María y Roberto y están divorciados.
Mis abuelos están casados. Mi hermana está separada de su marido y vive en Madrid.
Tengo los ojos azules y soy bastante cariñoso según mi madre. [5 marks]

At School

You must be able to:

- Discuss school subjects, your likes, dislikes and preferences
- Talk and write about your school, its buildings and your day.

School Subjects

el arte / dibujo	art	**la historia**	history
el baile	dance	**la informática**	ICT
el comercio	business	**los idiomas**	languages
los deportes	sports	**las matemáticas**	maths
el español	Spanish	**el teatro**	drama
la geografía	geography	**la tecnología**	technology

Estudio ocho asignaturas en total y mi asignatura preferida es la historia.
I study eight subjects in total and my favourite subject is history.

No me gustan nada las ciencias dado que son difíciles.
I really don't like science because it is difficult.

Useful Verbs

aguantar	to stand / put up with	**estudiar**	to study
alegrar	to make happy	**aprender**	to learn
disfrutar	to enjoy	**interesar**	to interest
elegir	to choose	**molestar**	to annoy
encantar	to love	**preferir**	to prefer
enseñar	to teach	**tener**	to have

Giving and Justifying Opinions

Phrases

Use the following phrases to give your opinion on school subjects:

Me gusta(n)...	I like...
Me encanta(n)...	I love...
Me molesta(n).	It (they) annoys me.
Prefiero...	I prefer...
No aguanto...	I can't stand...
Disfruto...	I enjoy...
Me alegra(n).	It (they) makes me happy.
Me interesa(n).	It (they) interests me.

Adjectives

Use adjectives to describe your opinion:

difícil(es)	hard / difficult	**divertido/a(s)**	fun
duro/a(s)	hard	**educativo/a(s)**	educational
emocionante(s)	exciting	**estupendo/a(s)**	great
fácil(es)	easy	**fuerte(s)**	strong
guay	cool	**interesante(s)**	interesting
malo/a(s)	bad	**necesario/a(s)**	necessary

> ## Key Sound
>
> The **ñ** sounds like an 'n' followed by a 'y' as in 'any':
>
> **español** Spanish
> **enseño**   I teach

> ## Key Point
>
> When using impersonal verbs such as **me gusta / me molesta** you must use the definite article:
>
> **Me encanta (el/la)…**
> I love…
> **Me gustan (los/las)…**
> I like…

obligatorio/a(s)	compulsory	práctico/a(s)	practical / useful
útil(es)	useful	HT estricto/a(s)	strict

Estudio español ya que será muy útil en el futuro.
I study Spanish because it will be very useful in the future.

A mi hermana le gustan mucho las matemáticas, pero yo no las aguanto.
My sister really likes maths, but I can't stand it.

Opino que el inglés es necesario, aunque es difícil, y me molesta estudiarlo.
I think that English is necessary, however it is difficult, and it annoys me.

Preferiría estudiar geografía en el futuro porque sería muy práctica.
I would prefer to study geography in the future because it would be very practical.

El año pasado estudié teatro, pero lo dejé porque no era obligatorio.
Last year I studied drama, but I dropped it because it wasn't compulsory.

About My School

En mi colegio hay…	In my school there is / are
el colegio / instituto	(secondary) school
la escuela	(primary) school
el edificio	the building
el patio	the yard / playground
el comedor	the dining room / canteen
el gimnasio	the gymnasium
la biblioteca	the library
las aulas	the classrooms
la sala de profesores	the staffroom
el salón de actos	the assembly hall
los vestuarios	the changing rooms
la sala de informática	the ICT room
la cancha de tenis	the tennis court
HT el campo de fútbol	the football pitch
HT el laboratorio de idiomas	the language lab
HT los laboratorios	the (science) laboratories
HT el teatro	the drama studio

> **Key Point**

If the subject is plural, e.g. **las ciencias** (science), then the opinion phrase using **me** and the adjective also need to be plural:

Me gustan las ciencias porque son interesantes.
I like science because it is interesting.

Me gusta el inglés porque es interesante.
I like English because it is interesting.

> **Key Point**

To get more marks, don't forget to explain your opinion:

Me encanta la historia porque la profe es guay.
I love history because the teacher is cool.

> **Quick Test**

1. Are these subjects masculine or feminine, and singular or plural?
   a) **música**   b) **deportes**   c) **ciencias**   d) **inglés**
2. Complete these sentences using the correct definite articles:
   a) **Me gustan** .... **matemáticas.**
   b) **Me molesta estudiar** .... **geografía.**
   c) **Me interesa mucho** .... **teatro.**
3. Translate the following into English:
   Me molesta estudiar el español porque es bastante difícil.
4. Translate the following into Spanish:
   I really like maths because it is interesting but I prefer science because it is more exciting, however I can't stand sports.

School Life

Quick Recall Quiz

Key Sound

You must be able to:

- Talk and write about life at school
- Discuss uniform and rules
- Use modal verbs in the present tense.

School

el alumno	pupil (boy)
la alumna	pupil (girl)
el Bachillerato	school leaving exam
el colegio (mixto)	(mixed) school
los deberes	homework
el / la director(a)	headteacher
el / la estudiante	student
el examen	exam
la prueba	test
la pregunta	question
la regla	rule / ruler
¿Cómo es tu instituto?	What's your school like?

Mi instituto es mixto y bastante grande con unos novecientos alumnos.
My school is mixed and quite big with about 900 pupils.

Me gusta mi colegio porque tiene muchas instalaciones buenas como muchas aulas, un salón de actos grande y un comedor enorme.
I like my school because it has lots of nice facilities like lots of classrooms, a big hall, and an enormous dining room.

Las clases empiezan a las nueve menos veinte y terminan a las tres en punto.
Classes start at 8.40 and finish at 3 o'clock on the dot.

Me gustan mucho mis profes porque explican bien y me ayudan mucho.
I really like my teachers because they explain well and help me a lot.

Sin embargo, mi profe de inglés me cae fatal porque no me explica bien las cosas, y es muy estricto.
However, I can't stand my English teacher because he doesn't explain things well, and he is very strict.

Key Point

Lots of words associated with the topic of school are cognates or near-cognates (words that look or sound very similar to English):

la clase	class
el estudiante	student
el examen	exam

Key Sound

The word 'and' in Spanish is **y** and is pronounced as 'ee' as in 'see'.

Key Point

When describing uniform with colours make sure the colour agrees in both number and gender with the noun it describes:

una falda negra
a black skirt

unos pantalones negros
some black trousers

However, when a colour is made up of two words then it does not agree:

una falda azul oscuro
a dark blue skirt

una chaqueta rojo oscuro
a dark red jacket

School Uniform

Llevamos…	We wear…
una falda	a skirt
unos pantalones	some trousers
una camisa blanca	a white shirt
un jersey	a jumper
una corbata	a tie
una chaqueta	a blazer
unos zapatos negros	some black shoes
una blusa	a blouse

Tenemos que llevar uniforme escolar y diría que no me gusta nada porque no puedo mostrar mi individualidad.
We have to wear a school uniform and I really don't like it at all because I cannot show my individuality.

Creo que es mejor llevar uniforme escolar porque así todo el mundo parece elegante y también parece igual.
I believe it is better to wear a school uniform because then everyone looks smart and looks the same.

School Rules

Se debe respetar a los demás.	You must respect others.
No se puede llevar joyas.	You cannot wear jewellery.
Hay que hacer los deberes.	You have to do your homework.
No se permite comer chicle.	You are not allowed to chew gum in class.
No se debe llevar maquillaje.	You must not wear makeup.

Solo se puede usar el móvil durante la hora de comer y nunca en clase.
You are only able to use your mobile phone during lunch hour and never in class.

Quick Test

1. Translate into Spanish: I don't like maths because we always have lots of tests.
2. In Spanish, describe your uniform using colours.
3. Which sentence does not make sense?
   a) **Me gusta mi uniforme porque es muy feo.**
   b) **No me gusta mi uniforme porque no es muy elegante.**
   c) **Me gusta mi uniforme porque es bastante bonito.**
4. HT Translate into English: **En mi escuela primaria no llevábamos uniforme escolar.**

Post-16 Education and Work

Quick Recall Quiz

Key Sounds

You must be able to:

- Talk and write about your plans for study and work
- Say what you would like to do, or intend to do
- Discuss jobs and employment
- Express opinions about your future.

Post-16 Choices

Quiero…	I want…
estudiar Bachillerato	to study A-Levels
ir a la universidad	to go to university
encontrar un trabajo	to find a job
seguir estudiando	to continue studying
tomar un año sabático	to take a gap year
trabajar a tiempo parcial / completo	to work part-time / full-time
HT conseguir un aprendizaje	to get an apprenticeship

Después de terminar los exámenes, voy a buscar un trabajo a tiempo parcial y también voy a ir a la universidad para estudiar ciencias.

After finishing my exams, I'm going to look for a part-time job and I am going to go to university to study science.

Iré a la universidad para ser médico.

I will go to university in order to become a doctor.

Estudiaremos mucho para aprobar los exámenes.

We will study a lot in order to pass our exams.

HT Voy a conseguir un aprendizaje porque quiero trabajar en una compañía eléctrica.

I'm going to get an apprenticeship because I want to work in an electric company.

Part-Time Jobs

Los sábados trabajo en una tienda como dependiente.

On Saturdays I work in a shop as a sales assistant.

Los fines de semana trabajo como camarero en un restaurante. Me pagan bien.

At the weekends I work as a waiter in a restaurant. It is well paid.

Antes y después del colegio todos los días cuido a mi hermano menor.

Before and after school every day I look after my little brother.

Para ganar un poco de dinero, ayudo a mi madre a hacer las tareas domésticas en casa.

To earn a little money, I help my mum to do the chores at home.

Key Point

When talking about jobs we do not use the article in Spanish:

Soy camarero.
I am a waiter.

Trabajo como director de empresa.
I work as a company director.

Key Sounds

ce, **ci**, **ca**, **co** and **cu** – 'th' as in 'theatre' when followed by 'e' or 'i' (in mainland Spanish and the Balearics) but a soft 's' in the rest of the Spanish speaking world; hard 'c' sound as in 'cat' when followed by 'a', 'o' or 'u':

cine	cinema
centro	centre
hice	I did
practica	practises
contestando	answering

Work Experience

Hice mis prácticas laborales en una tienda / oficina / escuela primaria / un banco.

I did my work experience in a shop / office / primary school / bank.

Todos los días trabajaba de las nueve hasta las cuatro. Charlaba con los clientes, contestaba llamadas telefónicas, escribía correos y era bastante interesante, aunque un poco monótono a veces.

Every day I worked from nine until four. I chatted with the customers, answered telephone calls, wrote emails and it was quite interesting, although a little monotonous at times.

Me gustaron mis prácticas. Trabajé como profesor en una escuela primaria. Era muy útil y divertido y ahora sé que me gustaría ser profesor en el futuro.

I liked my work experience. I worked as a teacher in a primary school. It was very useful and fun and now I know that I would like to be a teacher in the future.

Trabajaba como camarera en un restaurante sirviendo a los clientes.

I worked as a waitress in a restaurant serving the customers.

Connectives and Expressing Opinions

Here are some useful connectives for linking your statements when giving opinions:

aunque	although, even though
como	as
mientras	while, whilst
o	or
pero	but
porque	because
que	that
si	if, whether
y	and

No tengo trabajo, pero quiero conseguir un empleo a tiempo parcial.

I don't have a job, but I would like to get a part-time job.

Espero ir a la universidad mientras trabajo los fines de semana.

I hope to go to university while working at weekends.

> ### Key Point
>
> Use the preterite tense to describe something that you did in the past with a specific time. Use the imperfect to describe habitual things that happened in the past:
>
> **Hice mis prácticas en una oficina.**
> I did my work experience in an office.
> **Cada día hacía fotocopias.**
> Every day I did photocopying.

> ### Key Point
>
> Use the gerund with the imperfect or the preterite tense to describe habitual activities in the past:
>
> **Pasé un día contestando llamadas telefónicas.**
> I spent a day answering telephone calls.
> **Pasaba todos los días de mis prácticas ayudando a un profesor en una escuela primaria.**
> I spent every day of my work experience helping a teacher in a primary school.

Quick Test

1. Translate into Spanish: I want to go to university to study maths.
2. Translate into English: **Los fines de semana trabajo en una tienda para ganar un poco de dinero.**
3. Are these sentences about work experience in the preterite or imperfect tense? Explain the difference between the two tenses.
   a) **Hice mis prácticas laborales en una oficina.**
   b) **Todos los días contestaba llamadas telefónicas.**
   c) **El trabajo era muy interesante y divertido.**
4. Which sentence is grammatically incorrect and why?
   a) **Soy camarero en un restaurante.**
   b) **Soy una profesora en una escuela.**
5. Name at least five connectives in Spanish.

Practice Questions

Education and Work

1 Rearrange the words into the correct order to form sentences.

    a) encanta me porque español el interesante es

    b) estudiar encanta me matemáticas aunque difíciles son

    c) estudio asignaturas ocho prefiero y ciencias las

    d) estudiando quiero inglés continuar porque útil es

    e) la universidad espero a ir para estudiar geografía

    f) aunque interesante es gusta no me estudiar historia   [6 marks]

 2 Read the following sentences aloud.

    a) Me gusta estudiar tecnología porque es interesante.

    b) Quiero conseguir un trabajo a tiempo parcial.

    c) Trabajo los fines de semana en una tienda.

    d) Hice mis prácticas laborales en una oficina.

    e) Cada día contestaba llamadas telefónicas.

    f) Hice mis prácticas en un restaurante sirviendo a los clientes.   [6 marks]

3 Translate the following sentences into Spanish.

    a) I am going to go to university to study languages.

    b) I did my work experience in an office in the town centre.

    c) Every day I wrote emails.

    d) I am going to continue studying Spanish and French.

    e) I would like to find a part-time job.

    f) I'm going to get an apprenticeship.

    g) I worked as a waiter in a restaurant serving customers.   [7 marks]

4 Read the sentences. Write **P** for a positive opinion, **N** for a negative opinion or **P+N** for a positive and negative opinion.

a) No me gusta nada mi trabajo a tiempo parcial porque no me pagan bien. ....

b) Me gusta trabajar como dependiente, pero no gano mucho dinero. ....

c) Me encanta trabajar en el hotel porque el trabajo es muy variado. ....

d) La oficina en la que trabajo es muy grande y la odio. ....

e) Me encanta mi empleo porque los clientes son amables. ....

[5 marks]

5 Change the following imperative statements using the modal verbs and phrases: **se debe**, **hay que**, **se puede**.

a) ¡No hables en clase!

b) ¡Escucha al profe!

c) ¡No comas chicle!

d) ¡No corras en el pasillo!

e) ¡Lleva uniforme!

f) ¡No lleves maquillaje!

g) ¡No uses el móvil!

h) ¡Haz los deberes!

i) ¡Escribe la fecha!

j) ¡No bebas en clase! [10 marks]

6 Complete the sentences to talk about your future plans for work or study.

a) Voy a ....

b) Me gustaría ....

c) Quisiera ....

d) Tengo la intención de ....

e) Iré ....

f) Cuando termine los exámenes...

g) Vamos a ....

h) Intentaremos ....

i) Espero... [9 marks]

Healthy Living and Lifestyle

1 Write the correct letters A–G to match the images with the correct statements.

A B C

D E F

G

a) **A mí me apetece algo caliente, un café con leche por favor.** ....

b) **Quiero comer algo tradicional, una tortilla española, por favor.** ....

c) **Es Navidad, toma un vaso de vino.** ....

d) **Quisiera algo dulce, un pastel de manzana, por favor.** ....

e) **Quiero algo sano, una naranja, por favor.** ....

f) **Tengo sed. Necesito un vaso de agua.** ....

g) **Tengo hambre. Necesito un bocadillo de jamón con ensalada.** .... [7 marks]

2 Decide which meal (breakfast, lunch or dinner) each person is talking about.

a) **Desayuno cereales con leche.**

b) **Almuerzo en el cole.**

c) **Ceno con mi familia en casa.**

d) **Normalmente como un sándwich de queso en la cantina.**

e) **De vez en cuando tomo pan tostado con una taza de café.**

f) **Cuando estamos de vacaciones tomamos paella o pescado con patatas fritas.**

g) **Los españoles cenan muy tarde.** [7 marks]

3 Choose the correct words from the box below to complete the sentences.

tarjeta	quisiera	mesa	primer plato	carta	yo
bocadillo	menú	camarero	el camarero	segundo plato	un año
postre	cuenta	me gustó	mí	de postre	tarjeta

a) Una _____ para cuatro personas.

b) La _____, por favor.

c) ¿Puedo pagar con _____?

d) _____ una paella de mariscos.

e) De _____, una tarta de helado.

f) Para _____, un vaso de vino. [6 marks]

4 Which of the following is healthy? Tick **one** box.

a) **No evito comer comida rápida.** ☐

b) **Nunca como mucha fruta y verdura.** ☐

c) **Como una dieta con mucha grasa.** ☐

d) **No como muchos caramelos.** ☐ [1 mark]

5 Translate the sentences into Spanish.

a) I follow a balanced diet.

b) I avoid eating fast food.

c) I eat lots of fruit and vegetables.

d) Sometimes I eat sweets.

e) I like to eat desserts.

f) I drink wine twice a week.

g) I eat salad every day.

h) For breakfast I eat a Spanish omelette.

i) For lunch I eat a ham sandwich.

j) I usually drink eight glasses of water a day.

[10 marks]

6 Make these sentences negative.

a) **Siempre como hamburguesas.**

b) **Hago mucho ejercicio.**

c) **Fumo.**

d) **Bebo alcohol.**

e) **Paso mucho tiempo relajándome.**

f) **Suelo seguir una dieta equilibrada.**

g) **La ensalada es buena para la salud.**

h) **Las tartas son muy sanas.** [8 marks]

7 Choose the correct word or phrase to fill each gap.

a) _____ mucha fruta y verduras. (como / bebo / hago)

b) _____ comer paella. (suelo / como / cocino)

c) Nunca _____ mucho alcohol. (beber / tomo / hago)

d) _____ desayunar pan tostado. (desayuno / como / me gusta)

e) Para _____ en forma hago ejercicio. (estar / hacer / ser) [5 marks]

Sport and Sporting Activities

You must be able to:

- Talk and write about sport and sporting activities
- Discuss which sports and activities you used to do
- Compare past and present activities
- Talk about activities you would like to try in the future.

Sport and Sporting Activities

el fútbol	football
Juego al fútbol.	I play football.
el ejercicio	exercise
la natación	swimming
el ciclismo	cycling
Hago ciclismo.	I do / go cycling.
el polideportivo	sports centre
el club de jóvenes	youth club
la montaña	mountain
el parque	park
la piscina	swimming pool
la playa	beach
el estadio	stadium
Voy al estadio.	I go to the stadium.
Voy a la piscina.	I go to the swimming pool.

- To say **what you used to do**, use the **imperfect** tense:
  Cuando era más joven, jugaba al fútbol todos los días.
  When I was younger, I used to play football every day.
  Hacía ciclismo cada fin de semana.
  I used to go cycling every weekend.
- To say **where you used to go**, use the **imperfect** tense:
  Cuando tenía once años, iba a la piscina tres veces por semana.
  When I was 11, I used to go to the swimming pool three times a week.

Opinions

activo (m) / activa (f)	active
Él es activo / Ella es activa	He / She is active
deportivo/a	sporty
Me gusta / No me gusta	I like it / I do not like it
Es…	It is…
divertido	fun(ny)
bueno	good
peligroso	dangerous
difícil	difficult
duro	hard
fácil	easy
emocionante	exciting
popular	popular
el peligro	the danger

Key Verbs

jugar	to play
hacer	to do
ir	to go

Key Point

jugar al + sport = to play a sport – **jugar al fútbol** (to play football)

hacer (no article) + activity = to do an activity – **hacer ciclismo** (to do cycling), **hacer ejercicio** (to do exercise), **hacer natación** (to do swimming)

ir a + place = to go to – **ir al parque** (to go to the park), **ir a la playa** (to go to the beach)

Key Sounds

ñ – **montaña** (mountain), **año** (year), **España** (Spain)
j – **jugar** (to play), **jamás** (never), **jefe** (boss)

Key Verbs

jugaba	I used to play
hacía	I used to do
era	I was
tenía	I had (but 'I was' when talking about your age)
iba	I used to go

el reto	the challenge
la participación	the participation
el éxito	the success
HT **la competencia**	the competition
HT **el riesgo**	the risk
HT **la velocidad**	the speed

Comparing Now and Then

dejar de	to stop	**tener ganas de**	to want to
tener miedo de	to be frightened of	**disfrutar de**	to enjoy
correr	to run	**bailar**	to dance
esperar	to hope to	**probar**	to try
ganar	to win	**participar en**	to take part in
preferir	to prefer	**interesarse en**	to be interested in
llevar	to lead		
HT **herir**	to injure	HT **comenzar a**	to start
HT **practicar**	to practise / do		

Useful Connectives and Phrases

antes	before	**cuando**	when
ahora	now	**pero**	but
hace … años	… years ago	**sin embargo**	however
en este momento	at the moment	**por lo tanto**	therefore
en el pasado	in the past	**aunque**	even if
hoy en día	nowadays	**luego**	then
en el futuro	in the future	**a pesar de**	despite

Antes bailaba todo el tiempo, pero ahora prefiero correr.
Before I used to dance all the time, but now I prefer running / to run.

Hace cinco años tenía miedo al peligro, sin embargo hoy en día me interesan muchísimo los deportes extremos.
Five years ago I was afraid of the danger, however nowadays I'm really interested in extreme sports.

Types of Sports to Try in the Future

los deportes de equipo	team sports
los deportes de invierno	winter sports
los deportes individuales	individual sports

En el futuro, voy a probar otros deportes.
In the future, I'm going to try (out) other sports.

Tengo ganas de practicar los deportes de invierno.
I want to do winter sports.

Me gustaría participar en La Vuelta a España.
I would like to take part in the Tour of Spain.

> ### Key Sound
>
> The word **montaña** (mountain) has three key sounds – **montaña**. Practise saying it out loud until you perfect each syllable. Then try **año** (year), **antes** (before) and **todos los días** (every day).

> ### Key Verbs
>
> | | |
> |---|---|
> | **Tengo ganas de…** | I want to… |
> | **Me gustaría…** | I would like to… |

> ### Quick Test
>
> 1. How do you say 'before', 'now' and 'in the future' in Spanish?
> 2. What is the difference between **juego al fútbol** and **jugaba al fútbol**?
> 3. Translate into English: **Iba al club de jóvenes.**
> 4. Translate into Spanish: I used to go swimming.
> 5. Translate into English: **Me gustaría probar los deportes extremos.**

Music

You must be able to:

- Discuss music and your opinions
- Talk and write about your favourite singer or group.

Music

la música	music
descargar música	to download music
escuchar música	to listen to music
tocar música	to play music
el músico / la música	musician
el piano	piano
el teclado	keyboard
el / la cantante	singer
la canción	song
la música clásica	classical music
la música popular	pop / popular music
la música tradicional	traditional music
el flamenco	flamenco music

Playing and Listening to Music

Sé tocar la guitarra.   I know how to play the guitar.

Me gusta escuchar música sobre todo cuando hago deberes.
I like to listen to music, above all when I'm doing homework.

Lo que más me gusta es la música para relajarme, aunque odio la música clásica.
What I like most is listening to music to relax me, although I hate classical music.

Sobre todo, me gusta la música de Juan Luis Guerra.
Above all, I like the music of Juan Luis Guerra.

A mi modo de ver, Shakira es la reina de la música pop.
In my opinion, Shakira is the queen of pop music.

Mi cantante preferida es Rosalía ya que me interesa la música pop y el flamenco.
My favourite singer is Rosalía since I'm interested in pop music and flamenco.

Mi modelo a seguir es influencer, es artista, es rey de los vídeos en línea.
My role model is an influencer, he's an artist, he's the king of online videos.

El famoso que me encanta graba desde hace una semana un nuevo álbum.
The famous person that I love has been recording a new album for a week.

Mi grupo preferido ha aparecido en un programa de telerrealidad. Fue un concurso de canciones y tenías que votar por el ganador.
My favourite group has recently appeared in a reality TV programme. It was a song contest and you had to vote for the winner.

Key Verb

Tocar is the verb to play an instrument.
Toco el piano.
I play the piano.
Anoche toqué la guitarra.
Last night I played the guitar.

Paso mucho tiempo escuchando a mi grupo preferido.
I spend lots of time listening to my favourite group.

Gasto mucho dinero comprando nueva música.
I spend lots of money buying new music.

Quisiera regalar una nueva canción para promover su nuevo álbum.
He would like to gift a new song to promote his new album.

Agradezco a mi influencer preferido que me haya ayudado a presentarme bien en mis recientes vídeos.
I am thankful to my favourite influencer who has helped me to present myself well in my recent videos.

HT **Mi cantante preferido es J Balvin porque me encanta la música latina.**
My favourite singer is J Balvin because I love Latin music.

HT **¿Sabes tocar un instrumento?**
Do you know how to play an instrument?

HT **Mi influencer favorita cuelga fotos y vídeos en su página web. Publica muchas fotos y vídeos cada día.**
My favourite influencer posts photos and videos on her webpage. She publishes many photos and videos every day.

HT **Shakira ha fundado una fundación caritativa para ayudar a los pobres en su país natal.**
Shakira has founded a charity foundation to help poor people in her country of birth.

HT **Comparto mucha música con mis amigos.**
I share lots of music with my friends.

HT **La semana pasada organizó un concierto caritativo para cobrar dinero para los sintecho.**
Last week she organised a charity concert to collect money for the homeless.

HT **Respeto mucho a los famosos que influyen en la moda en las redes sociales.**
I really respect some of the famous people who influence fashion on social media.

Key Sounds

When there is an accent on a letter then the stress in the word is where the accent lies. Try pronouncing the following words: **canción** (song), **álbum** (album), **organizó** (organised), **página** (page), **música** (music).

Quick Test

1. Translate into Spanish: I love listening to classical music because it relaxes me.
2. Say in Spanish that you know how to play the keyboard.
3. Translate into English: **Los famosos como cantantes e influencers me influyen mucho.**
4. Correct this sentence: **Anoche escuché música clásica en mi amigo's casa.**
5. Choose the correct verbs to complete the sentences:
   a) **(Colgar / Cuelgo / Colgó) fotos en línea.**
   b) **Escucho música cada noche para (relajarme / jugar / escuchar).**
   c) **¿(Saber / Sé / Sabes) tocar un instrumento?**

Film, Cinema and TV

You must be able to:

- Talk and write about TV, film and cinema
- Use comparatives to debate an issue and express an opinion
- Express preferences.

Film and Cinema

en el cine	at the cinema
alquilar	to hire / rent
una estrella de cine	a film star
una película de acción	an action film
una película del oeste	a western
una película de terror	a horror film
una película policíaca	a detective film
una comedia	a comedy
un dibujo animado	a cartoon
una película de aventura	an adventure film
una película romántica / de amor	a romantic film
una película histórica	an historical film
la actuación	the acting / performance
la escena	the scene / stage
la banda sonora	the soundtrack

A mí me gustan las películas de aventura y también las comedias, pero a mi padre le encantan las películas históricas.
I like adventure films and also comedies, but my dad loves historical films.

No me gustan nada las películas del oeste porque me parecen aburridas.
I really don't like westerns because they seem boring to me.

Anoche fui al cine con mis amigos, y vimos una película de James Bond que nos encantó.
Last night I went to the cinema with my friends, and we watched a James Bond film which we loved.

Se trata de un espía que trabaja para el gobierno británico. ¡Fue verdaderamente emocionante!
It was about a spy who works for the British Government. It was really exciting!

Yo prefiero descargar películas de la red y verlas en casa.
I prefer to download films from the Internet and watch them at home.

Para mí, el cine es algo especial sobre todo cuando voy con mis amigos.
For me, the cinema is something special, especially when I go with my friends.

HT **No me gusta ir al cine; prefiero alquilar una película en la red.**
I don't like going to the cinema. I prefer to hire a film from the Internet.

TV

en la tele	on TV
un montón de anuncios	a lot of adverts
una telenovela	a soap opera
un concurso	a quiz show

un espectáculo	a show
las noticias	the news
las series	series
los programas musicales	music programmes

¿Qué ponen en la tele esta noche? What's on TV tonight?

Hay un concurso muy entretenido a las nueve.

There's a very entertaining quiz show on at nine o'clock.

Vale. ¿Viste el documental en la 1? Fue muy informativo e interesante.

OK. Did you see the documentary on Channel 1? It was very informative and interesting.

Esta noche voy a ver mi serie preferida. Es una serie americana y la veré en mi portátil.

This evening I am going to watch my favourite series. It is an American series, and I will watch it on my laptop.

Making Comparisons

más... que...	more... than...
menos... que...	less... than....
mejor que	better than
peor que	worse than
tan... como...	as... as...

- Don't forget adjectives must agree:

  Me gustan las películas de acción porque son más divertidas que los documentales.

  I like action films because they are more fun than documentaries.

  Los dibujos animados son mejores que las telenovelas.

  Cartoons are better than soaps.

  Para mí, el cine es peor que la tele porque es más caro.

  For me, the cinema is worse than the TV because it is more expensive.

  Creo que leer una novela es menos interesante que navegar en Internet.

  I believe that reading a novel is less interesting than surfing the Internet.

- To make comparisons between two things you can use the infinitive:

  En mi opinión, ir al cine es mejor que ver la tele.

  In my opinion, going to the cinema is better than watching TV.

Quick Test

1. Complete the sentences with the correct definite article: **el, la, los, las**
   a) **Me gustan** _____ **comedias.**
   b) **Me encanta** _____ **banda sonora.**
   c) **No me gustan** _____ **documentales.**
   d) **No me interesa** _____ **concurso.**
2. Say in Spanish that you love watching adventure films.
3. Say in Spanish that you prefer watching TV.
4. Translate the following sentence: **Me gustan las telenovelas porque son más entretenidas que los dibujos animados.**
5. Correct the following sentences:
   a) **Me gustan los documentales porque son más informativa que los dibujos animados.** (1)
   b) **No me gusta las telenovelas porque son menos interesante que las películas.** (2)
   c) **Las películas de acción es tan emocionante como las comedia.** (3)

Key Point

Adjectives must agree with the noun they are describing.

el dibujo animado divertido (the funny cartoon), **la serie divertida** (the funny series), **los documentales informativos** (the informative documentaries), **las noticias informativas** (the informative news)

Key Point

When using verbs such as **gustar** (to like), the definite article must also be used:

Me gustan las comedias. (I like comedies.)

Me encanta el canal 2. (I love Channel 2.)

Key Sounds

Sounds '**ca**', '**co**', '**cu**' are all hard 'c' sounds as in 'cat'. Try pronouncing the following words:
casa (house), **concurso** (contest), **comedia** (comedy), **película** (movie), **costa** (coast), **espectáculo** (show)

Sounds '**ce**' and '**ci**' are hard 'th' sounds in the Balearics and mainland Spain but soft 's' sound in the rest of the Spanish speaking world. Try saying the following words:
cinco (five), **escena** (scene), **anuncio** (advert), **policíaca** (detective)

Practice Questions

Free-time Activities

1 Choose the correct form of the verb to complete the following sentences. Circle the correct option.

a) Ayer _____ a los videojuegos.	juego	jugué	jugaré
b) Por la mañana me gusta _____ natación.	hacer	hago	haré
c) Cuando era pequeña _____ mucho al fútbol.	juego	jugar	jugaba
d) Suelo _____ la tele el fin de semana.	ver	veo	veía
e) Mañana voy a _____ de compras en el centro comercial.	ir	voy	iba
f) Después de _____ música, duermo.	escuchar	escucho	escuché
g) _____ en mi dormitorio antes de acostarme.	leer	leo	leí
h) En el pasado _____ la guitarra.	toco	tocaba	tocar
i) Voy a _____ al tenis mañana.	jugar	juego	jugaré
j) Paso mucho tiempo _____ con mis amigos.	charlar	charlo	charlando

[10 marks]

2 Write the correct letters A–E to match the programmes with the descriptions.

A los concursos	C las noticias	E los documentales
B las telenovelas	D las emisiones deportivas	

a) Esta noche veré un partido entre los dos mejores equipos de la liga. _____

b) Se puede ganar un premio de un millón de euros. _____

c) No quiero perderme el capítulo hoy porque mi personaje favorito va a morir. _____

d) Esta noche ponen un programa muy entretenido sobre los tigres en India. _____

e) Tenemos que verlas para saber lo que ha pasado hoy en el mundo. _____

[5 marks]

3 Write the correct letters A–G to match the activities with the descriptions.

A Watching a play   **D** Watching a football match   **F** Reading

B Watching a TV programme   **E** Listening to music   **G** Playing an instrument

C Watching a film

a) **Mi hermana fue al cine la semana pasada.** ....

b) **Hoy voy a ver una telenovela.** ....

c) **Mi equipo preferido juega en rojo.** ....

d) **Prefiero el rock.** ....

e) **Sé tocar la guitarra.** ....

f) **Me encanta leer las revistas y los tebeos.** ....

g) **El espectáculo va a ser fascinante.** ....   [7 marks]

4 Translate the following sentences into English.

a) **Me encanta jugar al fútbol porque es muy divertido.**

b) **Voy a ver un documental esta noche sobre elefantes en África.**

c) **Anoche hice natación en la piscina.**

d) **En el pasado tocaba el piano, pero ahora toco la guitarra.**

e) **Hago windsurf en la playa en verano.**   [5 marks]

5 Translate the following sentences into Spanish.

a) I like to listen to pop music.

b) I hate action films because they are boring.

c) I prefer going to the cinema with my family.

d) Last Sunday I played tennis in the park.

e) I used to play football with my friends.   [5 marks]

Review Questions

Education and Work

1 Translate the following sentences into Spanish.

    a) I don't like science because we have a lot of homework.

    b) I love English although we have to write a lot.

    c) I like Spanish because the teacher is kind and fun.

    d) I hate maths because we have lots of tests. [4 marks]

2 Choose the correct adjective ending for each colour of the uniform items.

    a) Llevo unos pantalones negro / negra / negros / negras.

    b) Tengo que llevar una chaqueta rojo / roja / rojos / rojas.

    c) Los chicos llevan una corbata gris / grises.

    d) Las chicas llevan una camisa blanco / blanca / blancos / blancas.

    e) Todos llevan zapatos marrón / marrónes / marrones. [5 marks]

3 Which of the following sentences does **not** make sense?

    a) Me encanta mi uniforme, porque es muy bonito.

    b) Detesto mi uniforme, ya que es muy incómodo.

    c) No me gusta mi uniforme, dado que es muy cómodo.

    d) Me gusta llevar uniforme, aunque es caro. [1 mark]

4 Complete these sentences using the correct definite article: **el**, **la**, **los**, **las**.

    a) Me gustan .... **ciencias.**   **f) No me gusta nada** .... **teatro.**

    b) Me encanta .... **inglés.**   **g) Me encantan** .... **ciencias.**

    c) Odio .... **historia.**   **h) Me gustan** .... **matemáticas.**

    d) Me gusta .... **educación física.**   **i) Me molesta estudiar** .... **geografía.**

    e) Me interesa .... **español.**   **j) Detesto** .... **religión.** [10 marks]

5 Choose the correct verbs from the box below to fill in the gaps.

| enseñar | aprobar | sacar | repasar | repetir | aprender | hacer |

a) Como tengo exámenes, necesito .... todas las noches.

b) Tengo que .... muchos deberes.

c) Debo .... bien el vocabulario en la clase de español.

d) El profe tiene que .... bien la información.

e) Es necesario .... los exámenes si se quiere ir a la universidad.   [5 marks]

6 Draw lines to match the two sentence halves.

a) En el futuro quiero…   un trabajo.

b) Después de terminar los exámenes…   a casarme.

c) Me gustaría encontrar…   con mis estudios.

d) Intento hacer un…   ir a la universidad.

e) Lo mejor para mí sería continuar…   aprendizaje.

f) Creo que no voy…   quisiera ir al colegio mayor.   [6 marks]

7 Match the description with the correct picture.

a) Doy clases de español en un instituto. Soy…   A

b) Escribo novelas de aventura. Soy…   B

c) Trabajo en una tienda en el centro comercial. Soy…   C

d) Trabajo en aviones sirviendo a la gente. Soy…   D

e) Preparo la comida en un hotel de lujo. Soy…   E   [5 marks]

Customs and Festivals

Quick Recall Quiz

You must be able to:

- Describe festivals
- Describe different traditions and customs.

Festivals

el Día de Muertos	The Day of the Dead
el Día de Reyes	Three King's Day (Epiphany)
la plaza de toros	bullring
los Reyes Magos	The Three Wise Men
la Semana Santa	Easter / Holy Week
la corrida	bullfight
la costumbre	tradition
la Navidad	Christmas
la Nochebuena	Christmas Eve
la Nochevieja	New Year's Eve
la Tomatina	Tomatina (tomato throwing festival)
las doce uvas de la suerte	twelve lucky grapes
la tradición	tradition
mi cumpleaños	my birthday
el desfile	parade / procession
el disfraz	fancy dress costume
el matrimonio	marriage
la boda	wedding
el paso	religious image carried during Holy Week
el traje de luces	suit of lights (worn by a bullfighter)
las Fallas	Valencian tradition of burning papier-mâché models
las tapas	bar snacks / tapas
los Sanfermines	festival in Pamplona involving running with the bulls
celebrar	to celebrate
compartir	to share
participar	to participate
quemar	to burn
HT asistir	to attend
HT los fuegos artificiales	fireworks

Describing Customs and Festivals

Durante la Semana Santa hay un desfile con pasos al aire libre.
During Holy Week there is a parade in the open air with religious images.

En mi casa solemos celebrar la Nochevieja con las doce uvas de la suerte a medianoche.
In my house we usually celebrate New Year's Eve with the twelve lucky grapes at midnight.

Los niños en España reciben los regalos el Día de Reyes, el seis de enero.
Children in Spain receive presents on Three King's Day, the sixth of January.

Los parientes de los difuntos visitan el cementerio el Día de Muertos para decorar las tumbas con flores.
Family members of the deceased visit the cemetery on Day of the Dead to decorate the graves with flowers.

Durante los Sanfermines hay muchas corridas y cada día hay un encierro a las ocho de la mañana.
During the festival of San Fermín there are lots of bullfights and running with the bulls every day at eight o'clock in the morning.

Para celebrar la Nochevieja en España se toman uvas y se bebe champán.
To celebrate New Year's Eve in Spain they eat grapes and drink champagne.

Para celebrar la Nochebuena en España se come en familia.
To celebrate Christmas Eve in Spain they eat as a family.

Durante la Pascua se va a la iglesia, y se ven los desfiles de los pasos.
During Easter they go to church, and they watch the parades with the religious images being carried.

¿Te gustaría ir a los Sanfermines?
Would you like to go to the festival of San Fermín?

Sí, me gustaría ir a la fiesta de San Fermín, porque sería muy emocionante aunque peligroso a mi modo de ver.
Yes, I would like to go to the San Fermín festival, because in my opinion, it would be very exciting, although dangerous.

No se celebra el Día de Muertos en Inglaterra sino Halloween.
They don't celebrate Day of the Dead in England, but Halloween.

La costumbre de cantar villancicos es muy especial y se celebra tanto en España como en Latinoamérica.
The custom of singing Christmas carols is very special and happens in both Spain and Latin America.

Durante la Pascua se pasa mucho tiempo en familia comiendo chocolate y bebiendo.
During Easter they spend lots of time as a family eating chocolate and drinking.

HT **A mí me encantan las Fallas porque me apasionan los fuegos artificiales.**
I love las Fallas because I'm passionate about fireworks.

Key Point

Use the impersonal **se** and the third-person singular form of the verb to mean 'they' in general: **se come** (they eat), **se bebe** (they drink), **se canta** (they sing)

Key Point

The gerund – the 'ing' form of the verb – is made by taking the infinitive ending off the verb and adding either **-ando** or **-iendo**, e.g. **comiendo** (eating), **bebiendo** (drinking), **cantando** (singing), **celebrando** (celebrating). It can be used with the verb **estar** to talk about an action that is taking place, e.g. **Estoy celebrando mi cumpleaños.** I am celebrating my birthday.

Quick Test

1. Change the infinitive verbs into the gerund:
   a) **Estoy comer...** c) **Están cantar...** e) **¿Estás pasar...?**
   b) **Está beber...** d) **Estamos celebrar...**
2. Complete the sentences in **1.** with your own ideas.
3. Choose the correct form of the verbs for each sentence.
   a) **En España se come / comer / comiendo paella.**
   b) **El Día de Muertos decorar / se decoran / decorando las tumbas.**
   c) **Paso mucho tiempo se juega / jugar / jugando con mi familia.**
   d) **Me gustaría se va / ir / yendo a los Sanfermines.**
   e) **Quisiera ver / se ve / viendo las Fallas.**
4. Say in Spanish that you love to celebrate New Year's Eve.
5. Translate into Spanish: We decorate the house.
6. Translate into English: **Mi madre preparó un pastel muy rico.**

Birthday Celebrations

Quick Recall Quiz

Key Sound

You must be able to:

- Describe birthday celebrations including any traditions
- Use the present perfect tense to explain what happened at a birthday celebration.

Birthday Celebrations

¡Enhorabuena!	Congratulations!
el cumpleaños	birthday
un día de alegría	a happy day
una celebración especial	a special celebration
una costumbre tradicional	a traditional custom
una fiesta divertida	a fun party / festival
Recibo regalos.	I get presents.
Como muchos caramelos.	I eat lots of sweets.
Llevamos disfraces.	We wear fancy dress outfits.
Escuchamos música.	We listen to music.
Vemos una película.	We watch a film.
Bailamos.	We dance.
Invito a mis amigos.	I invite my friends.
Lo celebro con un evento tradicional.	I celebrate with a traditional event.
Me parezco a un rey / una reina.	I look like a king / queen.

Para celebrar mi cumpleaños, invito a mis amigos y bailamos y cantamos canciones.

To celebrate my birthday, I invite my friends and we dance and sing songs.

Es una tradición española recibir regalos el día de tu santo y también el día de tu cumpleaños.

It's a Spanish tradition to receive presents on your saint's day and on your birthday too.

Lo pasamos muy bien celebrando mi cumpleaños con una divertida fiesta.

We had a good time celebrating my birthday with a fun party.

Durante la celebración bebo vino, pero no bebo mucho.

During the celebration I drink wine, but I don't drink much.

El año pasado nos vestimos con ropa nueva, y participamos en una fiesta sorpresa.

Last year we wore new clothes, and we attended a surprise party.

Me gustaría cenar, el día de mi cumpleaños, mi plato favorito, paella y pan.

I would like to have for dinner, on the day of my birthday, my favourite meal, paella and bread.

Es muy tradicional dar besos.

It is very traditional to give kisses.

Nunca he compartido mi fiesta con alguien.

I have never shared my party with anyone.

HT **Siempre he asistido a un concierto para festejar.**
I have always been to a concert to celebrate.

HT **Suelo ver fuegos artificiales para celebrar mi día especial.**
I usually watch fireworks to celebrate my special day.

HT **Mis padres me han sorprendido con una fiesta.**
My parents have surprised me with a birthday party.

The Present Perfect Tense

- The present perfect tense in Spanish is formed using the present tense of the verb **haber** and a past participle. It is used to explain what has happened recently.
  Haber: he, has, ha (hay), hemos, habéis, han
- Past participles are formed by removing the infinitive ending from the infinitive verb and then adding the **ado / ido** ending.

He jugado.	I have played.
Hemos comido.	We have eaten.
Han venido.	They have come.

> **Key Sound**
>
> The silent 'h' is never sounded at the beginning of words in Spanish. Try pronouncing the following words: **hay** (there is), **hotel** (hotel), **hijo** (son), **hambre** (hunger), **he hecho** (I've done)

> **Quick Test**
>
> 1. Translate into English:
>   **Para celebrar mi cumpleaños como mi plato favorito, que es una hamburguesa con patatas fritas.**
> 2. Translate into Spanish:
>   I celebrate my birthday with a fun party, and I invite my friends.
> 3. Make the following infinitive verbs into past participles: **celebrar, llevar, recibir, invitar, comer, beber**
> 4. Choose the correct form of the verb for each sentence.
>   a) **Celebré / Celebrar / He celebrado una fiesta el año pasado.**
>   b) **Mi amigo me ha sorprender / sorpresa / sorprendido con una fiesta.**
>   c) **Comer / Como / Comido paella y bebo / beber / bebido vino.**
>   d) **Invito a mis padre / amigos / amigo.**

Describing a Family Event

You must be able to:

- Talk about family events such as wedding celebrations
- Explain what happens on the day of the celebration
- Use the preterite and imperfect tenses to describe events in the past.

Family Events

un evento nacional	a national event
un evento internacional	an international event
la boda	wedding
el traje	suit
el vestido blanco	white dress
las flores	flowers
la celebración	celebration
una comida	a meal
la iglesia	church
las fotos	photos
besar	to kiss
casarse	to get married
costar	to cost
dar	to give
disfrutar	to enjoy
divorciarse	to divorce
enviar	to send
organizar	to organise
gastar	to spend (money)
pasar	to spend (time)
querer	to want
HT asistir	to attend
HT cobrar	to charge (money)
HT expresar	to express

HT **Recientemente asistí a la boda de mi hermana y su novio.**
Recently I attended the wedding of my sister and her husband.

Mi hermana se casó en un vestido blanco y largo. Era muy bonito.
My sister got married in a long, white dress. It was very beautiful.

Su novio llevó un traje muy elegante.
Her husband wore a very elegant suit.

Disfruté el día porque había muchas personas de mi familia allá.
I enjoyed the day because there were a lot of people from my family there.

Fuimos a la iglesia en un coche lujoso y dentro de la iglesia había muchas flores de colores diferentes.
We went to the church in a luxurious car and inside the church there were lots of different coloured flowers.

Había una gran variedad de comida después de la misa, y yo elegí comer paella dado que es mi plato favorito.
There was a great choice of food after the mass, and I chose to eat paella given that it is my favourite meal.

Durante la boda mi hermana tuvo que besar a su novio.
During the wedding my sister had to kiss her husband.
El vestido de mi hermana costó muchísimo; fue muy caro.
My sister's dress cost a lot. It was very expensive.
Antes de la boda, mi hermana organizó muchas cosas: la música, la comida, la ropa y la iglesia.
Before the wedding, my sister organised a lot: the music, the food, the clothes, and the church.
Envió las invitaciones a cada persona y recibió las respuestas.
She sent out invitations to each person and received the replies.
El fotógrafo cobró más de quinientos euros, pero las fotos eran estupendas.
The photographer charged more than five hundred euros, but the photos were amazing.
Mi hermana y su novio gastaron mucho dinero, pero esperan estar juntos para siempre.
My sister and her husband spent lots of money, but they hope to be together forever.

Preterite v Imperfect Tenses

- There is a mnemonic that can be used to decipher when to use the preterite tense and when to use the imperfect tense in Spanish.
- For the preterite tense the mnemonic SIMBA can be used: Single action, Interruption, Main event, Beginning and ending, Arrivals and departures
- For the imperfect tense the mnemonic CHEATED can be used: Characteristics and descriptions, Health, Emotions, Age, Time, Endless actions, Date
- The imperfect tense is one of the simplest tenses to learn in Spanish as there are only three irregular verbs: **ser** (to be), **ir** (to go) and **ver** (to see). The imperfect tense refers to an ongoing activity in the past.
- The preterite tense has more irregular verbs and refers to a specific time in the past.

> ### Quick Test
>
> 1. Choose the correct form of the verb in Spanish.
>   a) **Ayer asistí / asistía a la boda de mi primo y su novia.**
>   b) **En el pasado hubo / había muchas celebraciones y eventos importantes.**
>   c) **Antes costaba / costó menos casarse, pero ahora es muy caro.**
>   d) **El año pasado mi madre se casaba / se casó otra vez con mi padrastro.**
> 2. Translate the phrase into English: **Las flores eran muy hermosas.**
> 3. Translate the phrase into Spanish: My brother's grey suit was very elegant.

Customs, Festivals and Celebrations

1 Match the sentence halves about celebrating Christmas and New Year's Eve in Spain.

a) La cena de Nochebuena en España

b) Esta cena se celebra

c) La Nochevieja se despide del año

d) Se comen las famosas

e) La costumbre de las 12 uvas

i) con fuegos artificiales.

ii) tiene su origen en el año 1909.

iii) en las casas de los españoles junto a toda la familia.

iv) tiene lugar el 24 de diciembre.

v) 12 uvas de la suerte.

[5 marks]

2 Read the following text aloud.

Cada año hay muchos festivales en España. Uno de los más conocidos es La Tomatina. En diciembre tenemos la Navidad. Mucha gente la celebra en familia. Normalmente los jóvenes reciben regalos el Día de Reyes.

[5 marks]

3 Choose the correct question word from the box for each gap.

Cuál	Dónde	Cuándo	Qué

a) ¿................... es tu opinión sobre las fiestas en tu país?

b) ¿................... haces durante las vacaciones de Navidad?

c) ¿................... es tu cumpleaños?

d) ¿................... te gusta pasar tu cumpleaños?

[4 marks]

4 Answer the questions in **3.** in Spanish.

....

....

....

....

[4 marks]

5 Translate the following sentences into English.

a) En Nochevieja siempre tomo las doce uvas a la medianoche en punto.

....

b) El nuevo año empieza con fuegos artificiales y fiestas en la calle.

....

c) Durante los Sanfermines en Pamplona, se permite correr con los toros.

....

d) En Semana Santa tienes que caminar durante horas para ver los desfiles.

....

e) A los turistas les encantan las fiestas españolas.

....

[5 marks]

6 Write the correct letters A–E to match the images with the descriptions.

A

B

C

D

E

a) Es una fiesta divertida, pero ¡tengo que comprar ropa nueva! ....

b) Vivo en Valencia y es una fiesta local. ....

c) Compramos un árbol y muchos regalos. ....

d) Visitamos el cementerio con flores. ....

e) Voy a cumplir dieciséis años. ....

[5 marks]

Review Questions

Free-time Activities

1 Match the sentence halves about free time.

a) **Me gustaría practicar**   i) **pero ahora prefiero nadar.**

b) **Antes hacía ciclismo**   ii) **es más interesante que ver la televisión.**

c) **Siempre escucho música**   iii) **los deportes extremos.**

d) **Leer un libro**   iv) **una película policíaca.**

e) **Fui al cine para ver**   v) **cuando hago mis deberes.** [5 marks]

2 What are these people talking about? Tick the correct box for each sentence.

	Sport and activities	Music	Film and cinema	TV
a) No me gustan las noticias porque son aburridas.				
b) No voy al gimnasio porque soy perezoso.				
c) Voy a ver mi serie preferida con mi familia en casa.				
d) Su nueva canción es triste.				
e) Pienso que ir al cine es muy caro.				
f) Cuando era más joven, jugaba al baloncesto.				

[6 marks]

3 Read the following text aloud.

No tengo mucho tiempo libre. Sin embargo, a veces saco fotos de mi perro en el jardín.
De vez en cuando escucho música en mi dormitorio mientras hago mis deberes.
Me encanta ver la tele o jugar videojuegos con mis amigos. [4 marks]

4 Three friends are making plans. Write the correct verb form in each gap, using the infinitives provided.

Nayara: **¿Chicos, nosotros .... (ir) a la playa el miércoles?**

Luca: **Personalmente, no .... (querer) ir a la playa porque va a .... (hacer) calor. Normalmente .... (preferir) ir al cine.**

Ariana: **Me encanta .... (ver) películas en el cine, pero ahora no .... (tener) mucho dinero, y hay demasiada gente. .... (pensar) que voy a ver la televisión.**

[7 marks]

5 Choose the correct form of the adjective to complete each sentence.

a) En mi opinión, los deportes extremos son muy _____ .   peligroso / peligrosa / peligrosos

b) Hago natación en la piscina, pero es un poco _____ .   pequeño / pequeña / pequeñas

c) Es mi cantante _____ y el rey de la música pop.   preferido / preferida / preferidos

d) Me gustaría escuchar su _____ canción.   nuevo / nueva / nuevas

e) Creo que las películas de aventura son muy _____ .   aburridos / aburrida / aburridas

f) Para mí, ir al cine es demasiado _____ .   caro / cara / caros

g) Los concursos son más _____ que las telenovelas.   divertido / divertidas / divertidos

h) Pienso que las noticias son bastante _____ .   informativo / informativas / informativos

[8 marks]

6 Answer the questions in Spanish. Try to use a maximum of ten words in each answer.

a) ¿Qué deportes haces?

_____

b) Cuándo eras más joven, ¿qué deportes hacías?

_____

c) ¿Qué tipo de música te gusta? ¿Por qué?

_____

d) ¿Sabes tocar un instrumento?

_____

e) ¿Te gusta ir al cine? ¿Por qué (no)?

_____

f) ¿Qué te gusta ver en la televisión? ¿Por qué?

_____

[6 marks]

Celebrities

You must be able to:

- Discuss the lives and lifestyles of celebrities
- Talk and write about their careers and personal life.

Celebrity Lifestyle

la personalidad	celebrity / personality
la estrella	star
famoso	famous / well-known

Hay muchas personalidades en el mundo del cine, del deporte, de la música y de la televisión.
There are lots of celebrities in the world of film, sport, music and TV.

Las estrellas son famosas / tienen una reputación nacional e internacional.
Stars are famous / have a national and international popularity / reputation.

Algunas personalidades son famosas por la telerrealidad.
Some personalities are known because of reality TV (shows).

Son conocidos a causa de los medios.
They are famous because of the media.

Son muy ricos y tienen mucho dinero.
They are very rich and have lots of money.

> **HT Las personalidades llevan una vida muy diferente a la nuestra.**
> Celebrities lead a very different life to our own.

The Media

los medios	the media
el periódico	newspaper
los periódicos	newspapers
HT la prensa	the press

Nos gusta ver sus casas grandes y sus coches rápidos.
We like to see their big houses and their fast cars.

Discutimos su(s) carrera(s) o su(s) vida(s) personales.
We discuss their career(s) or their personal life / lives.

> **HT Seguimos su estilo de vida en los periódicos.**
> We follow their lifestyle in the newspapers.
> **HT Leemos entrevistas en la prensa y en línea.**
> We read interviews in the press and online.
> **HT Nos interesa una manera de vivir diferente.**
> We are interested in a different way of living.

Key Sounds

Single vowel sounds – 'a', 'e', 'i', 'o', 'u' and 'y'. These are very common sounds that you know from very short words: 'a' as in **la**, 'e' as in **el**, 'i' as in **mi**, 'o' as in **son**, 'u' as in **tu**, 'y' as in **y**. Learn a word for each single vowel sound so that you can replicate the sound with all new words you come across.

Key Point

Su / sus translate as 'their' in English. **Su** is used for the singular and **sus** is used for the plural, e.g. **su estilo de vida** (their way of living); **sus casas grandes** (their big houses).

Describing the Career of a Celebrity

la carrera	career
el premio	prize
la gira	tour
HT **el torneo**	tournament
HT **la campaña**	campaign

Siempre he querido ser actor / actriz / cantante.
I always wanted to be an actor / singer.

Como niño / niña jugaba al / hacía…
As a child, I used to play … / used to do …

A la edad de dieciséis años, cantaba en un grupo.
At the age of 16, she / he was singing in a group.

Empecé en 2015 como…   I started in 2015 as…

Su primer equipo / papel / primera canción fue…
His / her first team / role / song was…

Mi último personaje (en la televisión) fue…
My last character (on TV) was…

En su nueva película, es el héroe / es la heroína.
In his / her new film, he is the hero / she is the heroine.

HT **Desde mi infancia…**   Since my childhood…

HT **Siempre ha querido ser deportista profesional.**
She always wanted to be a professional sportsperson.

Ganó un premio / un concurso.   He / she won a prize / a competition.

Ella lanzó su nuevo vídeo / su nueva canción.
She released her new video / her new song.

Hizo una gira europea / mundial.
He / she went on a European / world tour.

Ella lanzó un anuncio.   She launched an advert.

Transmitió su nueva serie.   He / she broadcast his / her new series.

Anunció que se separaba de su pareja.
He / she announced that he / she was separating from his / her partner.

Anunció que se casará el próximo mes.
He / she announced that he / she is going to get married next month.

Vive en Madrid / en España con su pareja / sus hijos.
He / she lives in Madrid / in Spain with his / her partner / children.

Esperamos con interés la próxima película / el próximo capítulo / la próxima temporada.
We await the next film / chapter / season with interest.

HT **Se dice que tendrá un futuro brillante.**
They say that she will have a bright future.

HT **Su marido / su mujer / su familia está muy orgulloso/a.**
His / her husband / wife / family is very proud.

Quick Test

1. Choose the correct word: **su / sus casas; su / sus amigos; su / sus familia**
2. Give the Spanish for: lifestyle; interviews; team; character; competition
3. Translate into English: **Anunció que se separaba de su esposa.**
4. Translate into Spanish: She always wanted to become a singer.

Online Influencers

You must be able to:

- Discuss different types of influencers
- Talk and write about their work
- Express your opinions regarding influencers.

Types of Influencers

los / las influencers	influencers
la moda	fashion
la salud	health
la comida	food
los animales	animals / pets
el deporte	sport
los viajes	travel
la tecnología	technology
los videojuegos	gaming / computer games
HT **el estilo de vida**	lifestyle
HT **la belleza**	beauty

Hay muchos tipos de influencers hoy / en este momento.
There are all sorts of influencers today / at the moment.
Cada vez hay más influencers.
There are more and more influencers.
Hablan de moda / salud. They talk about fashion / health.
HT **Cada vez tienen más influencia.**
    They are having more and more influence.

What Influencers Do

el sitio	website
el blog	blog
un artículo	article
un selfie	selfie
las redes sociales	social media
el seguidor	follower
HT **la influencia**	influence
HT **la tendencia**	tendency

Publican blogs / artículos en línea.	They post blogs / articles online.
Ponen vídeos divertidos en su sitio.	They put funny videos on their site.
Se comunican en las redes sociales.	They communicate on social media.
Dan consejos / su opinión sobre…	
They give advice about / their opinion on…	
Recomiendan ciertos productos.	They recommend certain products.
Pueden tener millones de fans.	They can have millions of fans.
Pueden ganar mucho dinero.	They can earn a lot of money.
HT **Anuncian marcas.**	They advertise brands.

Key Verbs

son	they are / are being
hacen	they do / are doing
van	they go / are going
tienen	they have / are having

Key Point

The phrase **cada vez más** (meaning 'more and more') is very useful when discussing trends. **Cada vez menos** (meaning 'less and less') can be used in a similar way.

Becoming Famous

¿Cómo te hiciste famoso? How did you become famous?

Vio un programa de televisión sobre los influencers.
He / She saw a TV programme about influencers.

Empezó a hacer vídeos. He / She started to make videos.

Decidió publicar blogs en línea. He / She decided to post blogs online.

Sacó fotos y las puso en su sitio.
He / She took photos and put them on his / her site.

Tuvo mucho éxito. He / She was very successful.

Se hizo muy popular. He / She became very popular.

HT Se convirtió en una de las influencers españolas más famosas.
She became one of the most famous Spanish (female) influencers.

Opinions on influencers

seguir to follow

seguido (de) followed (by)

sigo a I follow

Sigo a las influencers en las redes sociales.
I follow influencers on social media.

Leo los artículos. I read articles.

Me encanta leer blogs sobre animales.
I love reading blogs about animals.

Me encanta mirar fotos sobre moda.
I love looking at photos about fashion.

Prefiero influencers que comparten sus experiencias.
I prefer influencers who share their experiences.

A mi modo de ver los influencers son extraordinarios.
In my opinion, influencers are extraordinary.

No me gustan demasiado los vídeos 'divertidos' con niños.
I don't really like 'funny' videos with little children in them.

Los influencers me dan muchas ideas útiles.
Influencers give me lots of useful ideas.

Mi sueño es convertirme en influencer (yo mismo).
My dream is to become an influencer (myself).

Key Sounds

Notice the difference between the **ge** sound and the **gui** sound. Try pronouncing the following words: **geografía** (geography), **seguidor** (follower)

Quick Test

1. How do you say 'more and more' in Spanish?
2. Translate these verbs into Spanish: they are going; they are having; they are doing
3. Translate into English: **Ella ha publicado unos vídeos en línea y se hizo muy popular.**
4. Translate into Spanish: I follow fashion influencers on social media.

Celebrities and Their Role in Society

You must be able to:

- Talk and write about celebrities' contribution to society
- Express opinions on the advantages and disadvantages of being famous
- Discuss your favourite celebrities.

Effects on Society

la identidad	identity	**la diferencia**	difference
la verdad	truth	**bi(sexual)**	bi(sexual)
minusválido	disabled	**transgénero**	trans
hetero	straight / heterosexual		

HT **la diversidad** — diversity
HT **la igualdad** — equality
HT **la libertad** — liberty / freedom

Algunas celebridades hablan fácilmente de su identidad.
Some celebrities talk easily about their identity.

Se habla de sus diferencias y la diversidad en nuestra sociedad.
They talk about differences and diversity in our society.

Las diferencias se aceptan y se da igualdad a todo el mundo.
Differences are accepted and equality is given to everyone.

Se pueden expresar opiniones y empezar la conversación.
You can express opinions and open a conversation.

la salud mental	mental health	**los errores**	mistakes / errors
los fallos	mistakes / errors / faults		

HT **las preocupaciones** — worries

Otras celebridades hablan de sus problemas mentales y las soluciones posibles.
Other celebrities discuss their mental health problems and possible solutions.

Explican sus dificultades y cómo han tenido éxito.
They explain their difficulties and how they have succeeded.

Pueden inspirar a toda generación. They can inspire a generation.

Ha sido una inspiración para los jóvenes / las chicas / los minusválidos.
She has been an inspiration for young people / girls / people with disabilities.

la catástrofe	catastrophe / disaster	**la crisis**	crisis
la amenaza	threat		

HT **el escándalo** — scandal

Personajes famosos completan desafíos para apoyar diversas causas.
Famous people complete challenges to support various causes.

Para mejorar la vida de los demás / el medio ambiente.
To improve the lives of others / the environment.

HT **Para ayudar a las víctimas de violencia / de pobreza / de paro.**
To help victims of violence / poverty / unemployment.

HT **Participan en acciones políticas como manifestaciones o huelgas.**
They participate in political actions such as demonstrations or strikes.

Key Point

To describe the actions of others, use the third-person singular form of the verb with the impersonal pronoun **se** – e.g. **se habla de** (they talk about); **se discute** (they discuss); Where the verb is followed by an object, it should agree in number – e.g. **se expresan opiniones** (they express opinions).

Key Point

Para + the infinitive of the verb is a useful construction to include in your speaking and writing. It means 'to' when you can substitute 'in order to' in English and the sentence still makes sense. For example: **para ayudar a los demás** = in order to help others = to help others.

Advantages and Disadvantages of Being Famous

algunas ventajas	some advantages
Se es rico/a.	You are rich.
Se puede comprar lo que se quiera.	You can buy whatever you like.
Se puede viajar a todas partes.	You can travel everywhere.
Se es poderoso/a.	You are powerful.
El dinero da seguridad.	Money gives (you) security.
HT la riqueza	wealth
algunas desventajas	some disadvantages
Todos los aspectos de su vida son públicos.	
All aspects of your life are public.	
Se pueden recibir amenazas.	You can receive threats.
Se arriesga a escándalos.	You risk scandals.
Se puede perder la popularidad.	You can lose your popularity.
HT La vida nunca es secreta.	Life is never secret.
Es bueno ser famoso porque…	It's good to be famous because…
Por otro lado, no es tan bueno, dado que…	
On the other hand, it's not so good, given that…	
Para mí, el dinero no es tan importante.	
For me, money isn't that important.	

Your Favourite Celebrities

Mi celebridad preferida se llama…	My favourite celebrity is called…
Admiro su carácter / su personalidad / sus habilidades.	
I admire his / her character / personality / abilities.	
Me gustaría conocerlo / conocerla.	I would like to meet him / her.
Me gustaría pasar un día con él / ella.	
I would like to spend a day with him / her.	
Quisiera sacar fotos / selfies.	I would like to take photos / selfies.
Me encantaría ver su barco / su casa / sus hijos.	
I would love to see his / her boat / house / children.	

HT **Se lo / la conoce como artista / deportista.**
He / she is known as an artist / sportsperson.

HT **Si pudiera, iría de vacaciones con él / ella.**
If I could, I would go on holiday with him / her.

HT **Si tuviera la oportunidad, me gustaría ir al estreno de su última película.**
If I had the opportunity, I would like to go to the premiere of his / her new film.

HT **Sería mucho mejor ver la película con todos los actores allí.**
It would be so much better to watch the film with all the actors being there!

Key Sounds

The rolling 'r' and 'rr' sounds in Spanish do not exist in English, so you will need to practise to perfect them! Try pronouncing words beginning with 'r', such as **rico** (rich), **riesgo** (risk), **rápido** (fast). The simple future and conditional tenses of verbs also give a perfect opportunity to roll those 'r's! For example: **habrá** (there will be), **me gustaría** (I would like), **seré** (I will be), **hablaremos** (we will talk). The 'rr' is rolled longer, and it is found in the middle of words such as **perro** (dog), **arroz** (rice), **corregir** (correct).

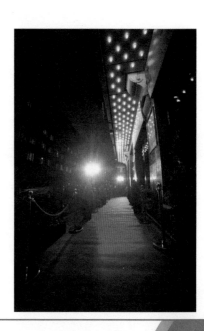

Quick Test

1. What is the Spanish for…? freedom, equality, truth, crisis, threat
2. What do these verbs mean in English: **expresan**; **hablan de**; **discuten**?
3. Translate into Spanish: in order to help; in order to improve; in order to support
4. Translate into English: **Quisiera pasar el día con él y sacar selfies.**

Celebrity Culture

1 Choose the correct word or phrase to complete each sentence.

a) El actor .... 20 años.   tengo / tiene / tenemos

b) La actriz .... española.   es / somos / soy

c) A ella .... tocar la guitarra.   me gusta / le gustan / le gusta

d) A ellos .... ver las películas de acción.   le gusta / les gusta / me gustan

e) Se puede .... a los demás.   ayudo / ayudan / ayudar

f) Ellos .... en un coche de lujo.   llegan / llegar / llega

g) Hace .... tiempo era dependiente.   muy / muchos / mucho

h) Cuando era más joven .... gordo.   fue / era / es

i) ¿Qué .... de la telerrealidad?   opinar / opinión / opinas

j) Vamos a hacer algo para ....   ayudar / ayuda / ayudo

[10 marks]

2 Rearrange the words into the correct order to form sentences about Jaime, a Mexican reality TV star.

a) un ganó concurso de Jaime cocina

b) en viven los una en donde serie selva participó famosos la

c) sabe batería la Jaime descubrí tocar que

d) subió social vi una el vídeo red que a

e) se la de llama Ricardo Jaime pareja   [5 marks]

3 Read the following text aloud.

Pilar Caramelo es una actriz argentina en muchas películas famosas. Es estrella del cine español y también inglés. Es la primera actriz en ganar un Oscar. Pilar habla cuatro idiomas con fluidez. Trabaja por buenas causas y da mucho dinero a obras benéficas.

[5 marks]

4 Choose the correct word from the box below to complete each sentence about celebrities' backgrounds and achievements.

guapas	ser	premios	interés
estudiaba	trabajo	gusta	estaba
gusta	ropa	actriz	tiene

a) Como niña quería ser bailadora y .... ballet.

b) De primer .... fue un vídeo de música pop.

c) Ahora tiene su propia marca de ....

d) Es una de las chicas más .... de Instagram.

e) Llegó a ser .... cuando tenía quince años.

f) Ha ganado muchos ....

g) Es modelo y .... millones de seguidores. [7 marks]

5 Answer the questions in Spanish. Try to use a maximum of ten words in each answer.

a) ¿Qué hacen los influencers?

....

b) ¿Por qué seguir a los influencers?

....

c) ¿Qué opinas de los influencers? ¿Por qué?

....

d) ¿Te gustaría ser influencer? ¿Por qué (no)?

....

e) ¿Quién es tu celebridad preferida? ¿Por qué?

....

f) ¿Cuáles son las ventajas de ser famoso?

....

g) ¿Cuáles son las desventajas de ser famoso?

....

[7 marks]

Review Questions

Customs, Festivals and Celebrations

1 Translate the sentences into English.

a) Para celebrar mi cumpleaños me gusta ir a un restaurante con mi familia.

b) El año pasado celebré mi cumpleaños con mis amigos.

c) Cada año en julio hay un festival de toros en Pamplona.

d) Me gustaría ver la Tomatina en Buñol, Valencia.

e) Siempre he querido participar en los Sanfermines, en Pamplona.

f) Durante la Tomatina se puede lanzar tomates a los amigos.

g) Se disfrazan durante el Día de Muertos en México.

h) La tradición de comer las doce uvas de la suerte a medianoche en Nochevieja
es muy importante para los españoles. [8 marks]

2 Read the following text aloud.

Cada mes hay una fiesta en España. Una de las más conocidas son Los Sanfermines.
En abril tenemos la Pascua. Mucha gente la celebra en familia. Normalmente los
jóvenes reciben huevos de chocolate. [5 marks]

3 Match up the sentence halves.

a) El año pasado

b) Cada año

c) Cuando era joven

d) En el futuro

e) Suelo celebrar

i) hay muchas fiestas en España.

ii) me gustaba participar en los desfiles.

iii) mi cumpleaños con mi familia.

iv) me gustaría participar en la Tomatina.

v) participé en un desfile en el sur de España. [5 marks]

4 Translate the following sentences into Spanish.

a) There are lots of festivals in Spain every year.

....

b) I like to celebrate my birthday with my friends.

....

c) Last year I visited Pamplona during the San Fermin festival.

....

d) In the future if I have money, I would like to visit Mexico to celebrate the Day of the Dead festival.

....

[4 marks]

5 Read the sentences about piñatas and choose the correct word for each gap.

a) La piñata .... **su origen en China.**   tiene / tienes / tengo

b) La piñata se llena con dulces y .... **juguetes.**   pequeño / pequeños / pequeñas

c) Los niños intentan .... **la piñata.**   romper / rompen / rompían

d) La piñata tiene un simbolismo ....   especiales / especial / especiala

e) La piñata puede representar .... **problemas en la vida.**   el / los / las   [5 marks]

6 Complete the sentences in Spanish.

a) Mi fiesta española favorita es ....

b) Me gustaría participar en ....

c) Durante las vacaciones de Pascua, me gusta ....

d) Para celebrar mi cumpleaños, ...

[4 marks]

Travelling Abroad

You must be able to:

- Talk about countries and nationalities
- Give the main details about a holiday
- Discuss types of transport.

Travelling Abroad

las vacaciones culturales	cultural holidays
las vacaciones en el extranjero	foreign holidays
hacer turismo	to visit the sights
Me encanta viajar al extranjero.	I love travelling abroad.
Las vacaciones me hacen feliz.	Holidays make me happy.

Me gustaría dar la vuelta alrededor del mundo.
I would like to go on a round the world trip.

Prefiero las vacaciones culturales porque me encanta visitar sitios interesantes y hacer turismo en verano.
I prefer cultural holidays because I like visiting interesting places and visiting the sights in summer.

Me gustan más las vacaciones en el extranjero con mi familia ya que nos gusta visitar países diferentes.
I prefer holidays abroad with my family because we like to visit different countries.

Nationalities

alemán / alemana	German
británico / británica	British
chino / china	Chinese
europeo / europea	European
francés / francesa	French
inglés / inglesa	English
italiano / italiana	Italian
el idioma	language

- Nationalities, just as for other nouns and adjectives, have both feminine and masculine forms. They do not start with a capital letter.

Es italiano.	He is Italian.
Es italiana.	She is Italian.

- Countries in Spanish are proper nouns and so need a capital letter at the start of the word.

Ella es de Italia.	She is from Italy.

- The language spoken in the country is usually the same as the masculine nationality:

español	Spanish
francés	French
Hablo español e italiano.	I speak Spanish and Italian.

Conozco a un hombre italiano que vive en España y prefiere ir de vacaciones deportivas.
I know an Italian man who lives in Spain and prefers to go on sporting holidays.

The Journey

en bicicleta	by bicycle
la estación	station
el aeropuerto	airport
en autobús	by bus
en avión	by plane
en barco	by boat
a pie	by foot / walking
el billete	ticket
el camino	journey
en coche	by car
el destino	destination
un vuelo directo	a direct flight
la distancia	distance
la llegada	arrival
la salida	departure / exit
barato	cheap
caro	expensive

Suelo viajar en avión porque es rápido, aunque es caro también.
I usually travel by plane because it's quick, although it is expensive too.

Prefiero ir en coche ya que podemos llegar a tiempo.
I prefer to travel by car since we are able to arrive on time.

Vamos a pie y en barco porque es más barato que ir en avión y más práctico que ir en autobús.
We go by foot and by boat because it is cheaper than going by plane and more practical than going by bus.

HT **El único problema es que siempre hay retrasos con los vuelos.**
The only problem is that the flight is always delayed.

Key Sound

'y' when followed by a word beginning with 'i' or 'hi' becomes 'e', e.g.:

Me encanta ir a España e Italia. Adoro las vacaciones culturales e históricas.
I love going to Spain and Italy. I love cultural and historical holidays.

Quick Test

1. Translate into Spanish:
   I usually go on foreign holidays with my family.
2. In Spanish, give an opinion on three modes of transport.
3. How do you say the following languages in Spanish?
   a) Spanish   **b)** French   **c)** English   **d)** Chinese
4. Translate into English:
   Prefiero viajar en tren porque es más barato que ir en avión.

Describing Holidays

You must be able to:

- Describe your holiday activities
- Describe the weather on holiday
- Use verbs in different tenses to discuss holidays.

Quick Recall Quiz

Key Sound

Describing Holidays

las vacaciones de aventura	adventure holidays
las vacaciones de verano	summer holidays
la excursión	trip / excursion
el recuerdo	souvenir
la maleta	suitcase
la mochila	rucksack
el espectáculo	show
el extranjero	abroad
el parque acuático	water park
el alojamiento	accommodation
HT **la exposición**	exhibition
HT **la arena**	sand

El año pasado fui de vacaciones a España, y lo pasé bien, yendo a la playa, disfrutando de las temperaturas altas. Fuimos a una corrida, pero no me gustó nada el espectáculo. Es una costumbre anticuada en mi opinión.
Last year I went on holiday to Spain, and I had a good time, going to the beach, enjoying the high temperatures. We went to a bullfight, but I really didn't like the show. It is an outdated custom in my opinion.

Barcelona es conocida como la capital de arte en España, y estoy de acuerdo porque he visitado muchas exposiciones de arte allí. Es una ciudad famosa, histórica y muy hermosa.
Barcelona is known as the capital of art in Spain, and I agree because I have visited lots of exhibitions there. It is a famous, historic, and very beautiful city.

Hace tres años, viajamos a los EE.UU. donde hicimos turismo; saqué muchas fotos, pero perdí mi pasaporte y mi cámara. Además, el hotel fue un desastre; fueron unas vacaciones horrorosas. También, el viaje duró unas diez horas en total. ¡Qué pena!
Three years ago, we travelled to the US where we visited the sights; I took lots of photos, but I lost my passport and my camera. In addition, the hotel was a disaster; it was a dreadful holiday. Also, the journey lasted ten hours in total. What a shame!

Cuando era joven, iba de vacaciones de verano con mis abuelos al País de Gales; jugábamos en la playa y nadábamos en la piscina.
When I was young, I used to go on summer holidays with my grandparents to Wales; we used to play on the beach and we used to swim in the pool.

En el futuro me gustaría visitar Australia. Siempre he querido ir a Sídney. Quiero visitar los monumentos y lo voy a pasar bien porque hará mucho sol.
In the future I would like to visit Australia. I have always wanted to go to Sydney. I want to visit the sights and I'm going to have a good time because it will be very sunny.

Key Point

Use imperfect for actions that were repeated or continuous without a beginning or end. Use preterite for actions that had a beginning and end or had a specific time when they happened.

Imperfect: **en el pasado** (in the past), **cuando era joven** (when I was young) Preterite: **ayer** (yesterday), **hace dos años** (two years ago)

Key Point

When using different tenses, signal to the examiner that you know you are using different tenses by using different time phrases.

Present: **normalmente** (normally), **en general** (in general)
Past tense preterite: **el año pasado** (last year), **hace dos años** (two years ago)
Past tense imperfect: **en el pasado** (in the past), **cuando era joven** (when I was young)
Past tense perfect: **recientemente** (recently)
Future tense: **en el futuro** (in the future), **el año próximo** (next year)

Holiday Weather

el tiempo	weather	**hace fresco**	it's cool
hace frío	it's cold	**llueve**	it rains / it's raining
hace calor	it's hot	**hace sol**	it's sunny
hace viento	it's windy		

En verano, cuando hace sol, me gusta tomar el sol en la playa.
In summer, when it's sunny, I like to sunbathe on the beach.

En primavera, llueve mucho, y me encanta dar un paseo; lo paso muy bien.
In spring, it rains a lot and I love to go for a walk; I have a great time.

En otoño, cuando hace fresco, disfruto de ir al bosque para caminar.
In autumn, when it's cool, I enjoy going to the woods to walk.

En invierno, cuando hace frío, no me gusta nada salir de la casa.
In winter, when it's cold, I really don't like leaving the house.

Todos los días hacía calor, pero el sábado hizo frío y llovió mucho.
It was hot every day, but on Saturday it was cold and it rained a lot.

Useful Verbs

beber	to drink	**coger**	to catch (transport)
comer	to eat	**comprar**	to buy
descansar	to relax	**nadar**	to swim
reservar	to reserve	**viajar**	to travel
visitar	to visit		
HT **alquilar**	to rent / hire	HT **divertirse**	to enjoy oneself
HT **merecer**	to be worthwhile	HT **quejarse**	to complain

Cojo el tren para ir a Madrid. — I catch the train to Madrid.

Me divierto en las playas en España.
I enjoy myself on the beaches in Spain.

Compro recuerdos para mis amigos. — I buy souvenirs for my friends.

Comí paella y bebí sangría. — I ate paella and I drank sangria.

Quisiera pasarlo bien. — I would like to have a good time.

HT **Merece la pena visitar Barcelona.**
It is worthwhile visiting Barcelona.

HT **Me quejé de la habitación porque estaba sucia.**
I complained because the room was dirty.

HT **Quiero alquilar una bicicleta para hacer un recorrido de la ciudad.**
I want to hire a bicycle to do a tour of the city.

Key Sound

'qu' is a 'k' sound. Try pronouncing the following words: **quisiera** (I'd like), **¿qué?** (what?), **queso** (cheese), **porque** (because)

National and International Holidays

Quick Recall Quiz

Key Sounds

You must be able to:

- Use idioms when discussing holidays
- Talk about needs and problems when staying abroad
- Discuss reasons for going abroad.

Holidays

un vuelo directo	a direct flight	**el retraso**	delay
la maleta	suitcase	**el alojamiento**	accommodation
el paisaje	scenery	**el recuerdo**	souvenir
el camping	campsite		

HT **la frontera**		border
HT **el hotel de lujo**		luxury hotel
HT **la arena**		sand

Idioms

- In Spanish, idioms are more in use in general daily conversation than in English. Understanding idioms is important because they require a deeper familiarity of the language we are speaking. Idioms may seem complicated at first, but they can actually be a lot of fun to learn.

No hay color.	There is no comparison.
Es la leche.	It's the GOAT / the best.
Tirar la casa por la ventana.	To throw money away.
Tener más lana que un borrego.	To be loaded. / To have lots of money.
Es pan comido.	It's a piece of cake.
Hacer un frío que pela.	To be freezing.
Echarle leña al fuego.	To make matters worse.

Opinions about Holidays

Prefiero pasar las vacaciones en el extranjero. Es la leche.
I prefer to spend the holidays abroad. It's the GOAT / the best.

Pienso que comprar recuerdos es como tirar la casa por la ventana.
I think that buying souvenirs is like throwing money away.

Me encantaría alojarme en un hotel de lujo, pero hay que tener más lana que un borrego para quedarse en un hotel de cinco estrellas.
I would love to stay in a luxury hotel but you need to be loaded to stay in a five-star hotel.

Hacer camping es pan comido. Camping is a piece of cake.

Me gustan más los vuelos directos que los vuelos con muchas escalas.
I prefer direct flights to flights with lots of stopovers.

En lugar de volar a sitios exóticos suelo pasar las vacaciones en casa.
Instead of flying to exotic locations, I usually spend the holidays at home.

Las vacaciones en casa son mejores que unas vacaciones caras en el extranjero.
Staycations (holidays at home) are better than expensive holidays abroad.

Me encanta visitar sitios donde se puede caminar sobre la arena y descansar.
I love visiting places where you can walk on the sand and relax.

El avión está retrasado.   The plane is delayed.

Cuando era joven me gustaba pasar las vacaciones en el país de Gales, pero ahora prefiero pasar las vacaciones con mis amigos en el extranjero.
When I was younger I used to like to spend holidays in Wales, but now I prefer to spend holidays with my friends abroad.

Siempre cuando hago camping hace un frío que pela porque en Inglaterra nunca hace calor y para echarle leña al fuego mis padres no quieren nunca quedarse en un hotel o un apartamento.
It's always freezing when I go camping because it's never hot in England, and to make matters worse my parents never want to stay in a hotel or apartment.

Toda mi vida he querido ir de vacaciones al extranjero, pero para echarle leña al fuego, mis padres solo quieren pasar las vacaciones en casa o haciendo camping.
All my life I have wanted to go abroad on holiday but to make matters worse my parents only want to spend the holidays at home or go camping.

HT **Para pasar la frontera y entrar en otro país, es necesario tener un pasaporte.**
To cross the border and enter another country you need a passport.

HT **Hace dos años fui de vacaciones y fueron unas vacaciones de pesadilla, tuve un retraso del vuelo y perdí mi maleta en el aeropuerto.**
Two years ago I went on holiday and it was a nightmare holiday, I had a delay and I lost my suitcase in the airport.

HT **En cuanto al alojamiento me gusta más algo barato como hacer camping en vez de alojarme en un hotel de lujo o un parador.**
With regards to accommodation I prefer something cheap like camping instead of a luxury hotel or a *parador* (a Spanish state-run hotel, usually in an artistic or historic monument).

HT **Si tuviera la oportunidad, me gustaría pasar las vacaciones en el extranjero. Sería la leche.**
If I had the opportunity, I would like to spend the holidays abroad. It would be the GOAT / the best.

HT **Haría un frío que pela si pasara las vacaciones en Inglaterra en vez de ir al extranjero.**
It would be freezing cold if I spent my holidays in England instead of going abroad.

HT **Cuando sea mayor, me gustaría pasar las vacaciones en el extranjero.**
When I am older, I would like to spend the holidays abroad.

HT **Si pudiera, me gustaría trabajar como voluntario durante las vacaciones.**
If I could, I would like to work as a volunteer during the holidays.

Key Sounds

The **ch** sound in Spanish is like the 'ch' sound in the English word 'church'. Try pronouncing the words **churros** (churros), **fecha** (date), **techo** (ceiling).
The **ll** sound in Spanish is like the 'y' sound in the English word 'year'. Try pronouncing the words **llave** (key), **me llamo** (I am called), **se llama** (he / she is called), **calle** (street)

Quick Test

1. What is the Spanish for…? sand, accommodation, souvenir, flight, scenery
2. What do these verbs mean in English: **volar**; **quedarse**; **comprar**?

Practice Questions

Travel and Tourism

1 Write each word in the correct category.

el espectáculo	el sol	el aeropuerto	la carne
en coche	ir de compras	el calor	nadar
el museo	hace fresco	el vino	un vuelo directo
las patatas fritas	el avión	llueve	la cena

Transport	Activities	Weather	Food and drink

[16 marks]

2 Write the correct first-person singular (**yo**) verb forms of the infinitive provided.

a) **Normalmente** .... **a España, pero el año pasado** .... **a Francia y el año que viene** .... **a Chile. (ir)**

b) **En general** .... **mucha fruta, pero ayer** .... **paella y esta noche** .... **pescado. (comer)**

c) **Ahora** .... **agua, pero esta mañana** .... **un café y más tarde** .... **vino. (beber)**

[9 marks]

3 Write the correct third-person singular verb forms of the infinitive provided.

En mi país .... **fresco, pero la semana pasada** .... **calor y la semana que viene** .... **sol. (hacer)**

[3 marks]

4 Read the sentences. Write **P** for a positive experience, **N** for a negative experience or **P+N** for a positive and negative experience.

a) **Fui de vacaciones con mi familia y perdimos las maletas y las mochilas.** ....

b) **El paisaje era bonito y compré unos recuerdos interesantes.** ....

c) **La paella era deliciosa pero el restaurante estaba sucio.** ....

d) **Me gusta el arte español y me gustó mucho ir al museo.** ....

e) **No merece la pena visitar la playa porque hace mucho viento.** .... [5 marks]

5 Match to make phrases.

a) tomar   i) en el extranjero

b) dar   ii) turismo

c) hacer   iii) un billete

d) viajar   iv) el sol

e) organizar   v) un paseo

f) comprar   vi) una excursión   [6 marks]

6 Write a sentence of your own for each noun/verb phrase above. Remember to conjugate the verbs correctly.

a) ....

b) ....

c) ....

d) ....

e) ....

f) ....

[6 marks]

7 Write your own answers to the questions in Spanish. Try to use a maximum of ten words in each answer.

a) **¿Adónde vas de vacaciones normalmente?** ....

b) **¿Qué tipo de vacaciones te gusta?** ....

c) **¿Qué tipo de vacaciones no te gusta?** ....

d) **¿Qué haces normalmente cuando estás de vacaciones?** ....

....

e) **¿Por qué las vacaciones son importantes?** ....

f) **¿Adónde te gustaría ir de vacaciones?** ....

g) **¿Qué hiciste durante las vacaciones de verano el año pasado?** ....

....

h) **¿Qué vas a hacer durante las vacaciones de verano el año que viene?**

....

[8 marks]

Celebrity Culture

1 Match up to make phrases.

a)	ganar	i)	vídeos
b)	leer	ii)	experiencias
c)	compartir	iii)	selfies
d)	subir	iv)	dinero
e)	escribir	v)	entrevistas
f)	sacar	vi)	artículos

[6 marks]

2 Read the following text aloud.

**En México, hay muchos famosos. A unas personas les gusta ver vídeos graciosos.
Otras son seguidoras de jugadores de tenis. Vemos a gente famosa en la televisión.
La mayoría gana mucho dinero.**

[5 marks]

3 Read the sentences. Write **P** for a positive opinion, **N** for a negative opinion or **P+N** for a positive and negative opinion.

a) **La vida de una celebridad nunca es secreta.** ....

b) **Los influencers dan consejos útiles.** ....

c) **Muchos famosos ayudan a los demás, sin embargo, algunos no quieren.** ....

d) **Las celebridades pueden inspirar a los jóvenes.** .... [4 marks]

4 Translate the following sentences into English.

a) **Las redes sociales tienen una gran influencia en los niños.**

b) **A muchos jóvenes les gusta imitar a los famosos.**

c) **Es mejor tener un modelo a seguir que conoces personalmente.**

d) **Deberíamos identificar a personas que han hecho algo impresionante.**

e) **Todos cometemos errores, incluso las personas famosas.** [5 marks]

5 Translate the following sentences into Spanish.

a) I would like to be rich and famous.

b) He won a prize for his first film.

c) I follow some influencers who talk about sport and health.

d) In future I will become an influencer.

e) Celebrities have lots of money, but their lives are not easy.

f) She is trans and her identity is very important.   [6 marks]

6 Complete the sentences in Spanish. Try to use a maximum of ten words in each answer.

a) Mi famoso preferido se llama

....

b) Mi famoso preferido se conoce como

....

c) Sigo a los influencers que

....

d) No me gustan los influencers que

....

e) Un buen modelo a seguir es

....

f) Es bueno ser famoso porque

....

g) No es bueno ser famoso porque

....

[7 marks]

Media and Technology

Quick Recall Quiz

Key Sounds

You must be able to:

- Say how you use different forms of media
- Say how you use different forms of technology
- Compare media and technology now and in the past.

Different Forms of Media

el artículo	article
el Internet	the internet
los medios de comunicación	media
el sitio web	website
la tele / la televisión	TV / television
buscar	to look for / to search
grabar	to record
HT **el blog**	blog
HT **el diario**	newspaper / diary / journal
HT **digital**	digital
HT **la prensa**	the press
HT **la radio**	radio
HT **navegar**	to surf / to browse

Ayer leí un artículo interesante. I read an interesting article yesterday.

A veces grabo mis programas favoritos.

I sometimes record my favourite programmes.

HT **Nunca escucho la radio.** I never listen to the radio.

HT **Navego por Internet durante horas.**

I surf the internet for hours on end.

Technology

la aplicación	app
la cámara	camera
el móvil	mobile phone
el ordenador	computer
la pantalla	screen
la tableta	tablet
el teclado	keyboard
el teléfono	phone / telephone
funcionar	to function / to work
llamar	to call / to phone
romper	to break
HT **el dispositivo**	device / gadget
HT **el emoticón**	emoji
HT **el portátil**	laptop
HT **fabricar**	to manufacture

Uso mi móvil para hacer mis deberes. I use my mobile to do my homework.

Siempre saco fotos con mi cámara. I always take photos with my camera.

Mi televisión tiene una pantalla muy grande.

My TV has a really big screen.

Key Sounds

Accents affect pronunciation – if you see an accent, this is where you stress (place emphasis on) the word. Try pronouncing the following words with the correct stress: **artículo** (article), **televisión** (TV), **cámara** (camera), **tecnología** (technology), **rápido** (quick / fast).

Mi hermano rompió su tableta. My brother broke his tablet.

HT **Tengo un portátil pero es viejo y lento.**
I have a laptop but it is old and slow.

HT **La empresa fabrica muchos dispositivos.**
The company makes a lot of devices.

Old v New Media and Technology

el anuncio	advert
la tecnología	technology
rápido	quick / fast
HT **la generación**	generation
HT **la memoria**	memory

Key Verbs	
tenía(n)	used to have / had
era(n)	used to be / were
(no) había	there was / were (no)

Los medios de comunicación han cambiado mucho en los últimos 25 años.
Media has changed a lot in the last 25 years.

Los móviles son más pequeños y rápidos y tienen más funciones.
Phones are smaller and faster and they have more functions.

La tecnología es más importante para los jóvenes.
Technology is more important for young people.

No había móviles – mis padres tenían que llamar por teléfono.
There were no mobiles – my parents had to call by telephone.

HT **Las televisiones son más grandes y hay un montón de canales.**
TVs are bigger and there are lots of channels.

HT **Los ordenadores tenían poca memoria.**
Computers didn't have much memory.

Quick Test

1. How do you say in Spanish…?: the press, keyboard, advert
2. Translate these verbs into Spanish: they used to have; it used to be; there were no
3. Translate into English: **Leo un diario online cada día.**
4. Translate into Spanish: It is easier to take photos with a mobile phone.

Quick Recall Quiz

Social Media

You must be able to:

- Explain how technology and social media are used
- Discuss the positives and negatives of social media.

Technology

bajar	to download
comunicar	to communicate
enviar	to send
funcionar	to work
grabar	to record
guardar	to save
mandar	to send
recibir	to receive
subir	to upload
HT **cargar**	to charge (e.g. phone)
HT **colgar**	to post
HT **conectar**	to connect
HT **navegar**	to surf
HT **publicar**	to publish

Suelo usar las redes sociales cada día para conectarme con mis amigos que viven en España.
I usually use social media every day to connect with my friends who live in Spain.

Generalmente paso tres horas navegando la Red cada noche.
Generally, I spend three hours surfing the net every night.

Prefiero usar mi consola X-Box para jugar videojuegos.
I prefer to use my X-Box console to play video games.

En vez de escribir cartas tradicionales, suelo escribir y mandar correos electrónicos.
Instead of writing traditional letters, I usually write and send emails.

HT **A mí me encanta bajar y publicar fotos con mi portátil.**
I love to upload and publish my photos with my laptop.

Mobile Phones

Mando mensajes a mis amigos.
I send messages to my friends.

Saco fotos y las publico en mi página web.
I take photos and publish them on my webpage.

Navego por Internet con mi móvil.
I surf the Internet with my mobile.

Uso mi móvil en el autobús llegando al colegio para escuchar música.
I use my mobile on the bus on the way to school to listen to music.

Para mí, mi móvil es un dispositivo práctico; lo uso para todo.
For me, my mobile is a practical device; I use it for everything.

Social Media

Me encanta usar las redes sociales como Instagram y Snapchat.
I love using social media like Instagram and Snapchat.

Suelo colgar mis fotos para mandarlas a mis amigos en otros países.
I usually post my photos to send them to my friends in other countries.

Anoche publiqué unas fotos de mi cumpleaños.
Last night I published some photos of my birthday.

Las redes sociales son útiles para buscar información.
Social media is useful to search for information.

Las redes sociales nos informan de lo que pasa en nuestro barrio.
Social media informs us of what is happening in our neighbourhood.

Revise

Key Point

When talking about a brand name, for example PlayStation, the name of the brand stays the same. The same goes for social network sites such as Instagram and TikTok.

Positives and Negatives of Social Media

Las redes sociales nos ayudan a conectar con los otros.
Social media helps us connect with others.

Las redes sociales nos educan.
Social media educates us.

Las redes sociales ayudan a las compañías a ganar nuevos clientes.
Social media helps companies to gain new clients.

La tecnología y las redes sociales pueden ser muy adictivas, y pueden causar problemas de sueño y concentración.
Technology and social media can be very addictive, and they can cause sleep and concentration problems.

He bajado muchas aplicaciones diferentes porque son útiles.
I have downloaded lots of different apps because they are useful.

HT **Publicar tu número de teléfono en redes sociales puede ser peligroso.**
Publishing your telephone number on social media can be dangerous.

HT **El ciberacoso es un problema grave actualmente.**
Cyberbullying is a serious problem now.

HT **Aunque disfruto las redes sociales, temo los comentarios de mis publicaciones.**
Although I enjoy social media, I fear the comments on my posts.

Quick Test

1. Translate into Spanish:
   I spend two hours surfing the net on my mobile every day.
2. What is the Spanish for...?   email   social media
3. Say in Spanish that you use your laptop to do your homework.
4. Translate into English:
   Suelo colgar fotos en las redes sociales cada día.

Social Media Influencers

You must be able to:

- Discuss social media influencers and how they became famous
- Give opinions about social media influencers.

Influencers

el / la influencer	influencer
gay	gay
heterosexual	heterosexual
bisexual	bisexual
transgénero	transgender
conocido	well-known
soltero	single
casado	married
divorciado	divorced
la marca	brand
telerrealidad	reality TV
la compra / las compras	shopping
HT **el aficionado**	fan
HT **desconocido**	unknown

Aunque no es la mejor influencer de España, me encanta Rosalía.
Although she is not the best influencer in Spain, I love Rosalía.
Rosalía es cantante, influencer, y actriz y es heterosexual.
Rosalía is a singer, influencer, and actress and is heterosexual.
Estaba prometida pero ahora está soltera.
She was engaged but is now single.
Jedet es el influencer transgénero más popular de España; trabaja para promover los derechos de toda la gente transgénera de España.
Jedet is the most popular transgender influencer in Spain; she works to promote the rights of all transgender people in Spain.
Georgina Rodríguez es la influencer más conocida de España. Es de origen argentino y nació en Buenos Aires, pero vivió toda su vida en el norte de España. Es modelo y empresaria y conoció a su pareja actual, Cristiano Ronaldo, en una tienda en Madrid.
Georgina Rodriguez is the most well-known influencer in Spain. She is of Argentinian origin and was born in Buenos Aires, but she lived her whole life in the north of Spain. She is a model and businesswoman and met her current partner, Cristiano Ronaldo, in a shop in Madrid.
En 2018 se convirtió en la española más seguida de la red social Instagram, con la que comenzó su nueva carrera como influencer. Tiene más de 35 millones de seguidores.
In 2018 she became the most followed Spanish person on the social media platform Instagram, which began her career as an influencer. She has more than 35 million followers.

Key Point

The verb **estar** is used to describe the state of a relationship in Spanish: single, engaged, married or divorced.

Key Point

Ser is used to describe sexuality in Spanish: **hetero** (heterosexual), **bi** (bisexual), **trans** (transgender).

Key Point

When describing what job someone does you do not need to use the article in Spanish.

Soy modelo.
I am a model.

Es embajadora de Save the Children y utiliza su influencia sensibilizar sobre los niños que viven en pobreza y también ha donado fondos a otras organizaciones benéficas.

She is an ambassador for Save the Children and uses her influence to raise awareness for children living in poverty, and she has also donated money to other charity organisations.

Usa las redes sociales para promover información y conciencia sobre la situación difícil de los niños necesitados.

She uses social media to promote information about and raise awareness of the difficult situation of children in need.

Ha trabajado para las marcas Gucci, Prada y Chanel.

She has worked for brands such as Gucci, Prada and Chanel.

Influye lo que pensamos que queremos comprar.

She influences what we think we want to buy.

Mucha gente quiere copiar su estilo de vida porque tiene mucha influencia.

Lots of people want to copy her lifestyle because she has lots of influence.

Opinions

En mi opinión…	In my opinion…
Diría que…	I would say that…
Para mí…	For me…
Creo que…	I think that…
Pienso que…	I think that…
Prefiero…	I prefer…

> **Key Point**
>
> Brand names do not change in Spanish.

> **Key Point**
>
> Try to vary your opinion phrases to make your speaking and writing more interesting.

> **Quick Test**
>
> 1. Translate into English: **Soy cantante, modelo e influencer.**
> 2. Choose the correct form of **ser** or **estar** to complete the sentences.
>   a) _____ divorciado.
>   b) _____ jugador de videojuegos.
>   c) _____ bisexual.
>   d) _____ prometida.
> 3. Translate into Spanish: They were married, but now they are single.
> 4. Describe your favourite influencer in Spanish.

> **Key Sounds**
>
> Spanish vowels are pronounced like:
>
> 'a' like in 'father', 'e' like in 'ten', 'i' like 'ee' in 'see', 'o' like 'o' in 'bottle', 'u' like 'oo' in 'soon'. Try pronouncing these words: **el gato** (the cat), **el elefante** (the elephant), **el ídolo** (the idol), **junto** (together).

Practice Questions

Media and Technology

1 Translate the key verbs into Spanish by completing the gaps.

  a) to upload = **s** _ _ _ _

  b) to download = **b** _ _ _ _

  c) to share = **c** _ _ _ _ _ _ _ _

  d) to send = **m** _ _ _ _ _

  e) to send = **e** _ _ _ _ _

  f) to communicate = **c** _ _ _ _ _ _ _ _

  g) to surf (the internet) = **n** _ _ _ _ _ _

  h) to look for = **b** _ _ _ _ _

[8 marks]

2 Read these people's experiences of technology. Write **P** for a positive experience, **N** for negative or **P+N** for positive and negative.

  a) El año pasado mi amigo sufrió ciberacoso. ....

  b) La tecnología siempre me ayuda con mis deberes. ....

  c) Me encanta charlar con mis amigos, sin embargo es adictivo. ....

  d) Es útil leer las noticias online para descubrir lo que pasa en todo el mundo. ....

  e) Alguien me robó los datos personales, por ejemplo, mi contraseña. ....

[5 marks]

3 Match the sentence halves about media and technology.

  a) Me encanta conectarme

  b) Normalmente uso mi móvil

  c) No me interesan las redes sociales

  d) Mi portátil no funciona

  e) En el pasado tenía

  i) para escuchar música.

  ii) porque lo he roto.

  iii) con mis amigos que viven en el extranjero.

  iv) un ordenador muy grande.

  v) porque son adictivas. [5 marks]

4 Read the following text aloud.

Los influencers utilizan su influencia en las redes sociales para promover productos y ganar dinero. Los más conocidos tienen millones de seguidores y por lo tanto trabajan con marcas muy famosas. Mucha gente quiere copiar sus vidas.

[3 marks]

5 Choose the correct form of the verb to complete each sentence.

a) _____ mi móvil y mi portátil cada día.   uso / usas / usan

b) Mis abuelos me _____ correos electrónicos.   envía / enviamos / envían

c) Necesitamos más espacios _____   verde / verdes / verdos

d) Creo que _____ el mejor influencer de España.   están / es / son

e) Los famosos _____ mucha influencia online.   tiene / tienen / tenemos

f) La tecnología ha _____ mucho durante mi vida.   cambiando / cambiaba / cambiado

g) Me gusta _____ los artículos en este sitio web.   leo / leyendo / leer

h) Cuando era joven, no _____ tableta.   tenía / tenías / tenían

[8 marks]

6 Answer the questions in Spanish. Try to use a maximum of 10 words in each answer.

a) ¿Cómo usas tu móvil?

_____

b) ¿Cómo usas la tecnología?

_____

c) ¿Qué hiciste online ayer?

_____

d) ¿Cuántas veces por semana usas las redes sociales?

_____

e) ¿Qué opinas de las redes sociales?

_____

f) ¿Cuáles son las ventajas de las redes sociales?

_____

[6 marks]

Review Questions

Travel and Tourism

1 Match the sentences with the correct topic.

A accommodation   **C** sightseeing   **E** complaints

B weather   **D** languages   **F** staycations

a) **Es importante hablar y comunicarse con todo el mundo.** ....

b) **Me gusta ir de vacaciones en verano porque hace calor.** ....

c) **La habitación está sucia y la comida está fría.** ....

d) **Me gustaría alojarme en un hotel de cinco estrellas.** ....

e) **No me gusta volar pues normalmente paso las vacaciones en casa.** ....

f) **Mañana voy a visitar todos los lugares de interés cultural.** .... [6 marks]

2 Choose the correct words from the box below to complete each sentence.

tiempo	muchas	hacer	histórica
famosa	espectáculo	exposición	maleta
extranjero	hace	barco	interesantes

a) **Viajar en** .... **es más interesante que viajar en avión.**

b) **Es importante llegar al aeropuerto a** ....**.**

c) **No tengo una** .... **pero tengo una mochila.**

d) **Es una ciudad** .... **y por lo tanto hay muchos turistas.**

e) **Siempre saco** .... **fotos de los sitios históricos.**

f) **Me gustaría visitar la** .... **de arte en el museo.**

g) **A mis padres no les gusta** .... **camping.**

h) **Normalmente doy un paseo cuando** .... **sol.** [8 marks]

3 Rearrange the words into the correct order to form sentences.

a) viajar   rápido   prefiero   en   avión   porque   es

b) el   países   diferentes   todo   visitar   gusta   en   mundo   me

c) playa   cuando   descanso   hace   sol   la   en

d) futuro   en   España   a   ir   me   gustaría   el

e) mi   camping   es   con   barato   familia   hago   porque

f) recuerdos   para   amigos   siempre   compro   mis   [6 marks]

4 Write sentences in Spanish giving your opinion about and comparing each set of words.

a) **el avión / el tren** ....

b) **un museo / la playa** ....

c) **un camping / un hotel** ....

d) **el sol / la lluvia** .... [4 marks]

5 Translate the following sentences into English.

a) **Hace dos años fui a Francia con mis amigos.**

b) **El año que viene me gustaría visitar a mi abuelo italiano.**

c) **Viajar en el extranjero es emocionante aunque no es barato.**

d) **En general voy en autobús porque es práctico.**

e) **Vamos a organizar una excursión a la playa.**

f) **Hacía calor cada día pero no me gusta nada el sol.**   [6 marks]

6 Translate the following sentences into Spanish.

a) Last year I went on holiday to South America.

b) Next year I am going to spend the holidays at home.

c) Cultural holidays are more interesting than adventure holidays.

d) In summer there are a lot of tourists in the airport.

e) I swam in the sea with my sisters and our dog.

f) We went to the beach but it was very cold.   [6 marks]

Where I Live

Quick Recall Quiz

Key Sounds

You must be able to:

- Describe your home and bedroom
- Use prepositions to describe where things are located
- Give opinions about your home.

My Home

Donde vivo yo…	Where I live…
un piso	an apartment
una casa	a house
un cuarto	a room
una habitación	a room / bedroom
un dormitorio	a bedroom
un jardín	a garden
un baño	a bathroom
una cocina	a kitchen
un salón	a living room
un árbol	a tree
la planta baja	the ground floor
la primera planta	the first floor
HT **mi hogar**	my home
HT **de madera**	of wood
HT **de piedra**	of stone

Vivo en una casa pequeña de dos plantas.
I live in a small house with two floors.

En mi casa hay un salón y una cocina en la planta baja y tres dormitorios en la primera planta.
In my house there is a living room and a kitchen on the ground floor and three bedrooms on the first floor.

En mi casa hay ocho habitaciones y, en el jardín, hay muchos árboles.
In my house there are eight bedrooms, and, in the garden, there are lots of trees.

No me gusta mi casa porque no tengo ni piscina ni cine.
I don't like my house because I don't have a swimming pool or a cinema.

HT **En mi hogar ideal tendríamos de todo, una piscina, un cine y un jardín enorme.**
In my ideal home we would have everything, a swimming pool, a cinema and an enormous garden.

Key Point

After a negative expression the article is <u>not</u> needed.

Tengo un cine.
I have a cinema.

No tengo cine.
I don't have a cinema.

Describing your Bedroom

una puerta	a door
una pared	a wall
una mesa	a table
una silla	a chair
una cama	a bed
una ventana	a window
un reloj	a clock

HT el rincón	the corner
HT el suelo	the floor

Prepositions

debajo de	under
entre	in between
a la izquierda	to the left
a la derecha	to the right

Mi dormitorio es bastante grande, con una cama, una mesa y una silla.
My bedroom is quite big, with a bed, a table and a chair.

Los muebles en mi dormitorio son bastante anticuados y me gustaría tener unos más modernos.
The furniture in my bedroom is quite old and I would like to have more modern furniture.

Antes tenía un dormitorio muy feo, pero ahora es más bonito.
Before I used to have a very ugly bedroom, but now it is prettier.

HT **La cama está entre la puerta y la ventana y en el rincón, hay una mesa.**
The bed is between the door and the window and in the corner, there is a table.

de + el and de + la

de + el = del	**Mi casa está cerca del parque.**
	My house is close to the park.
de + la = de la	**Mi casa está al lado de la piscina.**
	My house is next to the pool.

Giving Opinions

- When giving opinions always try and give a reason for your opinion to gain a better mark.
  Me gusta mi casa (I like my house) will gain you some marks but **me gusta mi casa porque es bastante grande** (I like my house because it is quite big) will gain you a better mark.

Key Sounds

Single 'r' is slightly rolled. Double 'r' has a slightly longer roll. Try and pronounce these words: **pared** (wall), **pero** (but), **primera** (first), **perro** (dog), **pizarra** (board).

Quick Test

1. Describe your house in Spanish, naming the rooms.
2. Describe your bedroom in Spanish.
3. Complete these sentences using **del** or **de la**.
   a) **Mi casa está al lado** _____ **piscina.**
   b) **Mi dormitorio está al lado** _____ **baño.**
   c) **Mi casa está cerca** _____ **colegio.**
4. Translate into Spanish:
   My bedroom is on the first floor.
5. Translate into English:
   Mi piso está en la planta baja.

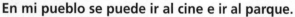

Town Versus Country

You must be able to:

- Describe where you live
- Give a description of the local area
- Discuss the advantages and disadvantages of living in a town versus in the countryside.

Quick Recall Quiz

Key Sound

Where I Live

en la costa	on the coast
en la capital	in the capital
en la ciudad	in the city / town
en las montañas	in the mountains
en las afueras	in the suburbs / on the outskirts
en un barrio industrial	in an industrial area
en el campo	in the countryside
en el centro	in the centre

My Local Area

En mi pueblo hay…	In my town there is / are…			
un centro comercial	a shopping centre			
un supermercado	a supermarket			
una zona peatonal	a pedestrianised area			
una biblioteca	a library	**una estación**	a station
una fábrica	a factory	**una piscina**	a swimming pool
una playa	a beach	**una plaza**	a square
una tienda	a shop	**un aeropuerto**	an airport
un banco	a bank	**un castillo**	a castle
un bosque	a forest	**un colegio**	a school
un cine	a cinema	**un café**	a cafe
muchos edificios	lots of buildings	**un estadio**	a stadium
espacios verdes	green spaces	**un hotel**	a hotel
un hospital	a hospital	**un mercado**	a market
un instituto	a high school	**un parque**	a park
un museo	a museum	**un puerto**	a port
un puente	a bridge	**un río**	a river
un restaurante	a restaurant	**unos servicios**	some toilets

En mi pueblo se puede ir al cine e ir al parque.

In my town you can go to the cinema and go to the park.

Se puede ir de compras porque hay tiendas, un mercado y unos supermercados.

You can go shopping because there are shops, a market and some supermarkets.

Hay mucho que hacer para los turistas en mi pueblo; hay un barrio antiguo, un centro comercial moderno y una playa bonita, hay museos y mercados cada lunes y sábado.

There is lots to do for tourists in my town; there's an old quarter, a modern shopping centre and a pretty beach, there are museums and markets every Monday and Saturday.

Advantages and Disadvantages

La ciudad donde vivo yo es muy animada, es bonita, bastante moderna, y enorme.

The town where I live is very lively, it is pretty, quite modern, and enormous.

El pueblo donde vivo yo es el peor porque es feo y no hay nada que hacer para los jóvenes.

The town where I live is the worst because it is ugly and there is nothing to do for young people.

Una ventaja de vivir en el campo es que conozco a todos mis vecinos y siempre estamos al aire libre porque no hay contaminación.

An advantage of living in the countryside is that I know all of my neighbours and we are always outside because there is no pollution.

Una desventaja de vivir en el campo es que falta un cine.

A disadvantage of living in the countryside is that there isn't a cinema.

Hay ventajas y desventajas de vivir en la ciudad: por un lado, hay mucha industria y hay menos paro, pero por otro lado no es tan limpio como el campo.

There are advantages and disadvantages of living in the city: on the one hand there is a lot of industry and there is less unemployment, but on the other hand it's not as clean as the countryside.

El problema de vivir en el campo para mí es que la arquitectura no es tan bonita como en la capital.

The problem with living in the countryside for me is that the architecture is not as beautiful as in the capital.

Se puede ver mucho más las diferencias entre la riqueza y la pobreza en la ciudad.

You can see a lot more differences between wealth and poverty in the city.

La naturaleza y el paisaje en el campo son hermosos.

Nature and the scenery in the countryside are beautiful.

Mi pueblo está situado entre la capital y el campo, cerca de la playa, pero lejos de las montañas.

My town is situated between the capital city and the countryside, close to the beach, but far from the mountains.

Key Verbs

The verb **vivir** (to live) is a regular **ir** verb and follows all of the rules for regular **ir** verbs. Learn the patterns for the verb **vivir** and you have learnt the pattern for all regular **ir** verbs.

vivir: vivo, vives, vive, vivimos, vivís, viven

Key Sound

'v' and 'b' sound like a 'b' in Spanish like in the English word 'big'. Try pronouncing these words: **vivir** (to live), **vive** (lives), **voy** (I'm going), **vamos** (let's go), **viaje** (trip).

Quick Test

1. Describe your town in Spanish. Use the verbs **vivir**, **estar**, **ser**.
2. Complete the sentences using **un**, **una**, **unos** or **unas**.
   a) **En mi pueblo hay** _____ **museo.**
   b) **Vivo cerca de** _____ **montaña.**
   c) **Está lejos de** _____ **tiendas.**
   d) **Una ventaja es que hay** _____ **mercados.**
3. Translate into Spanish: I live in an industrial town on the coast.
4. Translate into English: **Hay muchas fábricas en mi ciudad.**

Helping the Environment

Quick Recall Quiz

Key Sounds

You must be able to:

- Discuss different aspects of the environment
- Use different verbs to describe how you can help the environment
- Use modal verbs confidently.

The Environment

el aire	air
la basura	rubbish
la contaminación	pollution
el daño	damage
la energía	energy
una bolsa de plástico	a plastic bag
el cambio climático	climate change
la campaña	campaign
una organización benéfica	a charity organisation
los animales en peligro de extinción	animals in danger of extinction
el medio ambiente	the environment
la Tierra	the Earth
los productos químicos	chemical products
HT **los recursos naturales**	natural resources
HT **el planeta**	planet
HT **la calefacción**	central heating
HT **un desastre natural**	a natural disaster
HT **el desarrollo**	development
HT **los incendios forestales**	forest fires

Environment Verbs

limpiar	to clean	**recoger**	to collect
ayudar	to help	**respetar**	to respect
dañar	to damage	**salvar**	to save / rescue
mejorar	to improve	**tirar**	to throw
participar	to participate	HT **luchar**	to fight
aumentar	to increase	HT **matar**	to kill
apagar	to turn off	HT **promover**	to promote
contaminar	to pollute	HT **amenazar**	to threaten
proteger	to protect	HT **contribuir**	to contribute
reducir	to reduce	HT **conservar**	to conserve
reutilizar	to reuse	HT **desarrollar**	to develop
reciclar	to recycle	HT **desaparecer**	to disappear
encender	to turn on	HT **sobrevivir**	to survive

Looking After the Environment

Para reducir la contaminación, hay que tomar el autobús o ir a pie en vez de ir en coche.
To reduce pollution, you have to take the bus or walk instead of going by car.

Es mejor llevar una bolsa a la compra en vez de pedir una bolsa de plástico.
It is better to take a bag to do the shopping, instead of asking for a plastic one.

Es necesario reducir, reutilizar y reciclar para ayudar el medio ambiente.
It is necessary to reduce, reuse and recycle to help the environment.

Yo siempre apago las luces cuando salgo de una habitación.
I always turn off the lights when I leave a room.

Hay que promover el reciclaje en una campaña mundial.
We have to promote recycling in a worldwide campaign.

La contaminación del aire es un efecto muy grave de la fabricación.
Air pollution is a very serious effect of manufacturing.

> **HT** **Se debe bajar la calefacción.**
> You must turn down the central heating.
>
> **HT** **Se debe reciclar todo lo posible como el vidrio, el plástico, la ropa, el papel y el cartón y meterlo todo en los contenedores de reciclaje.**
> You must recycle as much as possible such as glass, plastic, clothes, paper and card, and put it all into the recycling containers.
>
> **HT** **El sobreuso de los recursos naturales daña el medioambiente.**
> The overuse of natural resources damages the environment.
>
> **HT** **El daño al medio ambiente es culpa NUESTRA.**
> The damage to the environment is OUR fault.
>
> **HT** **¿Hay una solución para el planeta?**
> Is there a solution for the planet?

Modal Verbs

- **Poder** (to be able to) and **deber** (to have to) are modal verbs. This means that they must be followed by a verb in the infinitive form.
  Se debe reducir la basura en las calles porque amenaza a los animales.
  You must reduce litter in the streets because it threatens animals.

Key Point

Use your knowledge of vocabulary to help you work out other words, e.g. **mejor** is 'better', **mejorar** is 'to improve'; **utilizar** is 'to use', **reutilizar** is 'to reuse'.

Key Sounds

The 'g' sound in Spanish: 'j' when in front of an 'i' or 'e'. Try pronouncing these words: **gente** (people), **gimnasio** (gymnasium), **Egipto** (Egypt).
'g' as in 'get' when followed by a 'u'. Try pronouncing these words: **guerra** (war), **guitarra** (guitar).
'g' as in 'get' when followed by an 'a' or 'o'. Try pronouncing these words: **garaje** (garage), **gordo** (fat).

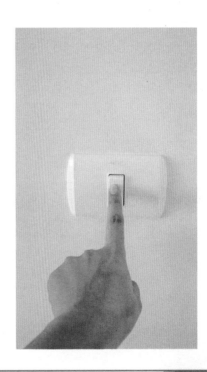

Quick Test

1. In Spanish, give five environmental problems.
2. Translate into English: **Mi pueblo está muy contaminado.**
3. Suggest two solutions starting with **Se debe** and **Hay que**.
4. Translate into Spanish: We must improve the environment.

The Environment and Where People Live

1 Match the sentence halves about where people live.

a) **Pienso que mi dormitorio**   i) **en la planta baja.**

b) **Hay una cocina**   ii) **pero hay un jardín.**

c) **Tengo una cama grande**   iii) **es feo y pequeño.**

d) **No tenemos una piscina**   iv) **con ocho cuartos.**

e) **Vivo en una casa pequeña**   v) **debajo de la ventana.**   [5 marks]

2 Choose the correct form of the adjective to complete each sentence.

a) **El pueblo donde vivo es muy** ....   **animado / animada / animados**

b) **Creo que mi ciudad es bastante** ....   **moderno / moderna / modernos**

c) **Necesitamos más espacios** ....   **verde / verdes / verdos**

d) **En el centro hay muchos restaurantes** ....   **bueno / buenos / buenas**

e) **Vivo en las montañas y son** ....   **bonita / bonitos / bonitas**

f) **Se puede hacer turismo en el barrio** ....   **antiguo / antigua / antiguos**

g) **La naturaleza en el bosque es** ....   **hermoso / hermosa / hermosos**

h) **Hay unos servicios públicos, pero están** ....   **sucio / sucios / sucias**

[8 marks]

3 Translate the key verbs into Spanish by completing the gaps.

a) to build   =   **c** _ _ _ _ _ _ _ _

b) to throw   =   **t** _ _ _ _

c) to save   =   **s** _ _ _ _ _

d) to destroy   =   **d** _ _ _ _ _ _ _

e) to clean   =   **l** _ _ _ _ _

f) to pollute = **c** _ _ _ _ _ _ _ _

g) to recycle = **r** _ _ _ _ _ _ _

h) to protect = **p** _ _ _ _ _ _ _   [8 marks]

4 Read the following text aloud.

Vivo en un piso grande en el centro de la ciudad. Me gusta mi barrio porque hay mucho que hacer para los jóvenes, pero una desventaja de vivir aquí es que hay mucho tráfico. Es importante proteger el medio ambiente y reducir la contaminación.

[3 marks]

5 Translate the following sentences into English.

a) Tenemos un jardín grande con muchos árboles hermosos.

b) Mi casa está cerca del parque y de mi colegio.

c) Vivo en las afueras en un barrio industrial.

d) Hay museos interesantes pero las tiendas son pequeñas.

e) En casa se debe reciclar y reutilizar.

f) Es mejor ir a pie en vez de ir en coche.   [6 marks]

6 Translate the following sentences into Spanish.

a) In my house there is a living room, but there is no garden.

b) In my bedroom I have a table and a chair.

c) I live on the coast next to the beach.

d) There is a swimming pool, but we do not have a cinema.

e) I participate in a campaign to help the earth.

f) My city is very polluted because there are lots of cars.   [6 marks]

Review Questions

Media and Technology

1   Write the correct letter A–E to match the images with the vocabulary.

A   B   C   D   E

a)   el móvil ....   c)   el portátil ....   e)   la tableta ....

b)   el teclado ....   d)   el ordenador ....

[5 marks]

2   Create your own sentences in different tenses for each infinitive provided.

	Past	Present	Future
a) enviar			
b) recibir			
c) usar			

[9 marks]

3   Match the questions and answers about media and technology.

a)   ¿Qué haces con tu móvil?   i)   Por la tarde.

b)   ¿Cuándo usas la tecnología?   ii)   Los móviles tienen más funciones.

c)   ¿Sigues a los influencers?   iii)   Escucho música.

d)   ¿Cómo ha cambiado la tecnología?   iv)   Sí, pero son un poco adictivas.

e)   ¿Usas las redes sociales?   v)   No, porque no me interesan.

[5 marks]

4 Choose the correct word from the box below to complete each sentence.

videojuegos	teclado	redes	todo
sueño	carrera	teléfono	ordenador

a) **Pienso que mi móvil es muy práctico, lo uso para** ....

b) **La tecnología causa problemas de** ....

c) **Comenzó su nueva** .... **como influencer.**

d) **El** .... **de mi portátil no funciona.**

e) **Hago mis deberes en mi habitación en mi** ....

f) **Mis abuelos siempre me llaman por** ....   [6 marks]

5 Translate the following sentences into English.

a) **En vez de mandar correos electrónicos, mando SMS.**

b) **Las redes sociales pueden ser muy adictivas y causan problemas.**

c) **Mi influencer favorito ha trabajado con muchas marcas famosas.**

d) **Hay demasiados anuncios en este sitio web.**

e) **Mi portátil es viejo y no funciona muy bien.**   [5 marks]

6 Translate the following sentences into Spanish.

a) I save a lot of photos on my mobile phone.

b) Last night I downloaded a new app.

c) He is an influencer, therefore he is very well-known.

d) I want to watch television but the screen is broken.

e) Young people think that technology is very important.   [5 marks]

Gender, Plurals and Articles

You must be able to:

- Use the correct gender of nouns
- Use definite and indefinite articles
- Make nouns plural.

Indefinite Articles and Nouns

- **un**   a / an (for a masculine word)
  un gato   a cat
  un perro   a dog
  un hombre   a man
- **una**   a / an (for a feminine word)
  una casa   a house
  una abuela   a grandmother
  una mujer   a woman

Definite Articles and Nouns

- **el**   the (for a masculine word)
  el gato   the cat
  el perro   the dog
  el hombre   the man
- **la**   the (for a feminine word)
  la casa   the house
  la abuela   the grandmother
  la mujer   the woman

Rules and Exceptions

- Words ending in **-o, -or, -ón, -és** and many ending in **-ma** are usually masculine, except:
  la mano   hand
  la radio   radio
  la cama   bed
  la pluma   feather
- Words that end in **-a, -sión, -ción, -dad, -tad, -tud, -umbre** are usually feminine, except:
  el día   day
  el mapa   map
  el planeta   planet
  el sofá   sofa

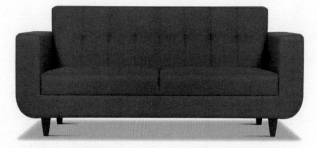

> ### Key Point
>
> When you learn nouns in Spanish you have to learn whether they are masculine or feminine. There are some general rules which may help.

> ### Key Point
>
> When using impersonal verbs such as **gustar** (to like), the definite article has to be used:
>
> **Me gusta el fútbol.**
> I like football.
> **No me gustan las películas de acción.**
> I don't like action movies.

Using Articles

- The definite article is sometimes used in Spanish where we wouldn't use it in English:

  El francés es genial.   French is great.

  Me gusta el español.   I like Spanish.

- The indefinite article is sometimes not used in Spanish where we would use it in English:

  Soy profesor.   I am a teacher.

  No tenemos cine.   We don't have a cinema.

- Where a job title is qualified by an adjective, the indefinite article is used:

  Es un buen profesor.   He's a good teacher.

Plurals

- To make a noun plural, you need to apply the following rules:
  - Add an **s** if the word ends in a vowel.
  - Add an **es** if the word ends in a consonant.
  - If the noun ends in **-ón** or **-ción**, drop the accent before adding **-es**.
  - If the noun ends in **-z**, change the **-z** to **-c** before adding **-es**.
- Remember that the article must also become plural:

unos	some (for masculine plural nouns)
unos gatos	some cats
unas	some (for feminine plural nouns)
unas casas	some houses
los	the (for masculine plural nouns)
los gatos	the cats
las	the (for feminine plural nouns)
las casas	the houses

> **Quick Test**
>
> 1. Are the following words masculine or feminine?
>   **ciudad   atleta   universidad   natación   ejercicio**
> 2. Make the following words plural:
>   **lápiz   marrón   cama   fresa   director**
> 3. Make the following words singular:
>   **peces   gatos   televisiones   pelotas   ojos**
> 4. Are these sentences correct? If not, then correct them:
>   a) **Me gusta historia.**
>   b) **Soy un profesor.**
>   c) **Me gustan las matemáticas.**
>   d) **Es buen actor.**

Adjectives, Comparatives and Superlatives

You must be able to:

- Use adjectives correctly: agreements and position
- Use comparative and superlative adjectives
- Use indefinite adjectives.

Adjectives

- When describing something in Spanish the adjective must agree with the noun. The ending of the adjective changes depending on whether the noun is masculine, feminine, singular or plural.
- Here is the pattern for regular adjectives:

Masculine singular	Feminine singular	Masculine plural	Feminine plural	English
bonito	**bonita**	**bonitos**	**bonitas**	pretty
amable	**amable**	**amables**	**amables**	friendly
trabajador	**trabajadora**	**trabajadores**	**trabajadoras**	hard-working
azul	**azul**	**azules**	**azules**	blue

- Most adjectives come after the noun they are describing, for example:

Es una mujer graciosa.   She is a funny woman.
Es un hombre tímido.   He is a shy man.

Some Exceptions

- Some adjectives come before the noun. When this happens, the masculine singular form if it ends in **o**, is shortened. The feminine form doesn't change. For example, **bueno** becomes **buen**.

Es un buen amigo.   He is a good friend.
Es una buena actriz.   She is a good actress.

- The following adjectives follow this pattern:

bueno	good	**segundo**	second
malo	bad	**alguno**	some / any
primero	first	**ninguno**	none

- Adjectives of quantity always come before the noun:

poco   few
Hay muy poca gente.   There are very few people.
mucho   a lot / lots of
Hay mucha gente.   There are lots of people.

- **Grande** is shortened before both masculine and feminine nouns, and its meaning changes too.

un gran amigo   a great friend
un amigo grande   a big friend
una gran amiga   a great friend
una amiga grande   a big friend

Comparatives and Superlatives of Adjectives

- To compare two things, use the following words and an adjective where indicated by "…":

más … que	more … than
menos … que	less … than
tan … como	as … as
mejor que	better than
peor que	worse than

  Mi padre es menos divertido que tu padre.
  My dad is less fun than your dad.
  Los documentales son más interesantes que las películas de terror.
  Documentaries are more interesting than horror films.

- To use the superlative, you put **el / la/ los / las** in front of **más / menos**:
  Las películas de terror son las más emocionantes.
  Horror films are the most exciting.

- Common irregulars are:

el / la mejor	the best
el / la peor	the worst
el / la mayor	the biggest / oldest
el / la menor	the youngest
Mi padre es el mejor.	My dad is the best.

- To form the absolute superlative add **-ísimo/a** to the end of the adjective after removing the final vowel.
  La película es aburridísima.   The film is extremely boring.

- Remember that you still need to make adjectives agree with the noun(s) in number and gender.

Indefinite Adjectives

- Indefinite adjectives such as **cada** (each), **otro** (other / another), **todo** (all), **mismo** (same), **alguno** (some), **ninguno** (none) don't always follow the patterns we would expect.
  - **cada** never changes:
    cada sábado   every Saturday   **cada noche**   every night
  - **todo**, **mismo** and **otro** agree with the noun:
    todos los días   every day
  - **otra** does not use the indefinite article:
    Tengo otro libro. I have another book. (not **tengo un otro libro**)

> ### Quick Test
>
> 1. Translate into Spanish: **a)** The old dog
>   **b)** The pretty girl
>   **c)** The hard-working boys
> 2. Translate into English: **a) Los jóvenes habladores**
>   **b) La chica tímida**
>   **c) Las mujeres altas**
> 3. Complete the sentences.
>   **a) Mi madre es más inteligente _____ yo.**
>   **b) Soy la _____ interesante.**
>   **c) Mi hermano es _____ mayor.**
> 4. Say in Spanish: The book is extremely good.

Adverbs, Interrogatives and Por v Para

You must be able to:

- Use adverbs with the correct ending and in the correct position
- Form interrogatives
- Use **por** and **para** in the correct situation.

Adverbs

- Adverbs describe verbs e.g. slowly, quickly, always. They often end in '-ly' in English.
- In Spanish, adverbs are formed by adding **-mente** onto the feminine form of the adjective:

lento	slow	**lentamente**	slowly
probable	probable	**probablemente**	probably

- Some irregulars that don't follow the pattern:

ahora	now	**allí**	there
aquí	here	**bien**	well
demasiado	too / too much	**mal**	badly
bastante	quite	**mucho**	a lot
muchas veces	often	**siempre**	always
ya	already		

- Adverbial phrases to make your speaking and writing sound more interesting:

dentro de poco	soon
por todas partes	everywhere
en otra parte	elsewhere

Position of Adverbs

- Adverbs usually follow the verb they describe:
  Caminamos lentamente.   We walk slowly.
- Sometimes they come before the verb to add emphasis:
  Siempre jugamos al fútbol.   We always play football.

Comparatives and Superlatives of Adverbs

- Comparatives and superlatives of adverbs are formed in the same way as comparatives and superlatives of adjectives, using **más … que**, **menos … que** etc.
  Mi madre habla más rápido que mi padre.
  My mum talks more quickly than my dad.

Interrogatives

- There are two ways of forming a question in Spanish: using intonation and using question words. Take a straightforward sentence and then use intonation at the end of the sentence to turn the sentence into a question:
  ¿El gato es grande?   Is the cat big?

Key Point

Try to learn adverbs in pairs of opposites:
bien / mal
good / bad
allí / aquí
here / there

- You can also form a question by using a question word or interrogative word. Here are the most common:

¿Cómo?	What / How?	**¿Cuándo?**	When?
¿Dónde?	Where?	**¿Por qué?**	Why?

¿Cuándo es tu cumpleaños?   When is your birthday?
¿Dónde vives?   Where do you live?

Por v Para

- **Por** and **para** can both mean 'for' but are used in different situations.
- **por** can be used to say…
  - 'for' / 'in' when talking about time:
    Salí por la noche.
    I went out for the night.
  - 'through' when talking about locations:
    Camino por el pueblo.
    I walk through town.
  - 'in exchange for':
    Le di 30 euros por la camiseta.
    I gave him 30 euros for the T-shirt.
  - 'on behalf of':
    Lo hizo por ti.
    He / She did it for you.
- **para** can be used to say…
  - 'by' / 'in time for':
    Tengo que hacerlo para mañana.
    I have to finish it for / by tomorrow.
  - 'in order to' when followed by an infinitive:
    Reciclo para proteger el medioambiente.
    I recycle (in order) to protect the environment.
  - 'for' a purpose / recipient:
    Lo compró para su amiga.
    He / She bought it for his / her friend.
  - 'in my opinion':
    Para mí es importante.
    For me it is important.
  - 'for what reason':
    ¿Para qué quieres el agua?
    What do you want the water for?

Quick Test

1. What do the following adverbs mean in English?
   a) **lentamente**   c) **saludablemente**
   b) **rápidamente**   d) **absolutamente**
2. Change the following adjectives into adverb:
   a) **fácil**   c) **frecuente**
   b) **posible**   d) **verdadero**
3. What does the following question mean: **¿Cuántos años tienes?**
4. Would you use **por** or **para** in the gaps?
   a) _____ **ir al cine, necesito coger el autobús.**
   b) **Vamos a pasar** _____ **el parque** _____ **llegar al colegio.**

Present Tense, Regular and Reflexive Verbs and Negatives

Quick Recall Quiz

You must be able to:

- Use the present tense correctly
- Use reflexive verbs correctly
- Make verbs negative.

The Present Tense

- Use the present tense to talk about what you usually do, e.g. 'I eat lunch every day'.

-ar Verbs

hablar	to speak
hablo	I speak
hablas	you speak
habla	he / she / you (polite) speak
hablamos	we speak
habláis	you speak
hablan	they / you (polite) speak
Hablo inglés y español.	I speak English and Spanish.

-er Verbs

comer	to eat
como	I eat
comes	you eat
come	he / she / you (polite) eat
comemos	we eat
coméis	you eat
comen	they / you (polite) eat
Comemos paella cada domingo.	We eat paella every Sunday.

-ir verbs

vivir	to live
vivo	I live
vives	you live
vive	he / she / you (polite) live
vivimos	we live
vivís	you live
viven	they / you (polite) live
Mis padres viven en Londres.	My parents live in London.

Infinitives

- Infinitives translate as 'to…' in English, for example, **beber** (to drink), **charlar** (to chat), **recibir** (to receive).
- Infinitives are used after phrases such as **me gusta** (I like) and after modal verbs such as:

poder	to be able to	**puedo**	I can
querer	to want	**quiero**	I want

> **Key Point**
>
> Make sure you can use and understand the correct form of the verb as the subject pronouns are often not used in Spanish.

preferir	to prefer	**prefiero**	I prefer

Puedo cantar bien. I can sing well.
Se puede ir al cine en mi pueblo. You can go to the cinema in my town.
Quisiera vivir en España. I would like to live in Spain.
Prefiero beber agua. I prefer to drink water.

Reflexive Verbs

- Reflexive verbs are often used when the verb involves doing something to yourself. Reflexive verbs are used for many actions involving daily routine and can also be used to convey emotions.

- The reflexive pronouns are:

me	myself	**nos**	ourselves
te	yourself	**os**	yourselves
se	his / herself / oneself	**se**	themselves

- Some examples of reflexive verbs:

lavarse	to wash (oneself)
vestirse	to get (oneself) dressed
levantarse	to get (oneself) up
dormirse	to fall asleep
despertarse	to wake (oneself) up

Me despierto a las ocho y me levanto en seguida. Me visto rápidamente.
I wake up at eight o'clock and I get up straight away. I get dressed quickly.

Me duermo a las diez de la noche. I go to sleep at ten o'clock at night.
¿A qué hora te despiertas? At what time do you wake up?
Se viste en el baño. He / She gets dressed in the bathroom.

Negatives

- To make a verb negative in Spanish, put **no** before the verb:
No hablo francés. I don't speak French.

- Sometimes the negative is in two parts and sometimes in one. If the negative is in two parts, then the two parts go around the verb:

No hablo nunca francés. I never speak French.
Nunca hablo francés. I never speak French.
No hablo francés tampoco hablo italiano.
I don't speak French, nor do I speak Italian.
No hablo ni francés ni italiano. I speak neither French nor Italian.
No conozco a nadie. I don't know anyone.
No juego jamás al fútbol. I never play football.
No tengo ningún trabajo. I don't have a job.

> **Key Point**
>
> Remember to check where you place negative words.

> ### Quick Test
>
> 1. Conjugate the following verbs in the first, second and third person singular present tense.
>   a) **charlar**　　b) **beber**　　c) **recibir**
> 2. Add the correct reflexive pronoun to these verbs. (Hint – look at the ending of the verb to help you.)
>   a) _____ **vistes**　b) _____ **levanta**　c) _____ **lavo**
> 3. Translate the following sentences into Spanish:
>   a) I never play volleyball.
>   b) I don't eat meat.
>   c) I don't watch documentaries either.

Practice Questions

Grammar 1

1 Make each of the following nouns and their definite articles plural.

a) el castillo ....

b) el hombre ....

c) el planeta ....

d) el agua ....

e) la naranja ....

f) la mujer ....

g) la estación ....

h) la luz .... [8 marks]

2 Make each of the following nouns and their indefinite articles singular.

a) unas catedrales ....

b) unos bolígrafos ....

c) unos balcones ....

d) unos autobuses ....

e) unas motos ....

f) unos árboles ....

g) unas habitaciones ....

h) unos cines .... [8 marks]

3 Choose the correct adjective from the box below to complete each sentence.

gran	impacientes	graciosas	simpático	rubio	habladora

a) Mi hermano es muy ....

b) Mi madre es muy ....

c) Mis padres pueden ser muy ....

d) En mi opinión, mis amigas son muy ....

e) Mi amiga Pilar tiene el pelo ....

f) Creo que mi tío es un .... hombre.   [6 marks]

4 Match the interrogatives on the left with the correct endings of the questions on the right.

a) ¿Cómo…   es tu cumpleaños?

b) ¿Cuál…   quieres ir, en autobús o en tren?

c) ¿Cuándo…   significa eso?

d) ¿Cuánto…   es el mío, el verde o el azul?

e) ¿Cuántos…   es aquella mujer, Señora Watson o Señora Woods?

f) ¿Dónde…   dices eso?

g) ¿Por qué…   está mi móvil?

h) ¿Qué…   cuestan los zapatos?

i) ¿Quién…   años tiene tu hermana?   [9 marks]

5 Choose the correct reflexive pronoun for each sentence.

a) Mi hermana siempre .... levanta muy temprano.   me / nos / se

b) Normalmente .... lavo antes de desayunar.   me / os / se

c) Mis padres .... duchan por la mañana.   os / nos / se

d) Nosotros .... ponemos en el uniforme escolar.   me / nos / te

e) ¿A qué hora .... acostáis el fin de semana?   os / te / nos

f) ¿Y tú Manolo, a qué hora .... despiertas durante la semana?   me / te / os

[6 marks]

Review Questions

The Environment and Where People Live

1 Write each word in the correct category.

un piso	una silla	una cocina	una mesa
la planta baja	un salón	un baño	una cama	una casa

Buildings	Rooms	Furniture

[9 marks]

2 Read the text and complete the sentences in English.

Mi habitación no es grande, pero es cómoda. Hay una mesa debajo de la ventana. En el rincón hay una silla. La cama está entre la mesa y la puerta. A la izquierda hay una televisión. Mi habitación está al lado del baño.

a) The room is .... but not ....

b) The window is .... the table.

c) The chair is ....

d) The bed is between the .... and the ....

e) The TV is on the ....

f) The room is .... the bathroom.

[8 marks]

3 Are these people's opinions of where they live positive (**P**), negative (**N**), or positive and negative (**P+N**)?

a) **Vivo en un pueblo feo donde no hay muchos espacios verdes.** ....

b) **Mis vecinos son simpáticos y hay mucho que hacer.** ....

c) **Es una ciudad muy animada, sin embargo, no es tan limpia como el campo.** ....

d) **Hay muchas fábricas y por lo tanto es muy fácil encontrar un trabajo.** ....

e) **El ayuntamiento en mi región no quiere gastar dinero.** .... [5 marks]

4 Answer the questions in Spanish. Try to use a maximum of ten words in each answer.

a) **¿Dónde vives?** ....

b) **¿Cómo es tu casa / tu piso?** ....

c) **¿Cómo es tu habitación?** ....

d) **¿Cómo es tu pueblo?** ....

e) **¿Cuáles son las ventajas y las desventajas de vivir en una ciudad?** ....

....

f) **¿Cuáles son las ventajas y las desventajas de vivir en el campo?** ....

....

g) **¿Dónde te gustaría vivir en el futuro?** ....

[7 marks]

5 Match to make phrases.

a)	**apagar**	i)	**la basura**
b)	**proteger**	ii)	**la contaminación**
c)	**recoger**	iii)	**el aire**
d)	**contaminar**	iv)	**la luz**
e)	**reducir**	v)	**una bolsa de plástico**
f)	**utilizar**	vi)	**el medioambiente**

[6 marks]

6 Write a sentence of your own for each phrase above. Remember to conjugate the verbs correctly.

a) ....

b) ....

c) ....

d) ....

e) ....

f) ....

[6 marks]

Common Irregular Verbs, Present Continuous and Conjunctions

Quick Recall Quiz

You must be able to:

- Use common irregular verbs
- Use verbs in the present continuous tense
- Use conjunctions in your sentences.

Common Irregular Verbs

- The nine most common irregular verbs in the present tense in Spanish are:

Infinitive	First person singular	Second person singular	Third person singular	First person plural	Second person plural	Third person plural
ser (to be)	soy (I am)	eres (you are)	es (he / she / it is)	somos (we are)	sois (you are)	son (they are)
estar (to be)	estoy (I am)	estás (you are)	está (he / she / it is)	estamos (we are)	estáis (you are)	están (they are)
tener (to have)	tengo (I have)	tienes (you have)	tiene (he / she / it has)	tenemos (we have)	tenéis (you have)	tienen (they have)
hacer (to do)	hago (I do)	haces (you do)	hace (he / she / it does)	hacemos (we do)	hacéis (you do)	hacen (they do)
ir (to go)	voy (I go)	vas (you go)	va (he / she / it goes)	vamos (we go)	vais (you go)	van (they go)
dar (to give)	doy (I give)	das (you give)	da (he / she / it gives)	damos (we give)	dais (you give)	dan (they give)
saber (to know)	sé (I know)	sabes (you know)	sabe (he / she / it knows)	sabemos (we know)	sabéis (you know)	saben (they give)
decir (to say)	digo (I say)	dices (you say)	dice (he / she / it says)	decimos (we say)	decís (you say)	dicen (they say)
poder (to be able to)	puedo (I can)	puedes (you can)	puede (he / she / one / you / it can)	podemos (we can)	podéis (you can)	pueden (they can)

- Some of these verbs involve vowel changes in certain forms:
    - e > ie group:

      querer   to want   **quiero**   I want

      pensar   to think   **pienso**   I think
    - o > ue group:

      volver   to return   **vuelvo**   I return

      soler   to usually   **suelo**   I usually
    - e > i group:

      decir   to say   **digo**   I say

      pedir   to ask for   **pido**   I ask for

The Present Continuous Tense

- The present continuous tense is used to describe actions taking place at the moment. This can be used in the exam to describe what is happening in a photo, for example:
  Está leyendo un periódico.   He / She is reading a newspaper.
- To form the present continuous tense, you need to form the present tense of the verb **estar** and add the gerund (in English this is the -ing form) of the action verb.
- The present tense of the verb **estar**:

estoy	I am	**estás**	you (sing.) are
está	he / she / it is	**estamos**	we are
estáis	you (pl.) are	**están**	they are

- The gerund in Spanish is formed as follows:

hablar	to speak	**hablando**	speaking
comer	to eat	**comiendo**	eating
recibir	to receive	**recibiendo**	receiving

Conjunctions

- Conjunctions are words and phrases that can be used to improve the flow of your language:
  Vamos a la playa ya que a mí me encanta.
  We go to the beach as I love it.
  Como helado si hace sol.   I eat ice cream if it is sunny.
  No hablo francés, sino español.   I don't speak French but (rather) Spanish.
  ¿Prefieres España o Francia?   Do you prefer Spain or France?
  Me encanta el español, pero es difícil aprenderlo.
  I love Spanish, but it is difficult to learn.
  Me encanta la música porque es relajante, aunque las suscripciones son caras.
  I love music because it is relaxing, although subscriptions are expensive.
- Use **y** in Spanish except when followed by a word beginning with **i** or **hi**, then change it to **e**:
  Hablo francés y español.   I speak French and Spanish.
  Hablo español e italiano.   I speak Spanish and Italian.

> **Quick Test**
>
> 1. Translate the following into Spanish:
>   a) I go to the cinema.   b) I have brown eyes.   c) I do yoga.
> 2. Translate the following into English: a) **Vamos al parque.**
>   b) **Tiene el pelo marrón.** c) **Hacemos natación.**
> 3. Change the following verbs into the present continuous form:
>   a) **Hago esquí.**   c) **Tomo el sol.**
>   b) **Como mucho chocolate.**   d) **Bebo coca-cola.**
> 4. Fill in the gap with the appropriate conjunction in brackets:
>   a) **Me gusta el español (sino / sin embargo / porque) es interesante.**
>   b) **No estudio geografía, (sino / sin embargo / porque) historia.**
>   c) **Juego al fútbol (sino / ya que / pero) me encanta.**

Past Tenses

You must be able to:

- Use the preterite tense
- Use the imperfect tense.

Quick Recall Quiz

The Preterite Tense

- There are two sets of endings for regular verbs in the preterite: **-ar** and **-er/-ir**.

-ar Verbs

hablar	to speak
hablé	I spoke
hablaste	you spoke **(tú)**
habló	he / she / it / you spoke **(Vd.)**
hablamos	we spoke
hablasteis	you spoke **(vosotros)**
hablaron	they / you spoke **(Vds.)**

-er and -ir Verbs

beber	to drink
bebí	I drank
bebiste	you drank **(tú)**
bebió	he / she / it / you drank **(Vd.)**
bebimos	we drank
bebisteis	you drank **(vosotros)**
bebieron	they / you drank **(Vds.)**

> ### Key Point
>
> The preterite tense is also known as the 'simple past' and is used to talk about completed actions in the past: 'I went', 'you ate' etc.

Irregular Verbs in the Preterite Tense

	ser (to be) / **ir** (to go)	**hacer** (to do)	**tener** (to have)	**ver** (to see)
(yo)	fui	hice	tuve	vi
(tú)	fuiste	hiciste	tuviste	viste
(él / ella / usted)	fue	hizo	tuvo	vio
(nosotros)	fuimos	hicimos	tuvimos	vimos
(vosotros)	fuisteis	hicisteis	tuvisteis	visteis
(ellos / ellas / ustedes)	fueron	hicieron	tuvieron	vieron

- Some verbs in the preterite tense involve irregular spellings in the first person (**yo**) form.
  - **jugar** (to play) – **jugué** (I played)
  - **sacar** (to take out / get) – **saqué** (I took out / got)
  - **llegar** (to arrive) – **llegué** (I arrived)
  - **tocar** (to play an instrument) – **toqué** (I played an instrument)

The Imperfect Tense

- To form the imperfect tense, add the following endings to the verb stem:

-ar Verbs

hablar	to speak
hablaba	I was speaking / used to speak
hablabas	you were speaking / used to speak (**tú**)
hablaba	he / she / it was / you were speaking / used to speak (**vd.**)
hablábamos	we were speaking / used to speak
hablabais	you were speaking / used to speak (**vosotros**)
hablaban	they / you were speaking / used to speak (**Vds.**)

-er and -ir Verbs

beber	to drink
bebía	I was drinking / used to drink
bebías	you drinking / used to drink (**tú**)
bebía	he / she / it was / you were drinking / used to drink (**vd.**)
bebíamos	we were drinking / used to drink
bebíais	you were drinking / used to drink (**vosotros**)
bebían	they / you were drinking / used to drink (**Vds.**)

- There are only three irregular verbs in the imperfect tense:

	ser (to be)	**ir** (to go)	**ver** (to see)
(yo)	era	iba	veía
(tú)	eras	ibas	veías
(él / ella / usted)	era	iba	veía
(nosotros)	éramos	íbamos	veíamos
(vosotros)	erais	ibais	veíais
(ellos / ellas / ustedes)	eran	iban	veían

- Two useful verbs in the imperfect tense are the verbs **haber** (**hay** in the present) and **soler**. These infinitives don't have direct English translations but their imperfect forms can be translated as 'there was / there were' and 'used to'.

Había mucha gente.	There were lots of people.
Solía jugar al tenis.	I used to play tennis.

> ### Key Point
>
> Irregular verbs in the preterite do not have accents. However, it is vital that accents are used correctly with regular verbs when writing, otherwise the meaning of the verb can change.
>
> **Hablo con el profesor.**
> I speak to the teacher.
> **Habló con el profesor.**
> He / She spoke to the teacher.

> ### Key Point
>
> The imperfect tense is used to describe what happened in the past, what something was like, what someone was doing, or what was happening.

> ### Quick Test
>
> 1. Translate into English: **Comieron paella ayer.**
> 2. Translate into Spanish:
>   a) I went
>   b) I played
>   c) I arrived
>   d) He drank
>   e) We did
> 3. Translate into Spanish: I took a lot of photos.
> 4. Translate into English: **Cuando era joven, me gustaba jugar al béisbol.**
> 5. Translate into Spanish: When I was young, I used to love to go the park on a Saturday.

Compound Past Tenses and The Passive

You must be able to:

- Use the present perfect and pluperfect tenses
- Use the passive.

Compound Past Tenses

- Compound past tenses are tenses which describe the past and use two verbs – a form of **haber** and a past participle.
- The verb **haber** means 'to have', but it is only used in specific phrases and tenses, and is not interchangeable with **tener**.
- Past participles in Spanish are formed by removing the verb ending (**-ar**, **-er**, **-ir**) and adding **-ado** (**-ar** verbs) or **-ido** (**-er** and **-ir** verbs).

The Present Perfect Tense

- The present perfect tense is used to say you 'have done' something.
- To form the present perfect tense, you need the present tense of **haber** and a past participle.

haber – to have (an auxiliary verb)	+ past participle
he	
has	**hablado** (spoken)
ha	
hemos	**bebido** (drunk)
habéis	
han	**vivido** (lived)

He hablado con mi profesor.	I have spoken with my teacher.
Ha bebido mucha agua.	She / He has drunk lots of water.
Han vivido en España.	They have lived in Spain.

- There are a number of irregular past participles in Spanish.

decir	to say	dicho	said
escribir	to write	**escrito**	wrote
hacer	to make / to do	**hecho**	made / did
poner	to put	**puesto**	put
ver	to see	**visto**	seen
volver	to return	**vuelto**	returned

The Pluperfect Tense

- The pluperfect tense is used to say you 'had done' something.
- To form the pluperfect tense, you need the imperfect tense of **haber** and a past participle.

haber – to have (an auxiliary verb)	+ past participle
había	
habías	**hablado** (spoken)
había	
habíamos	**bebido** (drunk)
habíais	
habían	**vivido** (lived)

Había hablado con mi profesor.   I had spoken with my teacher.
Había bebido mucha agua.   I / She / He had drunk lots of water.
Habían vivido en España.   They had lived in Spain.

- To say 'I have just' in Spanish, you don't need the verbs **haber** or **tener**. Use the construction **acabar de** + infinitive.

Acabo de terminar.   I have just finished.
Acabamos de llegar.   We have just arrived.

Key Point

Nothing comes between **haber** and the past participle. All pronouns and negatives come before **haber**.
No he visto a mi padre hoy.
I have not seen my father today.
Me he levantado muy tarde.
I have got up very late.

The Passive

- The passive is a 'voice' rather than a tense, as it can be used in any tense.
- The passive voice is used to say what is done to something, rather than who does it (the active voice):
  - They are reading a book – active voice
  - The book is read – passive voice
- The passive is formed in two different ways (the second is much more common):
  - **Ser** + past participle + **por**:
    El libro es leído por los chicos.   The book is read by the boys.
  - **Se** + third-person singular or plural verb:
    Se lee el libro.   The book is read.
    Se leen los libros.   The books are read.

Quick Test

1. Change these infinitives to past participles.
   a) **escuchar**
   b) **comer**
   c) **permitir**
2. Say in Spanish:
   a) I have just finished my homework.
   b) I have eaten chips.
   c) I had seen the film.
3. Change this active sentence to both forms of the passive voice.
   La tienda vende pan.

Pronouns

You must be able to:

- Understand how to use subject, direct and indirect pronouns
- Use pronouns with prepositions
- Use reflexive pronouns.

Subject Pronouns

- Subject pronouns (I, you, etc.) are not used very often in Spanish.
- In Spanish, the verb ending shows who is doing the action.
- Subject pronouns are normally added to add emphasis to a sentence.

yo	I	**nosotros/as**	we
tú	you (informal, singular)	**vosotros/as**	you (informal, plural)
él	he	**ellos**	they (masculine or mixed)
ella	she	**ellas**	they (feminine)
usted (often abbreviated to **Vd.**)	you (formal, singular)	**ustedes** (often abbreviated to **Vds.**)	you (formal, plural)

Quiero un café con leche.	I want a coffee with milk.
Yo quiero un café con leche.	I want a coffee with milk.
¿Qué opinas?	What do you think?
¿Qué opinas tú?	What do you think?

Direct and Indirect Object Pronouns

- Pronouns replace nouns to avoid repetition.
- Direct object pronouns are used to say 'it', 'me' or 'them'.
- Indirect object pronouns mean 'to me', 'to you', 'to them'.

  Me gusta la camiseta. ¿La tiene en verde?
  I like the T-shirt. Do you have it in green? (Direct object pronoun 'it')

  ¿Me puede dar la camiseta verde?
  Can you give (to) me the green T-shirt? (Indirect object pronoun '(to) me')

Key Point

The pronoun used must agree with the noun that it replaces.

¿Tienes estos zapatos en negro? Sí, los tengo en negro.

Do you have these shoes in black? Yes, I have them in black.

Direct object pronouns		Indirect object pronouns	
me	me	**me**	to me
te	you	**te**	to you
lo	him / it	**le**	to him / it
la	her / it	**le**	to her / it
lo / la	you (**Vd.**)	**le**	to you (**Vd.**)
nos	us	**nos**	to us
os	you	**os**	to you
los / las	them	**les**	to them
los / las	you (**Vds.**)	**les**	to you (**Vds.**)

- If both an indirect and a direct object pronoun are used, then the indirect object pronoun goes first.

  Mi padre me la dio.   My dad gave it to me.

- Object pronouns usually go before the verb. However, with the immediate future or the present continuous, they come either before the verb or attached to the end of the verbal phrase.

  Los voy a comprar. / Voy a comprarlos.

  I'm going to buy them.

  La estoy viendo. / Estoy viéndola. I'm watching it.

- This is the same for verbs such as **quiero** + infinitive:

  Lo quiero comprar. / Quiero comprarlo.

  I want to buy it.

- Pronouns are attached to the end of the imperative.

  ¡Cómpralo! Buy it!

Disjunctive Pronouns

- Disjunctive pronouns are pronouns used with a preposition, e.g. for me.

mí	me	**nosotros/as**	us
ti	you (informal, singular)	**vosotros/as**	you (informal, plural)
él	him / it	**ellos**	them (masculine)
ella	her / it	**ellas**	them (feminine)
usted	you (formal, singular)	**ustedes**	you (formal, plural)

Reflexive Pronouns

- Reflexive verbs describe an action that you do to yourself. They are accompanied by a reflexive pronoun. An example is the verb **lavarse** – to wash oneself / to get washed.

  me lavo   I wash (myself)

  te lavas   you wash (yourself) (**tú**)

  se lava   he / she / it washes (him / her / itself) / you wash (yourself) (**Vd.**)

  nos lavamos we wash (ourselves)

  os laváis   you wash (yourselves) (**vosotros**)

  se lavan   they wash (themselves) / you wash (yourselves) (**Vds.**)

The Personal A

- If the object of the verb is a person rather than a thing, the personal **a** is used.

  Veo la casa.   I see the house. (thing / object)

  Veo a la chica.   I see the girl.   (person)

> ## Quick Test
>
> 1. What do these subject pronouns mean in English?
>   a) tú   c) nosotros   e) usted
>   b) yo   d) ellos
> 2. Translate into English: **Me gustan las botas. ¿Las tienen en blanco?**
> 3. Translate into Spanish: I want to go out with you. (**tú**)

The Future Tenses, Subjunctive and Imperative Moods

You must be able to:

- Use verbs in the immediate, simple and conditional future tense
- Use the subjunctive mood
- Give commands or instructions using the imperative.

The Immediate, Simple and Conditional Future Tenses

- The immediate future tense is used to say what is **going to** happen. You form it using the present tense of the verb **ir** and add **a** and an infinitive verb. For example:

Voy a ir.	I am going to go.
Vas a salir.	You are going to go out.
Va a comer.	He / She is going to eat.
Vamos a bailar.	We are going to dance.
Vais a terminar.	You are going to finish.
Van a escribir.	They are going to write.

- The simple future tense is used to say what **will** happen.
- The conditional future tense is used to describe what **would** happen in the future.
- The simple and conditional future tenses are formed in a similar way. For regular verbs you take the full infinitive form of the verb and add the following endings:

hablar (to speak)	**Simple future tense**	**Conditional future tense**
yo	hablar**é**	hablar**ía**
tú	hablar**ás**	hablar**ías**
él / ella / usted	hablar**á**	hablar**ía**
nosotros/as	hablar**emos**	hablar**íamos**
vosotros/as	hablar**éis**	hablar**íais**
ellos / ellas / ustedes	hablar**án**	hablar**ían**

Si tengo suerte, mañana ganaré la lotería.
If I'm lucky, tomorrow I will win the lottery.
Si tuviera suerte, mañana ganaría la lotería.
If I were lucky, tomorrow I would win the lottery.

- The following verbs have irregular verbs stems in both the simple future tense and the conditional future tense.

Infinitive	Simple future tense		Conditional future tense	
decir	dir**é**	I will say	dir**ía**	I would say
hacer	har**é**	I will do	har**ía**	I would do
poder	podr**é**	I will be able to	podr**ía**	I would be able to
poner	pondr**é**	I will put	pondr**ía**	I would put
querer	querr**é**	I will want	querr**ía**	I would want
salir	saldr**é**	I will go out	saldr**ía**	I would go out
tener	tendr**é**	I will have	tendr**ía**	I would have
hay (haber)	habr**á**	there will be	habr**ía**	there would be

The Subjunctive Mood

- The subjunctive is a 'mood' or a 'voice' rather than a tense, as it can be used in different tenses.
- It is rare in English, but required in certain contexts in Spanish.
- You need to know the present tense singular forms of five key verbs in the subjunctive.

	yo	**tú**	**él / ella / usted**
hacer	haga	hagas	haga
ser	sea	seas	sea
ir	vaya	vayas	vaya
venir	venga	vengas	venga
tener	tenga	tengas	tenga

> **Key Point**
>
> You may also recognise the imperfect subjunctive **quisiera** (I would like). **Quisiera un kilo de naranjas, por favor.** I would like a kilo of oranges, please.

- You need to use the subjunctive in the following situations:
  - Referring to the future with **cuando**:
    Cuando tenga dinero, iré a España.
    When I have money, I will go to Spain.
  - After verbs of wishing, command, request and emotion:
    Espero que vengas.   I hope that you (will / can) come.
  - After the conjunction **que**:
    Es importante que lo hagas.   It's important that you do it.
  - Expressing purpose using **para que**:
    Mi madre ahorra para que mi hermano vaya a la universidad.
    My mum is saving up so my brother can go to university.

The Imperative

- The imperative is used to give commands or instructions.
- You need to know the imperative in the second person singular and plural forms.
- For the singular imperative, take the present tense **tú** form of the verb and remove the **-s**.
- For the plural imperative, take the infinitive form of the verb and replace the **-r** with **-d**.

You need to know the irregular forms of some common verbs in the **tú** form of the imperative.

> **Key Point**
>
> Remember to use opening and closing exclamation marks in your imperative phrase.

	Singular (tú)	**Plural (vosotros)**
hablar	¡Habla!	¡Hablad!
comer	¡Come!	¡Comed!
escribir	¡Escribe!	¡Escribid!

ser	to be	**¡Sé!**	Be!	**tener**	to have	**¡Ten!**	Have!
ir	to go	**¡Ve!**	Go!	**hacer**	to do / to make	**¡Haz!**	Do! / Make!
venir	to come	**¡Ven!**	Come!	**poner**	to put (on)	**¡Pon!**	Put (on)!
decir	to say / to tell	**¡Di!**	Say! / Tell!	**salir**	to leave / to go out	**¡Sal!**	Go out! / Leave!

> ### Quick Test
>
> 1. Translate into English: **hablaremos**; **iré**; **harás**; **saldrá**
> 2. Translate into Spanish: I would be; we would have; they would drink; she would listen
> 3. Translate into English: **No quiero que vayas conmigo**.
> 4. Translate into Spanish: Do your homework!
> 5. Change these infinitives into both imperative forms:
>   a) escuchar   b) trabajar   c) leer

Practice Questions

Grammar 2

1   Translate the following sentences into Spanish.

a)   Yesterday I played football with my brother.

....

b)   Last week, my parents spoke to my Spanish teacher.

....

c)   Last year we went to France.

....

d)   He travelled by bus.

....

e)   We ate in the kitchen.

....

f)   I bought a new mobile phone last Monday.

....

[6 marks]

2   Choose the correct form of the verb **haber** to complete the sentences.

he	has	ha	hemos	habéis	han

a)   **Mis padres** .... **hablado con mi profesor.**

b)   **Nosotros** .... **comida a la una.**

c)   **Yo** .... **visto la película antes.**

d)   **Marisa** .... **comido paella.**

e)   **¿Vosotros** .... **escrito al abuelo?**

f)   **¿Tú** .... **ido a la piscina esta semana?**

[6 marks]

3 Change the preterite verb into an imperfect verb, then translate the sentences into English.

a) Jugué con mi perro. ....

b) Nadé en el mar. ....

c) Viví en España. ....

d) Fui al parque. ....

e) Bebí un café. ....

[10 marks]

4 Choose the correct conditional verb to complete the sentences.

tendrías	estarían	podríamos	sería
tendría	iría	podría	irías

a) Yo .... contigo, pero no tengo tiempo.

b) Eso no .... ningún problema.

c) Tú .... que ir conmigo.

d) ¿Por qué no .... tú al cine con Paulo?

e) Juan .... estar aquí para las ocho.

f) Mi hermano nunca .... bastante dinero.

g) Ellos no .... en el restaurante.

h) Nosotros .... ver una película esta noche.

[8 marks]

5 Change the immediate future verb into a simple future verb, then translate the sentences into English.

a) Voy a jugar con mi perro. ....

b) Voy a nadar en el mar. ....

c) Voy a vivir en España. ....

d) Voy a ir al parque. ....

e) Voy a beber un café. ....

[10 marks]

Review Questions

Grammar 1

1 Choose the correct possessive adjective to complete the sentences.

a) **Mi / Mis cortinas son bonitas.**

b) **Vuestro / Vuestra dormitorio es muy pequeño.**

c) **¿Cómo es tu / tus casa?**

d) **Nuestro / Nuestra casa es bonita.**

e) **Su / Sus armario es grande.**

f) **Nuestros / Nuestras paredes son azules.**   [6 marks]

2 Complete the table in Spanish. All three verbs are regular in the present tense.

	escuchar	comer	vivir
yo	escucho		vivo
tú		comes	
él / ella / usted	escucha		vive
nosotros / nosotras		comemos	
vosotros / vosotras	escucháis		vivís
ellos / ellas / ustedes		comen	

[9 marks]

3 Continue the sentences by using an infinitive and complete them with your own information.

a) **Prefiero** ....

b) **Me gusta** ....

c) **Voy a** ....

d) **Tengo que** ....   [4 marks]

4 Make these sentences negative.

a) **Hablo español.**   ....

b) **Juego al fútbol.**   ....

c) Tengo un perro. ....

d) Siempre bebo agua. .... **[4 marks]**

5 Write the correct form of the verb in brackets. They are all radical changing verbs.

a) Las clases .... a las ocho y media. (empezar)

b) Mi amigo .... ir al cine. (preferir)

c) Yo .... hablar contigo. (querer)

d) ¿A qué hora te ....? (acostarse)

e) Yo me .... en mi habitación. (vestirse) **[5 marks]**

6 Would you use **ser** or **estar** to translate the bold words into Spanish? Tick the correct box.

	ser	estar
a) I **am** Spanish.		
b) My mum **is** a doctor.		
c) My sister **is** trans.		
d) My parents **are** divorced.		
e) The school **is** next to the park.		
f) My brother **is** funny.		

[5 marks]

7 Match the sentence halves by choosing the correct conjunction.

a) En el futuro quiero ser médico

b) Me gustaría ser contable,

c) En casa tengo dos gatos, tres perros

d) Mi abuela tiene más de ochenta años,

e) Mi hermano no es agradable,

f) Mi amiga Elena es muy perezosa

g) Con respecto a mi padre es muy gracioso

h) Al fin y al cabo, hay que trabajar siete

i) porque nunca estudia en el colegio.

ii) y cuatro caballos.

iii) pero encuentro difíciles las matemáticas.

iv) e inteligente.

v) que es mucha edad.

vi) u ocho horas cada día.

vii) o enfermero.

viii) sino maleducado. **[8 marks]**

Review Questions

Grammar 2

1 Complete the following sentences with the correct form of the preterite tense.

a) A   comimos   B   comieron   C   comió

Anoche mi amiga y yo _____ en un restaurante en el centro.

b) A   hablo   B   habló   C   hablaron

El lunes, Marco _____ con Antonia por teléfono.

c) A   fui   B   fuimos   C   fueron

Mis padres _____ a España por dos semanas.

d) A   puedo   B   pude   C   podría

No _____ contestar la pregunta.

e) A   visteis   B   vieron   C   vi

¿Vosotros _____ la película ayer?

f) A   me visto   B   me vistí   C   me vestí

Ayer, yo _____ a las ocho.   [6 marks]

2 Choose the correct imperfect tense verbs to complete the sentences.

esquiaba	hablaban	gustaba	había
nadaba	veía	jugaba	íbamos

a) Cuando era pequeño yo siempre _____ al fútbol en el jardín.

b) Yo _____ cada verano en el mar.

c) Cada invierno Nayara _____ en las montañas.

d) Nosotros _____ todos los años de vacaciones.

e) Ellos siempre _____ muy bien el español.

f) Mi hermano _____ los partidos de fútbol todos los sábados.

g) A mí me _____ mucho visitar a mis abuelos.

h) En el pasado _____ muchas tiendas en el pueblo.   [8 marks]

3   Complete the table in Spanish with the infinitive and first-person singular (**yo**) verb forms.

Infinitive	Present	Preterite	Imperfect	Perfect
....	**hablo**	....	**hablaba**	....
comer	....	**comí**	....	**he comido**
....	**vivo**	....	**vivía**	....

[8 marks]

4   Change these sentences to the passive voice (impersonal **se**). An example has been done for you.

Example: **Los libros son leídos en la biblioteca. → Se leen los libros en la biblioteca.**

a) **Las películas son vistas en el cine.** ....

b) **Los bocadillos son comidos en la cantina.** ....

c) **Los refrescos son bebidos en el parque.** .... [3 marks]

5   Correct the mistake in each future tense sentence.

a) **Esta noche saliré con mis amigos al centro.**

b) **Mañana, después del instituto jugé al baloncesto en el polideportivo.**

c) **Para proteger el medio ambiente poneré el papel en el reciclaje.**

d) **Mi hermano tenerá que estudiar mucho para aprobar sus exámenes.**

e) **Terminé mis estudios en junio del año que viene.**

f) **Si saco buenas notas, poderé ir a la universidad.** [6 marks]

6   Match the imperative phrases with the correct English translation.

a) **¡Toma la segunda a la derecha!**   i)   Take the first left!

b) **¡Háblame!**   ii)   Talk to me!

c) **¡Escribid la fecha!**   iii)   Listen to me!

d) **¡Siga todo recto!**   iv)   Go straight ahead!

e) **¡Toma la primera a la izquierda!**   v)   Take the second on the right!

f) **¡Escúchame!**   vii)   Write the date!   [6 marks]

Speaking

1 Role-play

You are talking to your Colombian friend. Your teacher will play the part of your friend and will speak first. You should address your friend as **tú**. When you see this - ? - you will have to ask a question. In order to score full marks, you must include a verb in your response to each task.

    1. Say what your favourite celebrity does. (Give **one** detail.)

    2. Say what your favourite celebrity looks like. (Give **one** detail.)

    3. Describe your favourite celebrity's personality. (Give **one** detail.)

    4. Say what sort of TV programmes you like. (Give **one** detail.)

?   5. Ask your friend a question about films.

10 marks

2 Role-play

You are talking to your Spanish friend. Your teacher will play the part of your friend and will speak first. You should address your friend as **tú**. When you see this - ? - you will have to ask a question. In order to score full marks, you must include a verb in your response to each task.

    1. Say one activity you do in your free time. (Give **one** detail.)

    2. Give one opinion about sport. (Give **one** detail.)

    3. Say what you did at the weekend. (Give **one** detail.)

    4. Describe your best friend. (Give **one** detail.)

?   5. Ask your friend a question about music.

10 marks

3 Reading aloud

Read aloud the following text **in Spanish**.

> **Somos cinco en mi familia.**
>
> **A veces puedo ser hablador.**
>
> **Mis hermanos me molestan y no nos llevamos bien.**
>
> **Espero casarme en el futuro.**
>
> **Mis padres están divorciados.**

5 marks

You will then be asked four questions **in Spanish** that relate to the topic of **Identity and Relationships with Others**.

- **Describe tu personalidad.**
- **¿Qué te gusta hacer con tus amigos?**
- **¿Cómo es tu mejor amigo o amiga físicamente?**
- **¿Cuál es tu opinión sobre el matrimonio?**

10 marks

4 Reading aloud

Read aloud the following text in Spanish.

> **Mando mensajes a mis amigos.**
>
> **Las redes sociales nos ayudan a conectar con los demás.**
>
> **Hay cada vez más influencers.**
>
> **Todos mis amigos tienen un móvil.**
>
> **Uso mi portátil para hacer mis deberes.**

5 marks

You will then be asked four questions **in Spanish** that relate to the topic of **Media and Technology**.

- **¿Qué haces con tu móvil?**
- **¿Qué es lo bueno de la tecnología?**
- **¿Te gustaría ser influencer?**
- **¿Hay desventajas con las redes sociales?**

10 marks

5 Photo card

Look at the two photos. Talk about the content of these photos for approximately one minute. You must say at least one thing about each photo.

5 marks

Now answer these questions related to the theme of **Popular Culture**.

- **¿Cuál es tu día favorito de la semana?**
- **¿Cuál es tu celebración favorita?**
- **¿Cómo te gusta pasar tu cumpleaños?**
- **¿Qué tipo de comida te gusta?**
- **¿Cuál es tu opinión sobre las fiestas en tu país?**
- **¿Qué piensas de las fiestas españolas?**
- **¿Qué haces durante las vacaciones de Navidad?**
- **¿Qué piensas de los fuegos artificiales?**

15 marks

Mixed Exam-Style Questions

Reading

1 You see these headlines on a Spanish news site.

A	¡Protestamos contra la contaminación!
B	Beber suficiente agua para su bienestar
C	Nueva zona peatonal en el centro histórico
D	Estudiar en la universidad – cada vez más caro
E	Muchas oportunidades en la industria tecnológica

Match the headlines to the correct topics.

a) Local area

b) The environment

c) The world of work

3 marks

2 Read what these Spanish teenagers say about their employment and work experience.

Carlos: Trabajo en una oficina moderna y grande y mi jefe es simpático.

Elena: Hice mis prácticas laborales en un banco y el trabajo era un poco monótono

Raúl: Me gustan mucho los niños pero mi trabajo en una escuela primaria es duro.

Sonia: Los sábados trabajo en una tienda y me encanta.

Javier: Pasé una semana en un restaurante y los clientes no eran comprensivos.

What do these people think about their employment and work experience?

Write **P** for a positive opinion, **N** for a negative opinion or **P+N** for a positive and negative opinion.

a) Carlos

b) Elena

c) Raúl

d) Sonia

e) Javier

5 marks

3 Read Ana's online post about healthy living and answer the questions in English.

> Creo que estoy en forma. No fumo y nunca fumaría porque mi madre fuma veinte cigarrillos cada día y detesto el olor. Mis amigos no toman drogas porque todos entendemos los riesgos, y solamente bebo alcohol en una fiesta, con moderación – por ejemplo, bebí una copa de vino la semana pasada porque fue el <u>bautizo</u> de mi primo. En cuanto a mi régimen, sigo una dieta equilibrada. Además, intento reducir el estrés, o sea hago ejercicio tres veces por semana. Sin embargo, no me gusta ir al gimnasio porque es aburrido. Pienso que dormir bien es más importante para el bienestar.

a) Why would Ana never smoke? (Give **two** details.)

....

b) Why do Ana and her friends not take drugs?

....

c) When does Ana drink alcohol?

....

d) How does Ana reduce stress?

....

e) What does Ana think of going to the gym?

....

f) What does Ana think is more important than the gym?

....

g) Read the text again. What is a **bautizo**?

A	a drink
B	a celebration
C	a shop

☐

8 marks

4 Translate these sentences into English.

a) No como ni carne ni pescado porque soy vegetariano.

b) Me encantan las matemáticas, aunque son difíciles.

c) Mi hermano hacía ciclismo cada fin de semana.

d) No me gusta la música clásica pero esta canción me relaja.

e) La actriz ganó un premio por su primera película.

10 marks

Writing

1 Your friend in Mexico sends you this photo. What is in this photo? Write **five** sentences in Spanish.

....

....

....

....

....

10 marks

2 Write an email to your Venezuelan friend about your school. Write approximately **50** words in Spanish. You must write something about each bullet point.

Mention:

- subjects
- teachers
- uniform
- rules
- daily routine.

10 marks

Mixed Exam-Style Questions

3 Using your knowledge of grammar, complete the following sentences. Choose the correct Spanish word from the three options in the grid.

a)

como	come	coma

Mi amigo _____ un bocadillo con queso.

b)

pequeño	pequeña	pequeños

Hay una tienda _____ en el centro.

c)

ver	veo	viendo

Me gusta _____ las películas de guerra.

d)

se	os	nos

No _____ llevamos bien.

e)

es	está	tiene

Mi hermana _____ ocho años.

5 marks

4 Translate the following sentences into Spanish.

a) I have green eyes.

....

b) There is a lot of traffic in my city.

....

c) It is forbidden to use your mobile in class.

....

d) Yesterday I ate chips and I drank water.

....

e) Next year I will buy a car.

....

10 marks

5 You are writing an article about travel and tourism.

Write approximately **90** words in Spanish.

You must write something about each bullet point.

Mention:

- the positive aspects of going on holiday
- how you have spent time away from home recently
- a trip you would like to take in future

☐

15 marks

6 HT You are writing an article about the environment and where you live.

Write approximately **150** words in Spanish.

You must write something about each bullet point.

Mention:

- information about your local area
- what you will do to help the environment in future

☐

25 marks

Answers

Pages 6–7 Review Questions

1. 8 – ocho [1]
   10 – diez [1]
   13 – trece [1]
   15 – quince [1]
   25 – veinticinco [1]
   37 – treinta y siete [1]
   42 – cuarenta y dos [1]
   53 – cincuenta y tres [1]
   61 – sesenta y uno [1]
   74 – setenta y cuatro [1]
   86 – ochenta y seis [1]
   90 – noventa [1]
2. **a)** Monday 11th July 2013 [1]
   b) Thursday 31st May 2008 [1]
   c) Saturday 5th June 2011 [1]
   d) Friday 17th January 2015 [1]
   e) Sunday 8th October 2012 [1]
   f) Wednesday 29th November 2017 [1]
   g) Tuesday 13th June 2009 [1]
3. Son las ocho y media. – 8:30 [1]
   Es la una y veinte. – 1:20 [1]
   Son las nueve menos veinte. – 8:40 [1]
   Es la una menos cuarto. – 12:45 [1]
   Son las dos y veinticinco. – 2:25 [1]
   Son las diez y diez. – 10:10 [1]
   Es el mediodía en punto. – 12:00 [1]
   Son las siete y cinco. – 7:05 [1]
   Son las once y cuarto. – 11:15 [1]
   Son las tres. – 3:00 [1]
4. **a)** C [1]; **b)** E [1]; **c)** I [1]; **d)** F [1];
   e) H [1]; **f)** D [1]; **g)** A [1]; **h)** J [1];
   i) G [1]; **j)** B [1]

Pages 8–13 Revise Questions

Page 9 Quick Test
1. Answers will vary. Example answer:
   Me llamo Bob. Bob se escribe B-O-B. Tengo quince años.
2. ¿Cómo te llamas? ¿Cuántos años tienes?
3. My name is Sara and I am sixteen years old. I am normally shy, but my mum says I am nice. Sometimes I can be lazy. My best friend's name is Juan and he is fifteen years old. He is very talkative / chatty. I get along well with him because he is funny.

Page 11 Quick Test
1. Soy bastante bajo/a pero muy delgado/a. Tengo el pelo largo, liso y castaño, y los ojos verdes.
2. alta, tiene, marrones

Page 13 Quick Test
1. Mis padres están separados.
2. I love my husband.
3. el matrimonio
4. es, están

Pages 14–15 Practice Questions

1. **a)** bonita [1]
   b) blancos [1]
   c) habladoras [1]
   d) bajo y gordo [1]
   e) divorciados [1]

---

   f) guapa [1]
   g) simpáticos [1]
   h) casados [1]
   i) responsable [1]
   j) azules [1]
2. **a)** es / se llama [1]
   b) somos [1]
   c) me llaman [1], me llamo [1]
   d) están [1]
   e) tenemos [1]
   f) es / se llama [1]
   g) eres [1]
   h) son [1]
   i) está [1]
3. **a)** Mi primo tiene el pelo castaño, liso y corto. [1]
   b) Soy bastante bajo y tengo los ojos verdes. [1]
   c) Mi hermano es de estatura mediana. [1]
   d) Mis tíos están casados, pero mi hermana está separada de su marido. [1]
4.

tener	ser	estar
tengo [1]	soy	estoy
tienes [1]	**eres [1]**	estás
tiene	**es [1]**	**está [1]**
tenemos	somos	**estamos [1]**
tenéis	**sois [1]**	estáis
tienen [1]	son	**están [1]**

5. **a)** P [1]; **b)** P+N [1]; **c)** N [1]
6. **a)** ~~está~~ están [1]
   b) ~~es~~ está [1]
   c) ~~tiene~~ tienen [1]
   d) ~~bajo~~ baja [1]
   e) ~~mi~~ mis [1]
   f) ~~llama~~ llaman [1]

Pages 16–21 Revise Questions

Page 17 Quick Test
1. ¿Tienes una mesa para cuatro, por favor?
2. La carta, por favor.
3. I am a vegan and I eat fruit for breakfast.
4. **a)** como
   b) bebo
   c) tengo
   d) tengo
   e) bebo, bebo
5. **a)** bebí, bebió
   b) comí, comiste

Page 19 Quick Test
1. Every day I wake up at 7:45 and I get up straight away.
2. Todas las noches me acuesto a las diez y me duermo enseguida.
3. **a)** he; **b)** ha; **c)** has; **d)** hemos; **e)** han
4. Answers will vary.
5. Answers will vary.

Page 21 Quick Test
1. **a)** Me duele la cabeza.
   b) Tengo dolor de brazo.
   c) Me duelen los dientes.
   d) Me duele la pierna.
   e) Me duele el pie.
2. My hands hurt because I have played a lot of volleyball.
3. Estoy en forma porque como una dieta equilibrada, es decir / o sea como pescado y verduras todos los días y bebo mucha agua.
4. Answers will vary. Example answer: Creo que estoy en forma porque hago ejercicio tres veces a la semana y también como alimentos saludables. No bebo alcohol y nunca tomaría drogas.

Pages 22–23 Practice Questions

1. **a)** two glasses of wine [1]
   b) four bottles of water [1]
   c) a hamburger with chips / fries [1]
   d) lots of meat [1]
   e) a glass of milk [1]
   f) a plate / dish of rice with chicken and vegetables [1]
   g) a kilo of apples [1]
   h) half a kilo of oranges [1]
   i) three pineapples [1]
   j) fish with hard-boiled eggs [1]
2. **a)** v) [1]; **b)** vii) [1]; **c)** iii) [1];
   d) vi) [1]; **e)** i) [1]; **f)** iv) [1];
   g) ii) [1]
3. Read the sentences aloud then listen to the sentences to check. **(1 mark for each sentence read correctly)**
4. **a)** What do you normally eat for breakfast? [1]
   b) What do you eat for lunch (at midday)? [1]
   c) Where do you eat dinner and what do you eat? [1]
   d) What do you normally drink? [1]
   e) Do you prefer fish or hamburgers? [1]
   f) Are you fit? [1]
5. **a)** me acosté [1], estaba [1]
   b) me levanto [1]
   c) me gustaría [1]
   d) hay [1]
   e) prefieres [1]
   f) estoy [1]
   g) tengo [1]
   h) hago [1], estar [1]
6. **a)** Hay que evitar una dieta malsana. [1]
   b) Debes acostarte temprano. [1]
   c) Tienes que dormir al menos ocho horas cada noche. [1]
   d) Debes practicar deporte tres veces a la semana. [1]
   e) No se debe fumar ni tomar drogas. [1]
   f) Hay que tratar de evitar el estrés. [1]
   g) Debes escuchar música para relajarte. [1]

Pages 24–25 Review Questions

1. a) se llama [1]
   b) eres [1]
   c) somos [1]
   d) tienen [1]
   e) son [1]
   f) se llaman [1]
   g) tienes [1]
   h) soy [1]
   i) es [1]
   j) tengo [1]
2. a) Tiene el pelo marrón, corto y liso, y los ojos verdes. [1]
   b) Soy bastante alto y muy delgado y también soy comprensivo y amable. [1]
   c) Mi padre es de estatura mediana. [1]
   d) Mis hermanos menores son muy deportistas. [1]
3. a) P [1]; b) P+N [1]; c) N [1]
4. Read the sentences aloud then listen to the sentences to check. (1 mark for each sentence read correctly)
5. a) Hay cuatro personas en mi familia, mi madre, mi padrastro, mi hermano menor y yo. [1]
   b) Soy bastante deportista, pero a veces puedo ser muy perezoso. [1]
6. Read the text aloud then listen to the text to check. (1 mark for each sentence read correctly)

Pages 26–31 Revise Questions

Page 27 Quick Test
1. a) feminine singular
   b) masculine plural
   c) feminine plural
   d) masculine singular
2. a) las; b) la; c) el
3. Spanish annoys me because it is quite difficult.
4. Me gustan mucho las matemáticas porque son interesantes, pero prefiero las ciencias porque son más emocionantes, sin embargo no aguanto los deportes.

Page 29 Quick Test
1. No me gustan las matemáticas porque siempre tenemos muchas pruebas.
2. Answers will vary. Example answer: Llevamos un uniforme, pero no me gusta. Llevamos una falda negra, una camisa blanca y una chaqueta azul oscuro con unos zapatos negros.
3. a) ✓
4. In my primary school we did not (use to) wear a school uniform.

Page 31 Quick Test
1. Quiero ir a la universidad para estudiar matemáticas.
2. At the weekend I work in a shop (in order) to earn a bit of money.
3. The preterite is used for a specific action in the past, and the imperfect is used for habitual / ongoing actions in the past.

a) preterite
b) imperfect
c) imperfect
4. Sentence b) is incorrect because we do not use the article in Spanish when talking about jobs.
5. Answers will vary. Example answer: y, pero, porque, para, aunque, mientras

Pages 32–33 Practice Questions

1. a) Me encanta el español porque es interesante. [1]
   b) Me encanta estudiar matemáticas, aunque son difíciles. [1]
   c) Estudio ocho asignaturas y prefiero las ciencias. [1]
   d) Quiero continuar estudiando inglés porque es útil. [1]
   e) Espero ir a la universidad para estudiar geografía. [1]
   f) Aunque es interesante, no me gusta estudiar historia. [1]
2. Read the sentences aloud then listen to the sentences to check. (1 mark for each sentence read correctly)
3. a) Voy a ir a la universidad para estudiar idiomas. [1]
   b) Hice mis prácticas en una oficina en el centro de la ciudad. [1]
   c) Todos los días escribía correos electrónicos. [1]
   d) Voy a continuar estudiando español y francés. [1]
   e) Me gustaría encontrar un trabajo a tiempo parcial. [1]
   f) Voy a conseguir un aprendizaje. [1]
   g) Trabajé / trabajaba como camarero en un restaurante sirviendo a los clientes. [1]
4. a) N [1]; b) P+N [1]; c) P [1]; d) N [1]; e) P [1]
5. a) No se debe / no se puede hablar en clase. [1]
   b) Se debe / hay que escuchar al profe. [1]
   c) No se debe / no se puede comer chicle. [1]
   d) No se debe / no se puede correr en el pasillo. [1]
   e) Se debe / hay que llevar uniforme. [1]
   f) No se debe / no se puede llevar maquillaje. [1]
   g) No se debe / no se puede usar el móvil. [1]
   h) Se debe / hay que hacer los deberes. [1]
   i) Se debe / hay que escribir la fecha. [1]
   j) No se debe / no se puede beber en clase. [1]
6. Answers will vary. Example answers:
   a) Voy a ir a la universidad. [1]
   b) Me gustaría estudiar matemáticas. [1]
   c) Quisiera conseguir un aprendizaje. [1]
   d) Tengo la intención de tomar un año sabático. [1]
   e) Iré a Sudamérica para aprender español. [1]
   f) Cuando termine los exámenes voy a estudiar el Bachillerato. [1]
   g) Vamos a encontrar un trabajo. [1]
   h) Intentaremos estudiar mucho para aprobar los exámenes. [1]
   i) Espero ganar mucho dinero. [1]

Pages 34–35 Review Questions

1. a) D [1]; b) B [1]; c) G [1]; d) E [1]; e) C [1]; f) F [1]; g) A [1]
2. a) breakfast [1]
   b) lunch [1]
   c) dinner [1]
   d) lunch [1]
   e) breakfast [1]
   f) dinner [1]
   g) dinner [1]
3. a) mesa [1]
   b) cuenta [1]
   c) tarjeta [1]
   d) quisiera [1]
   e) postre [1]
   f) beber [1]
4. d) ✓ [1]
5. a) Sigo / tengo una dieta equilibrada. [1]
   b) Evito comer comida rápida. [1]
   c) Como muchas frutas y verduras. [1]
   d) A veces como dulces / caramelos. [1]
   e) Me gusta comer el postre. [1]
   f) Bebo vino dos veces por semana. [1]
   g) Como ensalada todos los días. [1]
   h) Para el desayuno como una tortilla española. [1]
   i) Para el almuerzo / a mediodía como un sándwich / bocadillo de jamón. [1]
   j) Normalmente bebo ocho vasos de agua al día. [1]
6. a) Nunca como hamburguesas. [1]
   b) No hago mucho ejercicio. [1]
   c) No fumo. [1]
   d) No bebo alcohol. [1]
   e) No paso mucho tiempo relajándome. [1]
   f) No suelo seguir una dieta equilibrada. [1]
   g) La ensalada no es buena / es mala para la salud. [1]
   h) Las tartas no son muy sanas / son muy malsanas. [1]
7. a) como [1]
   b) suelo [1]
   c) tomo [1]
   d) me gusta [1]
   e) estar [1]

Pages 36–41 Revise Questions

Page 37 Quick Test
1. antes, ahora, en el futuro
2. Juego is in the present tense and means 'I play', and jugaba is in the imperfect (past) tense and means 'I used to play'.
3. I used to go to the youth club.
4. Hacía natación.
5. I would like to try (out) extreme sports.

Page 39 Quick Test
1. Me encanta escuchar música clásica porque me relaja.
2. Toco el teclado. / Sé tocar el teclado.
3. Famous people / celebrities like singers and influencers influence me a lot.

Answers

4. ~~mi amigo's casa~~ la casa de mi amigo
5. **a)** Cuelgo
    b) relajarme
    c) Sabes

Page 41 Quick Test
1. a) las; **b)** la; **c)** los; **d)** el
2. Me gusta ver películas de aventura.
3. Prefiero ver la televisión.
4. I like soap operas because they are more entertaining than cartoons.
5. a) ~~informativa~~ informativos
    b) ~~gusta~~ gustan, ~~interesante~~ interesantes
    c) ~~es~~ son, ~~emocionante~~ emocionantes, ~~comedia~~ comedias

Pages 42–43 Practice Questions

1. a) jugué   **[1]**
    b) hacer   **[1]**
    c) jugaba   **[1]**
    d) ver   **[1]**
    e) ir   **[1]**
    f) escuchar   **[1]**
    g) leo   **[1]**
    h) tocaba   **[1]**
    i) jugar   **[1]**
    j) charlando   **[1]**
2. a) D **[1]**; **b)** A **[1]**; **c)** B **[1]**; **d)** E **[1]**;
    e) C **[1]**
3. a) C **[1]**; **b)** B **[1]**; **c)** D **[1]**; **d)** E **[1]**;
    e) G **[1]**; **f)** F **[1]**; **g)** A **[1]**
4. a) I love playing football because it's a lot of fun. **[1]**
    b) I'm going to watch a documentary tonight about elephants in Africa. **[1]**
    c) Last night I went swimming / swam in the pool. **[1]**
    d) In the past, I used to play / played the piano, but now I play the guitar. **[1]**
    e) I do windsurfing at the beach in summer. **[1]**
5. a) Me gusta escuchar música pop. **[1]**
    b) Odio las películas de acción porque son aburridas. **[1]**
    c) Prefiero ir al cine con mi familia. **[1]**
    d) El domingo pasado jugué al tenis en el parque. **[1]**
    e) Jugaba al fútbol con mis amigos. **[1]**

Pages 44–45 Review Questions

1. a) No me gustan las ciencias porque tenemos muchos deberes. **[1]**
    b) Me encanta el inglés aunque tenemos que escribir mucho. **[1]**
    c) Me gusta el español porque el profe / la profe es amable y divertido/a. **[1]**
    d) Odio las matemáticas porque tenemos muchas pruebas. **[1]**
2. a) negros **[1]**
    b) roja **[1]**
    c) gris **[1]**
    d) blanca **[1]**
    e) marrones **[1]**
3. c) ✓ **[1]**

4. a) las **[1]**; **b)** el **[1]**; **c)** la **[1]**; **d)** la **[1]**;
    e) el **[1]**; **f)** el **[1]**; **g)** las **[1]**; **h)** las **[1]**;
    i) la **[1]**; **j)** la **[1]**
5. a) repasar   **[1]**
    b) hacer   **[1]**
    c) aprender   **[1]**
    d) enseñar   **[1]**
    e) aprobar   **[1]**
6. a) En el futuro quiero ir a la universidad. **[1]**
    b) Después de terminar los exámenes quisiera ir al colegio mayor. **[1]**
    c) Me gustaría encontrar un trabajo. **[1]**
    d) Intento hacer un aprendizaje. **[1]**
    e) Lo mejor para mí sería continuar con mis estudios. **[1]**
    f) Creo que no voy a casarme. **[1]**
7. a) B **[1]**; **b)** E **[1]**; **c)** D **[1]**;
    d) C **[1]**; **e)** A **[1]**

Pages 46–51 Revise Questions

Page 47 Quick Test
1. a) comiendo
    b) bebiendo
    c) cantando
    d) celebrando
    e) pasando
2. Answers will vary. Example answers:
    a) Estoy comiendo paella.
    b) Está bebiendo vino.
    c) Están cantando canciones.
    d) Estamos celebrando mi cumpleaños.
    e) ¿Estás pasando la Navidad con tu familia?
3. a) come
    b) se decoran
    c) jugando
    d) ir
    e) ver
4. Me encanta celebrar la Nochevieja.
5. Decoramos la casa.
6. My mum made a really tasty / delicious cake.

Page 49 Quick Test
1. To celebrate my birthday I eat my favourite dish / meal which is hamburger with chips.
2. Celebro mi cumpleaños con una fiesta divertida, e invito a mis amigos.
3. celebrado, llevado, recibido, invitado, comido, bebido
4. a) celebré
    b) sorprendido
    c) como, bebo
    d) amigos

Page 51 Quick Test
1. a) asistí
    b) había
    c) costaba
    d) se casó
2. The flowers were very beautiful.
3. El traje gris de mi hermano era muy elegante.

Pages 52–53 Practice Questions

1. a) iv) **[1]**; **b)** iii) **[1]**; **c)** i) **[1]**;
    d) v) **[1]**; **e)** ii) **[1]**

2. Read the sentences aloud then listen to the sentences to check. **(1 mark for each sentence read correctly)**
3. a) Cuál   **[1]**
    b) Qué   **[1]**
    c) Cuándo   **[1]**
    d) Dónde   **[1]**
4. Answers will vary. Example answers:
    a) Me gustan las fiestas en mi país, sobre todo la Semana Santa. **[1]**
    b) Normalmente paso las vacaciones de Navidad con mi familia. **[1]**
    c) Mi cumpleaños es el dos de febrero. **[1]**
    d) Me gusta celebrar mi cumpleaños en un restaurante. **[1]**
5. a) On New Year's Eve I always eat the twelve lucky grapes at exactly midnight. **[1]**
    b) The new year begins with fireworks and parties in the street. **[1]**
    c) During the San Fermín festival, you are allowed to run with the bulls. **[1]**
    d) At Easter you have to walk for hours to see the parades. **[1]**
    e) Tourists love Spanish festivals. **[1]**
6. a) C **[1]**; **b)** E **[1]**; **c)** A **[1]**; **d)** B **[1]**;
    e) D **[1]**

Pages 54–55 Review Questions

1. a) iii) **[1]**; **b)** i) **[1]**; **c)** v) **[1]**;
    d) ii) **[1]**; **e)** iv) **[1]**
2.

		Sport and activities	Music	Film and cinema	TV
a)	No me gustan las noticias porque son aburridas.				✓ **[1]**
b)	No voy al gimnasio porque soy perezoso.	✓ **[1]**			
c)	Voy a ver mi serie preferida con mi familia en casa.				✓ **[1]**
d)	Su nueva canción es triste.		✓ **[1]**		
e)	Pienso que ir al cine es muy caro.			✓ **[1]**	
f)	Cuando era más joven, jugaba al baloncesto.	✓ **[1]**			

3. Read the sentences aloud then listen to the sentences to check. **(1 mark for each sentence read correctly)**

4. vamos **[1]**, quiero **[1]**, hacer **[1]**, prefiero **[1]**, ver **[1]**, tengo **[1]**, pienso **[1]**
5. a) peligrosos **[1]**
   b) pequeña **[1]**
   c) preferido **[1]**
   d) nueva **[1]**
   e) aburridas **[1]**
   f) caro **[1]**
   g) divertidos **[1]**
   h) informativas **[1]**
6. Answers will vary. Example answers:
   a) Hago ciclismo todos los fines de semana. **[1]**
   b) Cuando era más joven, jugaba al fútbol en el parque. **[1]**
   c) Me gusta la música clásica porque me relaja. **[1]**
   d) No sé tocar un instrumento, pero quiero aprender. **[1]**
   e) No me gusta ir al cine porque es muy caro. **[1]**
   f) Me gusta ver los concursos porque son divertidos. **[1]**

Pages 56–61 Revise Questions

Page 57 Quick Test
1. sus; sus; su
2. estilo de vida; entrevistas; equipo; carácter; concurso
3. He announced that he was separating from his wife / She announced that she was separating from her wife.
4. Siempre ha querido ser cantante.

Page 59 Quick Test
1. cada vez más
2. van; tienen; hacen
3. She posted some videos online and became very popular.
4. Sigo a los influencers de moda en las redes sociales.

Page 61 Quick Test
1. libertad, igualdad, verdad, crisis, amenaza
2. they express; they speak about; they discuss
3. para ayudar; para mejorar; para apoyar
4. I would like to spend the day with him and take selfies.

Pages 62–63 Practice Questions

1. a) tiene **[1]**
   b) es **[1]**
   c) le gusta **[1]**
   d) les gusta **[1]**
   e) ayudar **[1]**
   f) llegan **[1]**
   g) mucho **[1]**
   h) era **[1]**
   i) opinas **[1]**
   j) ayudar **[1]**
2. a) Jaime ganó un concurso de cocina. **[1]**
   b) Participó en una serie donde los famosos viven en la selva. **[1]**
   c) Descubrí que Jaime sabe tocar la batería. **[1]**

d) Vi el / su vídeo que subió a una red social. **[1]**
   e) La pareja de Jaime se llama Ricardo. **[1]**
3. Read the sentences aloud then listen to the sentences to check. **(1 mark for each sentence read correctly)**
4. a) estudiaba **[1]**
   b) trabajo **[1]**
   c) ropa **[1]**
   d) guapas **[1]**
   e) actriz **[1]**
   f) premios **[1]**
   g) tiene **[1]**
5. Answers will vary. Example answers:
   a) Los influencers promueven productos y marcas en las redes sociales. **[1]**
   b) Sigo a los influencers porque hablan de cosas que me interesan. **[1]**
   c) Me gustan los influencers porque son graciosos e interesantes. **[1]**
   d) No me gustaría ser influencer porque no tienen una vida privada. **[1]**
   e) Mi celebridad preferida es Erling Haaland porque tiene mucho talento. **[1]**
   f) Se puede ganar mucho dinero y viajar por todo el mundo. **[1]**
   g) Se puede recibir amenazas y los aficionados no siempre son simpáticos. **[1]**

Pages 64–65 Review Questions

1. a) To celebrate my birthday, I like to go to a restaurant with my family. **[1]**
   b) Last year, I celebrated my birthday with my friends. **[1]**
   c) Every year in July, there is a bull festival in Pamplona. **[1]**
   d) I would like to see the Tomatina [festival] in Buñol, Valencia. **[1]**
   e) I have always wanted to participate / take part in in the San Fermín festival in Pamplona. **[1]**
   f) During the Tomatina, you can throw tomatoes at your friends. **[1]**
   g) People dress up during the Day of the Dead in Mexico. **[1]**
   h) The tradition of eating the twelve lucky grapes at midnight on New Year's Eve is very important for Spanish people. **[1]**
2. Read the sentences aloud then listen to the sentences to check. **(1 mark for each sentence read correctly)**
3. a) v) **[1]**;   b) i) **[1]**;   c) ii) **[1]**;
   d) iv) **[1]**;   e) iii) **[1]**
4. a) Hay muchos festivales en España cada año. **[1]**
   b) Me gusta celebrar mi cumpleaños con mis amigos. **[1]**
   c) El año pasado visité Pamplona durante el festival de San Fermín. **[1]**
   d) En el futuro, si tengo dinero, me gustaría visitar México para celebrar el festival del Día de los Muertos. **[1]**
5. a) tiene **[1]**
   b) pequeños **[1]**
   c) romper **[1]**

d) especial **[1]**
   e) los **[1]**
6. Answers will vary. Example answers:
   a) Mi fiesta española favorita es la Semana Santa porque es una fiesta emocionante. **[1]**
   b) Me gustaría participar en las Fallas porque es una fiesta divertida. **[1]**
   c) Durante las vacaciones de Pascua, me gusta comer mucho chocolate. **[1]**
   d) Para celebrar mi cumpleaños, hago una fiesta con mis amigos. **[1]**

Pages 66–71 Revise Questions

Page 67 Quick Test
1. Normalmente voy de vacaciones al extranjero con mi familia.
2. Answers will vary. Example answer: Viajar en avión es caro, viajar en coche es cómodo, viajar en autobús es barato.
3. a) español
   b) francés
   c) inglés
   d) chino
4. I prefer to travel by train because it is cheaper than travelling by plane.

Page 69 Quick Test
1. I saw lots of interesting shows.
2. a) fuimos
   b) iba
   c) era
   d) vi
   e) sacaba
3. Fui a la playa y comí en un restaurante.
4. Answers will vary. Example answer: Normalmente voy a España para visitar a mis abuelos, pero el año pasado fui a Grecia con mis amigos y el año que viene me gustaría viajar por Francia con mi hermano.

Page 71 Quick Test
1. arena, alojamiento, recuerdo, vuelo, paisaje
2. to fly; to stay; to buy

Pages 72–73 Practice Questions

1. **Transport** en coche **[1]**
   un vuelo directo **[1]**
   el aeropuerto **[1]**
   el avión **[1]**
   Activities el museo **[1]**
   ir de compras **[1]**
   nadar **[1]**
   el espectáculo **[1]**
   Weather llueve **[1]**
   el calor **[1]**
   hace fresco **[1]**
   el sol **[1]**
   Food and drink las patatas fritas **[1]**
   la carne **[1]**
   la cena **[1]**
   el vino **[1]**
2. a) voy **[1]**, fui **[1]**, voy a ir / iré **[1]**
   b) como **[1]**, comí **[1]**, voy a comer / comeré **[1]**

Answers

c) bebo **[1]**, bebí **[1]**, voy a beber / beberé **[1]**

3. hace **[1]**, hizo **[1]**, va a hacer / hará **[1]**

4. **a)** N **[1]**; **b)** P **[1]**; **c)** P+N **[1]**; **d)** P **[1]**; **e)** N **[1]**

5. **a)** iv) **[1]**; **b)** v) **[1]**; **c)** ii) **[1]**; **d)** i) **[1]**; **e)** vi) **[1]**; **f)** iii) **[1]**

6. Answers will vary. Example answers:
a) No me gusta tomar el sol porque pienso que es aburrido. **[1]**
b) Me gusta dar un paseo temprano por la mañana cuando está todo tranquilo. **[1]**
c) Es importante tener nuevas experiencias cuando estoy de vacaciones. **[1]**
d) No me gusta viajar al extranjero porque tengo miedo a volar. **[1]**
e) El profe organiza una excursión para los estudiantes. **[1]**
f) ¿Dónde puedo comprar un billete de tren? **[1]**

7. Answers will vary. Example answers:
a) Normalmente voy a Italia con mi familia y viajamos en avión. **[1]**
b) Me gustan las vacaciones culturales porque me interesa la historia. **[1]**
c) No me gustan las vacaciones deportivas porque no soy muy deportista. **[1]**
d) Prefiero visitar sitios y monumentos interesantes. Doy un paseo cada día. **[1]**
e) Es importante relajarse y es interesante descubrir una cultura nueva. **[1]**
f) Me gustaría visitar Sudamérica para practicar mi español durante las vacaciones. **[1]**
g) El año pasado fui a Grecia con mi madre y hacía mucho sol. Me gustó mucho. **[1]**
h) Creo que voy a pasar un fin de semana en Londres con mis amigos porque vamos a ver un concierto. **[1]**

Pages 74–75 Review Questions

1. **a)** iv) **[1]**; **b)** v) **[1]**; **c)** ii) **[1]**; **d)** i) **[1]**; **e)** vi) **[1]**; **f)** iii) **[1]**

2. Read the sentences aloud then listen to the sentences to check. **(1 mark for each sentence read correctly)**

3. **a)** N **[1]**; **b)** P **[1]**; **c)** P+N **[1]**; **d)** P **[1]**

4. **a)** Social networks have a strong (big) influence on children. **[1]**
b) Many young people like to copy famous people. **[1]**
c) It is better to have a role model who you know personally. **[1]**
d) We should identify with people who have done something impressive. **[1]**
e) Everyone makes mistakes / we all make mistakes, even / including famous people. **[1]**

5. **a)** Me gustaría ser famoso/a y rico/a. **[1]**
b) Ganó un premio por su primera película. **[1]**
c) Sigo a unos influencers que hablan de deporte y salud. **[1]**
d) En el futuro voy a hacerme influencer. **[1]**
e) Los famosos tienen mucho dinero, pero sus vidas no son fáciles. **[1]**

f) Es transgénero y su identidad es muy importante. **[1]**

6. Answers will vary. Example answers:
a) Mi famosa preferida se llama Lady Gaga. **[1]**
b) A mi famoso preferido se le conoce especialmente como cantante. **[1]**
c) Sigo a los influencers que me inspiran y hablan de cosas importantes. **[1]**
d) No me gustan los influencers que promueven productos todo el tiempo. **[1]**
e) Un buen modelo a seguir es Greta Thunberg porque usa su fama para proteger el medioambiente. **[1]**
f) Es bueno ser famoso porque se puede comprar lo se que quiera. **[1]**
g) No es bueno ser famoso porque se arriesga uno a escándalos. **[1]**

Pages 76–81 Revise Questions

Page 77 Quick Test
1. la prensa, el teclado, el anuncio
2. tenían; era; no había
3. I read an online newspaper / a newspaper online every day.
4. Es más fácil sacar fotos con un móvil.

Page 79 Quick Test
1. Paso dos horas navegando la red en mi móvil todos los días.
2. correo electrónico, redes sociales
3. Uso mi portátil para hacer mis deberes.
4. I usually post photos on social media every day.

Page 81 Quick Test
1. I am a singer, a model and an influencer.
2. **a)** está; **b)** es; **c)** es; **d)** está
3. Estaban casados, pero ahora están solteros.
4. Answers will vary. Example answer: Mi influencer favorita es Georgina Rodríguez. Creo que es una persona simpática y generosa, y también es muy bonita. Tiene el pelo largo y castaño y los ojos marrones. Su pareja también es famoso.

Pages 82–83 Practice Questions

1. **a)** to upload = subir **[1]**
b) to download = bajar **[1]**
c) to share = compartir **[1]**
d) to send = mandar **[1]**
e) to send = enviar **[1]**
f) to communicate = comunicar **[1]**
g) to surf (the internet) = navegar **[1]**
h) to look for = buscar **[1]**

2. **a)** N **[1]**; **b)** P **[1]**; **c)** P+N **[1]**; **d)** P **[1]**; **e)** N **[1]**

3. **a)** iii) **[1]**; **b)** i) **[1]**; **c)** v) **[1]**; **d)** ii) **[1]**; **e)** iv) **[1]**

4. Read the sentences aloud then listen to the sentences to check. **(1 mark for each sentence read correctly)**

5. **a)** uso **[1]**
b) envían **[1]**
c) verdes **[1]**

d) es **[1]**
e) tienen **[1]**
f) cambiado **[1]**
g) leer **[1]**
h) tenía **[1]**

6. Answers will vary. Example answers:
a) Uso mi móvil para hablar con mis amigos y mis padres. **[1]**
b) Uso la tecnología para hacer mis deberes y leer artículos. **[1]**
c) Ayer jugué a los videojuegos con mi primo. **[1]**
d) Uso las redes sociales todos los días. **[1]**
e) Me gustan las redes sociales, pero sé que hay muchos riesgos. **[1]**
f) Se puede compartir cosas interesantes con los demás. **[1]**

Pages 84–85 Review Questions

1. **a)** D **[1]**; **b)** B **[1]**; **c)** E **[1]**; **d)** A **[1]**; **e)** F **[1]**; **f)** C **[1]**

2. **a)** barco **[1]**
b) tiempo **[1]**
c) maleta **[1]**
d) famosa **[1]**
e) muchas **[1]**
f) exposición **[1]**
g) hacer **[1]**
h) hace **[1]**

3. **a)** Prefiero viajar en avión porque es rápido. **[1]**
b) Me gusta visitar países diferentes en todo el mundo. **[1]**
c) Cuando hace sol descanso en la playa. **[1]**
d) En el futuro me gustaría ir a España. **[1]**
e) Hago camping con mi familia porque es barato. **[1]**
f) Siempre compro recuerdos para mis amigos. **[1]**

4. Answers will vary. Example answers:
a) El avión es más cómodo que el tren. **[1]**
b) Ir a la playa es menos interesante que ir al museo. **[1]**
c) Creo que un hotel es mejor que un camping. **[1]**
d) Pienso que la lluvia es peor que el sol. **[1]**

5. **a)** Two years ago I went to France with my friends. **[1]**
b) Next year I would like to visit my Italian grandfather. **[1]**
c) Travelling abroad is exciting although it is not cheap. **[1]**
d) Generally I travel by bus because it's practical. **[1]**
e) We are going to organise a trip / excursion to the beach. **[1]**
f) It was hot every day but I really don't like the sun. **[1]**

6. **a)** El año pasado fui de vacaciones a Sudamérica. **[1]**
b) El año que viene voy a pasar las vacaciones en casa. **[1]**
c) Las vacaciones culturales son más interesantes que las vacaciones de aventura. **[1]**
d) En verano hay muchos turistas en el aeropuerto. **[1]**

e) Nadé en el mar con mis hermanas y nuestro perro. **[1]**

f) Fuimos a la playa pero hacía mucho frío. **[1]**

Pages 86–91 Revise Questions

Page 87 Quick Test

1. Answers will vary. Example answer: Vivo en una casa bastante grande. Tenemos un jardín. En la planta baja hay una cocina, un salón y un comedor, y en la primera planta hay tres habitaciones y un baño.

2. Answers will vary. Example answer: Me gusta mi habitación porque es cómoda. Hay una mesa y una silla, y tengo una cama debajo de la ventana. En el rincón hay un sofá.

3. a) de la; b) del; c) del

4. Mi dormitorio / habitación está en la primera planta.

5. My flat is on the ground floor.

Page 89 Quick Test

1. Answers will vary. Example answer: Vivo en una casa en la costa. Está muy cerca de la playa y es un pueblo muy bonito.

2. a) un; b) una; c) unas; d) unos

3. Vivo en una ciudad industrial en la costa.

4. There are a lot of factories in my town.

Page 91 Quick Test

1. Answers will vary. Example answers: La contaminación, el cambio climático, los animales en peligro de extinción, los incendios forestales, los desastres naturales

2. My town is very polluted.

3. Answers will vary. Example answers: Se debe usar el transporte público, hay que reciclar la basura.

4. Debemos / se debe mejorar el medio ambiente.

Pages 92–93 Practice Questions

1. a) iii) **[1]**; b) i) **[1]**; c) v) **[1]**; d) ii) **[1]**; e) iv) **[1]**

2. a) animado **[1]**
   b) moderna **[1]**
   c) verdes **[1]**
   d) buenos **[1]**
   e) bonitas **[1]**
   f) antiguo **[1]**
   g) hermosa **[1]**
   h) sucios **[1]**

3. a) to build = construir **[1]**
   b) to throw = tirar **[1]**
   c) to save = salvar **[1]**
   d) to destroy = destruir **[1]**
   e) to clean = limpiar **[1]**
   f) to pollute = contaminar **[1]**
   g) to recycle = reciclar **[1]**
   h) to protect = proteger **[1]**

4. Read the sentences aloud then listen to the sentences to check. **(1 mark for each sentence read correctly)**

5. a) We have a big garden with lots of beautiful / lovely trees. **[1]**

b) My house is near / close to the park and my school. **[1]**

c) I live in the suburbs / outskirts in an industrial area. **[1]**

d) There are interesting museums but the shops are small. **[1]**

e) At home you should recycle and reuse. **[1]**

f) It is better to walk / go by foot instead of travelling by car. **[1]**

6. a) En mi casa hay un salón, pero no hay jardín. **[1]**

b) En mi dormitorio tengo una mesa y una silla. **[1]**

c) Vio en la costa al lado de la playa. **[1]**

d) Hay una piscina, pero no tenemos cine. **[1]**

e) Participo en una campaña para ayudar a la Tierra. **[1]**

f) Mi ciudad está muy contaminada porque hay muchos coches. **[1]**

Pages 94–95 Review Questions

1. a) C **[1]**; b) D **[1]**; c) A **[1]**; d) E **[1]**; e) B **[1]**

2. Answers will vary. Example answers:
   a) Ayer envié un correo electrónico a mi tía **[1]**; Envío SMS a mis amigos todos los días **[1]**; Te voy a enviar unas fotos **[1]**
   b) Anoche recibí un mensaje interesante **[1]**; Cada día recibo muchos mensajes **[1]**; No sé cuántas llamadas recibiré mañana **[1]**
   c) Cuando era joven no usaba Internet **[1]**; No uso mi móvil en el colegio **[1]**; Voy a usar mi portátil para hacer mis deberes **[1]**

3. a) iii) **[1]**; b) i) **[1]**; c) v) **[1]**; d) ii) **[1]**; e) iv) **[1]**

4. a) todo **[1]**
   b) sueño **[1]**
   c) carrera **[1]**
   d) teclado **[1]**
   e) ordenador **[1]**
   f) teléfono **[1]**

5. a) Instead of sending emails, I send text messages. **[1]**
   b) Social networks can be very addictive and [can] cause problems. **[1]**
   c) My favourite influencer has worked with many famous brands. **[1]**
   d) There are too many adverts on this website. **[1]**
   e) My laptop is old and doesn't work very well. **[1]**

6. a) Guardo muchas fotos en mi móvil. **[1]**
   b) Anoche bajé una nueva aplicación / app. **[1]**
   c) Es un influencer, por lo tanto, es muy conocido. **[1]**
   d) Quiero ver la televisión, pero la pantalla está rota. **[1]**
   e) Los jóvenes piensan que la tecnología es muy importante. **[1]**

Pages 96–103 Revise Questions

Page 97 Quick Test

1. feminine, masculine or feminine, feminine, feminine, masculine

2. lápices, marrones, camas, fresas, directores

3. pez, gato, televisión, pelota, ojo

4. a) Me gusta la historia.
   b) Soy profesor.

Page 99 Quick Test

1. a) el perro viejo
   b) la chica / niña bonita
   c) los chicos / niños / jóvenes trabajadores

2. a) the chatty boys
   b) the shy girl
   c) the tall women

3. a) que; b) má; c) el

4. El libro es buenísimo.

Page 101 Quick Test

1. a) slowly
   b) quickly
   c) healthily
   d) absolutely

2. a) fácilmente
   b) posiblemente
   c) frecuentemente
   d) verdaderamente

3. How old are you?

4. a) para; b) por, para

Page 103 Quick Test

1. a) charlo, charlas, charla
   b) bebo, bebes, bebe
   c) recibo, recibes, recibe

2. a) te; b) se; c) me

3. a) Nunca juego al vóleibol.
   b) No como carne.
   c) No veo documentales tampoco.

Pages 104–105 Practice Questions

1. a) los castillos **[1]**
   b) los hombres **[1]**
   c) los planetas **[1]**
   d) las aguas **[1]**
   e) las naranjas **[1]**
   f) las mujeres **[1]**
   g) las estaciones **[1]**
   h) las luces **[1]**

2. a) una catedral **[1]**
   b) un bolígrafo **[1]**
   c) un balcón **[1]**
   d) un autobús **[1]**
   e) una moto **[1]**
   f) un árbol **[1]**
   g) una habitación **[1]**
   h) un cine **[1]**

3. a) simpático **[1]**
   b) habladora **[1]**
   c) impacientes **[1]**
   d) graciosas **[1]**
   e) rubio **[1]**
   f) gran **[1]**

4. ¿Cómo quieres ir, en autobús o en tren? **[1]**
   ¿Cuál es el mío, el verde o el azul? **[1]**
   ¿Cuándo es tu cumpleaños? **[1]**

Answers

¿Cuánto cuestan los zapatos? **[1]**
¿Cuántos años tiene tu hermana? **[1]**
¿Dónde está mi móvil? **[1]**
¿Por qué dices eso? **[1]**
¿Qué significa eso? **[1]**
¿Quién es aquella mujer, Señora Watson
o Señora Woods? **[1]**

5. a) se **[1]**;　b) me **[1]**;　c) se **[1]**;
 d) nos **[1]**;　e) os **[1]**;　f) te **[1]**

Pages 106–107 Review Questions

1.

Buildings	Rooms	Furniture
un piso **[1]** una casa **[1]** la planta baja **[1]**	una cocina **[1]** un salón **[1]** un baño **[1]**	una mesa **[1]** una cama **[1]** una silla **[1]**

2. a) comfortable **[1]**, big **[1]**
 b) above **[1]**
 c) in the corner **[1]**
 d) table **[1]**, door **[1]** (any order)
 e) left / left-hand side **[1]**
 f) next to **[1]**
3. a) N **[1]**;　b) P **[1]**;　c) P+N **[1]**;　d) P **[1]**;
 e) N **[1]**
4. Answers will vary. Example answers:
 a) Vivo en una casa pequeña en el
 campo. **[1]**
 b) Me gusta mi casa porque es cómoda y
 bonita. **[1]**
 c) Mi habitación es bastante pequeña y
 moderna. **[1]**
 d) Mi pueblo es animado pero un poco
 feo. **[1]**
 e) En una ciudad hay mucho que hacer,
 sin embargo, puede ser ruidoso. **[1]**
 f) En el campo se puede estar al aire libre
 pero no hay muchas tiendas. **[1]**
 g) En el futuro me gustaría vivir en una
 casa grande cerca de la playa. **[1]**
5. a) iv) **[1]**;　b) vi) **[1]**;　c) i) **[1]**;
 d) iii) **[1]**;　e) ii) **[1]**;　f) v) **[1]**
6. Answers will vary. Example answers:
 a) Apago las luces cuando salgo de una
 habitación. **[1]**
 b) Es importante proteger el
 medioambiente. **[1]**
 c) Los fines de semana recogemos la
 basura en la playa. **[1]**
 d) Las fábricas en mi ciudad contaminan
 el aire. **[1]**
 e) Para reducir la contaminación se puede
 ir a pie. **[1]**
 f) Nunca utilizo una bolsa de plástico –
 llevo mi propia bolsa. **[1]**

Pages 108–116 Revise Questions

Page 109 Quick Test
1. a) Voy al cine.
 b) Tengo los ojos marrones.
 c) Hago yoga.
2. a) We are going to the park.
 b) He / she has brown hair.

 c) We go (do) swimming.
3. a) Estoy haciendo esquí.
 b) Estoy comiendo mucho chocolate.
 c) Estoy tomando el sol.
 d) Estoy bebiendo coca-cola.
4. a) porque
 b) sino
 c) ya que

Page 111 Quick Test
1. They ate paella yesterday.
2. a) fui
 b) jugué
 c) llegué
 d) bebió
 e) hicimos
3. Saqué muchas fotos.
4. When I was young, I used to like playing
 baseball.
5. Cuando era joven, me encantaba ir al
 parque los sábados.

Page 113 Quick Test
1. a) escuchado
 b) comido
 c) permitido
2. a) Acabo de terminar mis deberes.
 b) He comido patatas fritas.
 c) Había visto la película.
3. El pan es vendido por la tienda.
 Se vende pan.

Page 115 Quick Test
1. a) you (informal singular)
 b) I
 c) we (masculine or mixed)
 d) they (masculine or mixed)
 e) you (formal singular)
2. I like the boots. Do you have them in
 white?
3. Quiero salir contigo.

Page 117 Quick Test
1. we will talk; I will go; you will do;
 he / she will go out
2. sería; tendríamos; beberían; ella escucharía
3. I don't want you to go with me.
4. ¡Haz tus deberes!
5. a) ¡Escucha! ¡Eschuchad!
 b) ¡Trabaja! ¡Trabajad!
 c) ¡Lee! ¡Leed!

Pages 118–119 Practice Questions

1. a) Ayer jugué al fútbol con mi hermano. **[1]**
 b) La semana pasada, mis padres hablaron
 con mi profesor de español. **[1]**
 c) El año pasado fuimos a Francia. **[1]**
 d) Viajó en autobús. **[1]**
 e) Comimos en la cocina. **[1]**
 f) Compré un teléfono móvil nuevo el
 lunes pasado. **[1]**
2. a) han **[1]**;　b) hemos **[1]**;　c) he **[1]**;
 d) ha **[1]**;　e) habéis **[1]**;　f) has **[1]**
3. a) Jugaba con mi perro. **[1]** – I used to play
 with my dog. **[1]**
 b) Nadaba en el mar. **[1]** – I used to swim
 in the sea. **[1]**

 c) Vivía en España. **[1]** – I used to live in
 Spain. **[1]**
 d) Iba al parque. **[1]** – I used to go to the
 park. **[1]**
 e) Bebía un café. **[1]** – I used to drink a
 coffee. **[1]**
4. a) iría **[1]**
 b) sería **[1]**
 c) tendrías **[1]**
 d) irías **[1]**
 e) podría **[1]**
 f) tendría **[1]**
 g) estarían **[1]**
 h) podríamos **[1]**
5. a) Jugaré con mi perro. **[1]** – I will play
 with my dog. **[1]**
 b) Nadaré en el mar. **[1]** – I will swim in the
 sea. **[1]**
 c) Viviré en España. **[1]** – I will live in
 Spain. **[1]**
 d) Iré al parque. **[1]** – I will go to the
 park. **[1]**
 e) Beberé un café. **[1]** – I will drink (a)
 coffee. **[1]**

Pages 120–121 Review Questions

Grammar 1
1. a) Mis **[1]**;　b) Vuestro **[1]**;　c) tu **[1]**;
 d) Nuestra **[1]**;　e) Su **[1]**;　f) Nuestras **[1]**
2.

escuchar	comer	vivir
escucho	**como [1]**	vivo
escuchas [1]	comes	**vives [1]**
escucha	**come [1]**	vive
escuchamos [1]	comemos	**vivimos [1]**
escucháis	**coméis [1]**	vivís
escuchan [1]	comen	**viven [1]**

3. Answers will vary. Example answers:
 a) Prefiero comer patatas fritas. **[1]**
 b) Me gusta jugar al baloncesto. **[1]**
 c) Voy a ir al cine. **[1]**
 d) Tengo que hacer mis deberes. **[1]**
4. a) No hablo español. **[1]**
 b) No juego al fútbol. **[1]**
 c) No tengo perro. **[1]**
 d) Nunca bebo agua. **[1]**
5. a) empiezan **[1]**
 b) prefiere **[1]**
 c) quiero **[1]**
 d) acuestas **[1]**
 e) visto **[1]**
6.

		ser	estar
a)	I **am** Spanish.	✓ **[1]**	
b)	My mum **is** a doctor.	✓ **[1]**	
c)	My sister **is** trans.	✓ **[1]**	
d)	My parents **are** divorced.		✓ **[1]**
e)	The school **is** next to the park.		✓ **[1]**
f)	My brother **is** funny.	✓ **[1]**	

7. **a)** vii) **[1]**; **b)** iii) **[1]**; **c)** ii) **[1]**;
   d) v) **[1]**; **e)** viii) **[1]**; **f)** i) **[1]**;
   g) iv) **[1]**; **h)** vi) **[1]**

Pages 122–123 Review Questions

1. **a)** A comimos [1]
   b) B habló [1]
   c) C fueron [1]
   d) B pude [1]
   e) A visteis [1]
   f) C me vestí [1]
2. **a)** jugaba [1]
   b) nadaba [1]
   c) esquiaba [1]
   d) íbamos [1]
   e) hablaban [1]
   f) veía [1]
   g) gustaba [1]
   h) había [1]

3.

Infinitive	Present	Preterite	Imperfect	Perfect
hablar **[1]**	hablo	hablé **[1]**	hablaba	he hablado **[1]**
comer	como **[1]**	comí	comía **[1]**	he comido
vivir **[1]**	vivo	viví **[1]**	vivía	he vivido **[1]**

4. **a)** Se ven películas en el cine. **[1]**
   b) Se comen bocadillos en la cantina. **[1]**
   c) Se beben refrescos en el parque. **[1]**
5. **a)** ~~saliré~~ saldré **[1]**
   b) ~~jugé~~ jugaré **[1]**
   c) ~~poneré~~ pondré **[1]**
   d) ~~tenerá~~ tendrá **[1]**
   e) ~~terminé~~ terminaré **[1]**
   f) ~~poderé~~ podré **[1]**
6. **a)** v) **[1]**; **b)** ii) **[1]**; **c)** vii) **[1]**;
   d) iv) **[1]**; **e)** i) **[1]**; **f)** iii) **[1]**

Pages 124–131 Mixed Exam-Style Questions

Speaking

1. Role-play

TEACHER'S ROLE
- You begin the role-play.
- You should address the candidate as *tú*.
- You must read out the teacher's role shown below in italics **without any changes**.

You must begin the role-play by using the introductory text below.

Introductory text: *Estás hablando con tu amigo colombiano / tu amiga colombiana. Yo soy tu amigo / tu amiga.*

1 Ask the candidate what their favourite celebrity does. (Elicit **one** detail.)
   ¿Qué hace tu persona famosa favorita?
   Allow the candidate to say what their favourite celebrity does. Example answer: Mi persona famosa favorita es cantante y actriz.

2 Ask the candidate what their favourite celebrity looks like. (Elicit **one** detail.)
   ¿Cómo es tu persona famosa favorita físicamente?
   Allow the candidate to say what their favourite celebrity looks like. Example answer: Tiene el pelo rubio y los ojos verdes.

3 Ask the candidate to describe their favourite celebrity's personality. (Elicit **one** detail.)
   Describe la personalidad de tu persona famosa favorita.
   Allow the candidate to describe their favourite celebrity's personality. Example answer: Es muy simpática y un poco habladora.

4 Ask the candidate what sort of TV programme they like.
   ¿Qué tipo de programa te gusta?
   Allow the candidate to say what sort of TV programme they like. Example answer: Me gustan mucho las telenovelas.

5 **?** *Vale.*
   Allow the candidate to ask a question about films. Example answer: ¿Te gustan las películas de aventura?
   (Give an appropriate response)

2. Role-play

TEACHER'S ROLE
- You begin the role-play.
- You should address the candidate as *tú*.
- You must read out the teacher's role shown below in italics **without any changes**.

You must begin the role-play by using the introductory text below.

Introductory text: *Estás hablando con tu amigo español / tu amiga española. Yo soy tu amigo / tu amiga.*

1 Ask the candidate what they do in their free time. (Elicit **one** detail.)
   ¿Qué haces en tu tiempo libre?
   Allow the candidate to say what they do in their free time. Example answer: Voy al cine y escucho música.

2 Ask the candidate for their opinion about sport. (Elicit **one** detail.)
   ¿Cuál es tu opinión sobre el deporte?
   Allow the candidate to give their opinion about sport. Example answer: No me gusta el deporte pero es importante para estar en forma.

3 Ask the candidate what they did at the weekend. (Elicit **one** detail.)
   ¿Qué hiciste el fin de semana pasado?
   Allow the candidate to say what they did at the weekend. Example answer: El fin de semana pasado fui de compras con mis amigos.

4 Ask the candidate to describe their best friend. (Elicit **one** detail.)
   ¿Cómo es tu mejor amigo o amiga?
   Allow the candidate to describe their best friend. Example answer: Mi mejor amigo es gracioso y bastante tímido.

5 **?** *Vale.*
   Allow the candidate to ask a question about music. Example answer: ¿Te gusta la música pop?
   (Give an appropriate response)

3. Reading aloud
Answers will vary. Example answers:
- Soy muy artística y a veces puedo ser perezosa.
- Me gusta ver la televisión e ir al cine con mis amigos.
- Mi mejor amiga tiene los ojos azules y el pelo castaño.
- El matrimonio no me interesa y no quiero casarme.

4. Reading aloud
Answers will vary. Example answers:
- Hablo con mis amigos y escucho música.
- Se puede estar en contacto con los amigos y la familia todo el tiempo.
- Me gustaría ser influencer porque se puede ganar mucho dinero.
- Las redes sociales pueden ser peligrosas y adictivas.

5. Photo card
Answers will vary. Example answers:
- Mi día favorito de la semana es el sábado porque tengo mucho tiempo libre.
- Mi celebración favorita es mi cumpleaños porque recibo muchos regalos.
- Siempre paso mi cumpleaños con mis amigos porque es muy divertido.
- Me gusta la comida española tradicional, por ejemplo la paella y las tortillas.
- No hay muchas fiestas interesantes en mi país, pero me gusta celebrar la Nochebuena.
- Las fiestas españolas me interesan mucho, ¡sobre todo la Tomatina!
- Durante las vacaciones de Navidad visito a mis abuelos y paso tiempo con mi familia.
- Mi perro tiene miedo a los fuegos artificiales, pero creo que son bonitos.

Reading

1. **a)** C **[1]**; **b)** A **[1]**; **c)** E **[1]**
2. **a)** P **[1]**; **b)** N **[1]**; **c)** P+N **[1]**;
   d) P **[1]**; **e)** N
3. **a)** Her mum smokes **[1]** and she hates the smell **[1]**.
   b) They understand the risks. **[1]**
   c) at parties **[1]**
   d) by exercising **[1]**
   e) It's boring. **[1]**
   f) sleeping well **[1]**
   g) B **[1]**
4. **a)** I don't eat meat or fish / I eat neither meat nor fish because I am a vegetarian. **[2]**
   b) I love maths although it is difficult. **[2]**
   c) My brother used to cycle every weekend. **[2]**
   d) I don't like classical music but this song relaxes me. **[2]**
   e) The actress won a prize for her first film. **[2]**

Answers

Writing

1. Answers will vary. Example answers:
   - Hay un chico y una chica. **[2]**
   - Están de vacaciones. **[2]**
   - Hace sol. **[2]**
   - Tienen un plano. **[2]**
   - Están contentos. **[2]**

2. Answers will vary. Example answer:
   Estudio ocho asignaturas y mi asignatura preferida es la historia. Los profes pueden ser estrictos, pero también son simpáticos. Tenemos que llevar una falda negra y una camiseta blanca. En mi colegio no se puede usar el móvil en clase. Llego al colegio a las ocho y media y las clases empiezan a las nueve. **[10]**

3. a) come **[1]**; b) pequeña **[1]**; c) ver **[1]**;
   d) nos **[1]**; e) tiene **[1]**

4. a) Tengo los ojos verdes. **[2]**
   b) Hay mucho tráfico en mi ciudad. **[2]**
   c) No se puede / está prohibido usar el móvil en clase. **[2]**
   d) Ayer comí patatas fritas y bebí agua. **[2]**
   e) El próximo año / el año que viene compraré / voy a comprar un coche. **[2]**

5. Answers will vary. Example answer: Las vacaciones son importantes porque se puede visitar sitios interesantes y aprender sobre culturas diferentes. Es importante relajarse y las vacaciones nos ayudan a reducir el estrés. El año pasado fui a España con mi familia y visitamos muchas ciudades como Madrid y Valencia. Me gustaron los museos y las playas, y comimos comida típica española como paella de marisco. Afortunadamente hacía mucho calor. En el futuro me gustaría dar la vuelta alrededor al mundo porque sería genial visitar países diferentes. ¡Sería un sueño pero también sería muy caro! **[15]**

6. Answers will vary. Example answer: Vivo en una ciudad grande en el norte de Inglaterra. Vivo con mi familia en una casa bastante pequeña en las afueras. En mi ciudad hay mucho que hacer, sobre todo para los jóvenes. Por ejemplo, se puede ir al cine o visitar el estadio famoso donde juega el equipo de fútbol. También hay un centro comercial grande y la semana pasada fui de compras con mis amigos. Una desventaja de vivir aquí es que hay mucha contaminación.
   Creo que es muy importante proteger el medioambiente. En el futuro, para reducir la contaminación en mi ciudad, voy a tomar el autobús o ir a pie al colegio, en vez de ir en coche. También tengo la intención de participar en una manifestación contra el cambio climático, porque amenaza al planeta. En mi ciudad se debe reducir la basura en las calles porque todo parece sucio y feo. **[25]**

Appendix A: Spanish Sound–Symbol Correspondences (SSCs)

Spanish Sound–Symbol Correspondences (SSCs)

The table below specifies key differences in sound-spelling correspondences between Spanish and English. You will need to learn these at GCSE to be able to read out loud (for the Reading Aloud task in Paper 2: Speaking) and transcribe (for the Dictation task in Paper 1: Listening) with sufficient accuracy at this level, along with example words from this Revision Guide, taken from the AQA vocabulary list.

It is not an exhaustive list of the all sound-spelling correspondences in the Spanish language. Where a letter or combination of letters is pronounced (or a sound spelt) in approximately the same way in Spanish as in English, it is not listed.

You will be expected to pronounce words with stress patterns that allow your speech to be clear and comprehensible.

The use of hyphens indicates the position of the letters in a word, when position is relevant to the sound: xx- (at the beginning of a word); -xx- (in the middle of a word); -xx (at the end of a word).

Sound-symbol correspondence	Examples
a	alto, antes
o	dos, cinco
e	español, medio
i	idea, iglesia
u	universidad, instituto
ll	llamar, calle
ch	leche, ocho
c	casa, chica
co	coche, cocina
cu	escuchar, concurso
cu + vowel	cuerpo, cuidado
ce	cerca, doce
ci	concierto, diecisiete
z	zona, manzana
que	porque, querer
qui	tranquilo, equilibrado
ga	ganar, gato
go	largo, tengo
gu	preguntar, alguno
ge	gente, imagen
gi	gimnasio, región
gue	hamburguesa, juguete
gui	guitarra, seguir
j	ojo, naranja
ñ	mañana, cumpleaños
v	verde, verdad
-r-, -r	pero, hablar
rr, r-, -r-	cerrar, sonreír
silent h	hospital, hoy

Appendix B: The AQA Specification

The AQA Specification

The AQA GCSE Spanish subject content for teaching from September 2024 onwards and for GCSE exams from 2026 onwards is based on three main components:

1. **Vocabulary lists**
   - At Foundation Tier, the vocabulary list comprises 1,200 lexical items.
   - At Higher Tier, there are a further 500 lexical items (i.e. 1,700 in total).
   - This Revision Guide uses lexical items / vocabulary found on the AQA vocabulary lists as detailed in Section 3.3 of the AQA 8692 specification.
   - For the full lists provided in Appendices 2 and 3 of the AQA 8692 specification, visit the AQA website.

2. **Grammar requirements**
   - The grammar requirements are set out in two tiers: Foundation Tier and Higher Tier.
   - The requirements set out for Higher Tier include everything specified for Foundation Tier.
   - This Revision Guide uses solely the grammar requirements listed in Section 3.2 of the AQA 8692 specification.
   - For the full list of requirements, visit the AQA website.

3. **Sound-symbol correspondences**
   - Spanish sound-symbol correspondences are required at both Foundation and Higher Tiers and are listed in Appendix A of this Revision Guide (page 141).
   - This Revision Guide provides examples of sound-symbol correspondences on each spread under the 'Key Sounds' heading.
   - The full sound-symbol correspondences can also be found in Appendix 1 of the AQA 8692 specification (visit the AQA website).

To enhance teaching and learning, the AQA 8692 specification covers three distinct themes. You will be expected to use the prescribed vocabulary and grammar across a range of contexts and assessment tasks.

Index

Notes

Collins

AQA GCSE 9-1
Spanish

Workbook

Libby Mitchell, Sherrie A. Spinks
and Amy Bates

Preparing for the GCSE Exam

Revision That Really Works

Experts have found that there are two techniques that help you to retain and recall information and consistently produce better results in exams compared to other revision techniques.

It really isn't rocket science either – you simply need to:

- **test yourself** on each topic as many times as possible
- **leave a gap** between the test sessions.

Three Essential Revision Tips

1. **Use Your Time Wisely**

   - Allow yourself plenty of time.
   - Try to start revising six months before your exams – it's more effective and less stressful.
   - Don't waste time re-reading the same information over and over again – it's not effective!

2. **Make a Plan**

   - Identify all the topics you need to revise (this Complete Revision & Practice book will help you).
   - Plan at least five sessions for each topic.
   - One hour should be ample time to test yourself on the key ideas for a topic.
   - Spread out the practice sessions for each topic – the optimum time to leave between each session is about one month but, if this isn't possible, just make the gaps as big as realistically possible.

3. **Test Yourself**

   - Methods for testing yourself include: quizzes, practice questions, flashcards, past papers, explaining a topic to someone else, etc.
   - This Complete Revision and Practice book provides seven practice opportunities per topic.
   - Don't worry if you get an answer wrong – provided you check what the correct answer is, you are more likely to get the same or similar questions right in future!

Visit **collins.co.uk/collinsGCSErevision** for more information about the benefits of these revision techniques, and for further guidance on how to plan ahead and make them work for you.

QR Codes

A QR code in this Workbook section links to one or both of the following:

- a video working through the solution to one of the questions on that topic, indicated by the ▶ icon
- audio content to be used with a question, indicated by the ◀ icon.

Contents

Visit our website to download the audio material for the Listening Paper on pages 174–185 of this workbook.

1 Read the text then answer the questions.

> Me llamo José Luis y tengo 14 años. Voy a presentar a mi familia.
>
> Somos cinco en casa. Mi madre tiene 43 años. Es bastante alta y delgada. Es muy tolerante y casi nunca se enfada con nosotros. Es médica y muy trabajadora. Mi padre tiene 44 años. Es profesor de matemáticas y trabaja en un instituto.
>
> Tengo un hermano que se llama Carlos y una hermana que se llama Elisa. Carlos pronto va a cumplir 16 años. Es muy vago y poco hablador. Elisa tiene 10 años. Es baja. Se parece bastante a nuestra abuela porque tiene el pelo rubio y los ojos azules. Charla mucho y es muy graciosa. Nos reímos mucho con ella.
>
> ¿Y yo? Bueno, tengo el pelo castaño y los ojos marrones como mi padre y soy deportista, como mi madre. Mis padres dicen que soy un poco perezoso, ¡pero no estoy de acuerdo!
>
> Mis abuelos están jubilados y viven cerca de nosotros. Nos cuidan a veces. Son muy simpáticos y siempre están muy orgullosos de nosotros.

a) Which of these adjectives match José Luis's description of his mother? Tick **three** boxes.

slim ☐

ambitious ☐

patient ☐

hard-working ☐

b) How old is Carlos? ....

c) Who is talkative and funny? ....

d) Who does José Luis look like in his family? ....

e) Does José Luis think of himself as being sporty or a bit lazy? ....

f) What does José Luis say about his grandparents? Give **three** details.

....

....

[10 marks]

2 Match the beginnings and endings of the sentences below.

a) Mi cumpleaños es el 13 de julio y nací   **i)** y se relaciona bien con todos.

b) Mi hermana se parece a mi padre porque   **ii)** es alta y tiene el pelo negro.

c) No sé si quiero casarme en el futuro   **iii)** porque depende de muchas cosas.

d) Mi abuelo es muy simpático   **iv)** nos peleamos de vez en cuando.

e) Me llevo bien con mi hermana pero   **v)** en dos mil trece.

[5 marks]

3 Complete the text using the words from the box.

bien	comprensiva	gemelas	hermanos	llamo
llevamos	ojos	pelo	tía	tío

Soy hija única. No tengo _____ pero tengo muchos primos. Una de mis primas tiene la

misma edad que yo y nos _____ súper bien. Además, las dos tenemos el _____

castaño y los _____ verdes. Nuestra familia dice que somos como _____ . Su

nombre es Alba y yo me _____ Natalia. De carácter, Alba es artística, _____ y

sensible. Su madre, mi _____ , es artista y su padre, mi _____ es músico. Es una

familia agradable y muy interesante. Me entiendo muy _____ con ellos.   [10 marks]

4 Read the text in **3**. Then choose the correct options in the sentences below.

a) Natalia **has a sister / is an only child.**

b) She has **some cousins / one cousin**.

c) Natalia and Alba **look alike / are alike in personality**.

d) Their family says they are **like twins / sisters**.

e) Alba is **understanding and sensitive / clever and sensible.**

f) Natalia's uncle is **an artist / a musician.**   [6 marks]

5 Read Pablo's account of relationships in his family. Then write the correct letter in the boxes.

Mis padres están divorciados y vivo con mi madre pero a veces tengo que pasar el fin de semana en casa de mi padre y su mujer, mi madrastra. Ella es simpática pero tiene una hija que me molesta. Nos peleamos bastante y no quiere compartir nada conmigo. Además, mi padre y mi madrastra tienen un bebé y el bebé llora mucho. Prefiero quedarme en casa con mi madre pero también quiero a mi padre. Es complicado.

a) Pablo's parents are…

A	married.
B	separated.
C	divorced.

c) Pablo doesn't get on well with…

A	his stepmother.
B	his stepsister.
C	the baby.

b) Pablo spends most of his time with…

A	his mother.
B	his father.
C	his stepmother.

[3 marks]

Healthy Living and Lifestyle

1 Read the texts. Then choose one correct statement about each person. Write the letter in the box.

> Soy vegetariana pero a veces como pescado. No me gusta la comida con mucha grasa y no me gustan los postres muy dulces. Prefiero la fruta. No bebo vino. Prefiero agua o zumo de fruta.   Dalia

> Creo que es importante tener una dieta equilibrada. Prefiero comer alimentos saludables y casi nunca como comida basura. Sin embargo, cuando salgo a comer, muchas veces pido patatas fritas porque me encantan.
>
> Vicente

> Soy vegana. No como ni carne, ni pescado. Me gustan las ensaladas y los platos a base de arroz. La paella es mi plato preferido pero tiene que ser una paella con muchas verduras y sin carne. Sin embargo, nunca cenamos paella, porque es un plato fuerte y es más saludable comerlo a mediodía.   Raquel

> Si tengo mucha hambre, lo que más me gusta comer es una buena hamburguesa o una pizza enorme. Sé que no son platos muy sanos pero solo los como de vez en cuando y además, hago mucho deporte, bebo muy poco alcohol y no fumo. Es importante estar en forma.   Hugo

a) Dalia…

A	never eats fish.
B	doesn't like greasy food.
C	prefers sweet desserts.

b) Vicente…

A	thinks a balanced diet is important.
B	eats junk food.
C	never eats chips.

c) Raquel…

A	eats fish but not meat.
B	likes salads and rice dishes.
C	loves eating paella in the evening.

d) Hugo…

A	knows junk food isn't healthy.
B	doesn't do much exercise.
C	doesn't drink or smoke.

[4 marks]

▶ 2 Read the sentences. Then number them from 1–10 to put them in chronological order.

a) Luego cenamos y me acuesto sobre las nueve y media. _____

b) Salimos de clase por la tarde a las tres y media. _____

c) Llego al instituto a las ocho y media. _____

d) Salgo de casa a las ocho. _____

e) Después de desayunar, me lavo los dientes y me peino. _____

f) Me levanto y me ducho. _____

g) Desayuno pan tostado y un vaso de leche. _____

h) De lunes a viernes, me despierto a las siete y cuarto. _____

i) Antes de desayunar, me pongo el uniforme. _____

j) Llego a casa a las cuatro y hago los deberes. _____ [10 marks]

◀ 3 Read the sentences in **2**. aloud. [10 marks]

4 Complete the sentences with the words from the box.

| los pies | el estómago | cabeza | la pierna | los dientes | los ojos |

a) ¡Ay, me duelen _____ ! Tengo que ir al dentista.

b) Mi hermano se cayó de la bicicleta y creo que se ha roto _____ .

c) Comí demasiado y ahora me duele _____ .

d) Para el dolor de _____ hay que tomar una aspirina.

e) Debes llevar gafas de sol para proteger _____

f) Ayer corrí 20 kilómetros y ahora me duelen bastante _____ . [6 marks]

5 Match the answers to the questions.

a) ¿Qué hay que comer para tener una dieta equilibrada?

b) ¿Por qué es necesario comer fruta y verduras?

c) ¿Cómo debes proteger los dientes y evitar citas con el dentista?

d) ¿Por qué es importante dormir lo suficiente?

e) ¿Cuáles son los riesgos de fumar, beber alcohol y tomar drogas?

f) ¿Es importante evitar el sobrepeso?

g) ¿Qué debo hacer para estar en forma?

i) Una variedad de alimentos saludables.

ii) Para que el cuerpo y la mente descansen.

iii) Porque tu cuerpo necesita vitaminas y minerales para protegerse contra infecciones.

iv) Practicar un deporte regularmente.

v) No comer caramelos y refrescos altos en azúcar.

vi) Las malas costumbres son malas para la salud y pueden causar enfermedades.

vii) Sí, porque puedes bajar el riesgo de sufrir un cáncer.

[7 marks]

Education and Work

▶ **1** Choose the correct words from the box to complete the conversation.

ciencias	comercio	difíciles	emocionante	idiomas	tecnología

Oriol: ¿Qué asignaturas te gustan más, Elena?

Elena: Pues, me gustan las ciencias, la informática y la _____.

Oriol: Sí, las _____ son interesantes y la informática es necesaria.

Elena: ¿Te gustan las matemáticas?

Oriol: No me gustan mucho porque para mí son _____. Prefiero los idiomas y la historia.

Elena: A mí también me encantan los _____ porque en el futuro quiero viajar y conocer otros países.

Oriol: ¿Qué asignaturas no te gustan?

Elena: No me interesa mucho ni el _____ ni la geografía.

Oriol: A mí tampoco. ¿Pero sabes cuál es mi asignatura preferida?

Elena: ¿Los deportes?

Oriol: No, el teatro. ¡Es _____!

Elena: Entonces, vas a ser actor.

Oriol: ¡Ya veremos!

[6 marks]

2 Read the conversation in **1.** again. Then answer the questions.

a) Which four subjects does Elena like?

_____

b) What subject does Oriol not like and why?

_____

c) What subject does Elena like because she thinks it's useful for the future?

_____

d) What does Elena say about business studies and geography?

_____

e) What is Oriol's favourite subject and what does he say about it?

_____

[10 marks]

3 Read the clues about school facilities and write the words in the crossword.

Across

3 Charlo con mis amigos en el … durante el recreo.

4 Hay un concierto en el … esta noche.

6 Comemos en el … a mediodía.

7 Se puede estudiar en la … pero no se debe hablar en voz alta.

8 Dejé mi jersey y mi corbata en los … después de la clase de gimnasia y ahora no los encuentro.

Down

1 Hay un partido en el … de fútbol después de clase.

2 El … de ciencias tiene ventanas grandes y en verano no aguantamos el calor.

5 Mañana no hay clases de gimnasia porque se está reparando el … .

9 Los estudiantes que no hicieron los deberes tienen que ir a la … de profesores para hablar con la directora.

10 No se permite comer chicle en las … .

11 El examen de español es en el … de actos.

[11 marks]

4 Match the beginnings and endings of the sentences.

a) Hay que respetar

b) Es mejor llevar uniforme

c) Los mejores profes explican

d) Me gustaría hacer un aprendizaje porque

e) Me fastidia hacer los deberes

i) bien y son estrictos.

ii) aprendes mientras trabajas.

iii) sin embargo sé que nos ayuda a aprobar los exámenes.

iv) porque todo el mundo parece igual.

v) a los demás.

[5 marks]

Free-time Activities

▶ **1** Read the texts. Then write the correct name to answer each question below.

Me llamo Tomás, tengo 16 años y me apasiona el deporte. Cuando era más joven, hacía natación. Casi todos los días me levantaba a las cinco y media para ir a la piscina. Era bastante duro pero me gustaba. Sin embargo, hace unos meses decidí dejar la natación porque tenía que estudiar para los exámenes. Ahora, los fines de semana, salgo a correr o hago ciclismo. En el futuro me gustaría probar otros deportes, como los deportes de invierno y los deportes extremos.

Mi nombre es Sonia. Tengo 15 años y soy una persona activa y deportista. Empecé a jugar al fútbol cuando tenía 10 años. Jugaba con mis hermanos. Ahora creo que juego mejor que ellos. Me gusta porque es un deporte emocionante y divertido. Me encantan los deportes de equipo. Por otra parte, me gusta mucho la música y el baile. Fui a mi primera clase de ballet a los 4 años. Prefiero la música latina y la música pop. Son muy bailables. Shakira es mi cantante favorita.

Me llamo Omar. A decir verdad, no me interesa mucho el deporte. Cuando era pequeño aprendí a nadar pero ahora solo me baño cuando voy a la playa. La música es lo que más me interesa. Toco la guitarra y quiero aprender a tocar el teclado también. Me gusta escribir canciones. Escucho muchos tipos de música, desde el pop y el rap a la música clásica. También me interesa el cine, y me gustan sobre todo las películas de acción y las de aventura. En el futuro me gustaría componer música para las bandas sonoras de las películas. ¡Eso sería guay!

Who...

a) used to swim several times a week? ....

b) only swims when at the beach? ....

c) thinks football is exciting and fun? ....

d) gave up a sport to focus on school work? ....

e) started dancing when very young? ....

f) goes running and cycling? ....

g) likes team sports? ....

h) plays a musical instrument? ....

i) likes watching films? ....

j) would like to do winter sports in the future? ....

[10 marks]

2 Match the words and phrases from the text in **1.** with the English translations.

a) **Me apasiona el deporte.**

b) **Era duro pero me gustaba.**

c) **Me gustaría probar otros deportes.**

d) **Es un deporte emocionante.**

e) **Es muy bailable.**

f) **Quiero aprender a tocar el teclado.**

g) **Me gustan las películas de acción.**

h) **¡Eso sería guay!**

i) It's very good to dance to.

ii) I love sport.

iii) I want to learn to play the keyboard.

iv) I would like to try other sports.

v) That would be cool!

vi) I like action films.

vii) It was hard but I liked it.

viii) It's an exciting sport.　　　　[8 marks]

3 Where would you see these signs? Match the signs to the places.

A　**El ballet *Lago de los Cisnes*, a las 7.30**	a) **en el cine**
B　**Superficie mojada, es peligroso correr**	b) **en el estadio**
C　**Película de horror** 　　**No apta para menores de 12 años.**	c) **en la piscina**
D　**Partido hoy entre Real Madrid y Barcelona FC**	d) **en el teatro**
E　**Actividades para esta tarde:** 　　**tenis de mesa, ajedrez, arte y dibujo**	e) **en el polideportivo**
F　**Se puede alquilar canchas de tenis y de pádel**	f) **en el club de jóvenes**

[6 marks]

4 Read what Raúl says about his free time. Then answer the questions below.

> **En mi tiempo libre me gusta salir con mis amigos al parque a jugar al fútbol o a la piscina a nadar. Cuando estoy en casa, lo que más me gusta es escuchar música y leer. Cuando era más joven, me encantaba ver dibujos animados en la tele pero ahora no veo mucho la tele porque no me interesan ni los concursos, ni las telenovelas, ni los programas de telerrealidad. Además, los anuncios me fastidian. Prefiero descargar películas y series de la red porque puedo elegir las que me gustan.**
>
> **El fin de semana pasado, salí al teatro con mi familia para celebrar el cumpleaños de mi hermana. Vimos un espectáculo de teatro musical. A mí no me apasiona este tipo de música, pero a mi hermana, sí. Después fuimos a comer pizza. Así que en general lo pasamos bien y mi hermana se quedó muy contenta. El mes que viene, voy a cumplir 16 años y quiero ir a un festival de música con mis amigos.**

a) What activities does Raúl do when he goes out with his friends? ....

b) What does he like doing at home? ....

c) What kind of TV programmes did he enjoy when he was younger? ....

d) Why doesn't he watch much TV now? Give **one** detail. ....

e) Why does he prefer to download films? ....

f) Why did he go to the theatre last weekend? ....

g) Who enjoyed the theatre trip most, Raúl or his sister? ....

h) How is Raúl planning to celebrate his next birthday? ....　　[8 marks]

Customs, Festivals and Celebrations

1 Read the texts, then match them to the photos. Write the correct letter in each box.

A

B

C

a) En España se celebra Semana Santa con desfiles religiosos. En mi pueblo, por ejemplo, hay un desfile que pasa por la Calle Mayor y que termina en la iglesia. Mucha gente participa y los que no están en el desfile, esperan en la iglesia para ver la llegada. Otra tradición de Pascua es que un grupo de niños y adultos del pueblo va de casa en casa a cantar canciones tradicionales. Las canciones son divertidas y alegres.

Alicia

☐

b) En agosto suelo ir a la Fiesta Mayor en el pueblo de mis abuelos. Todo el mundo participa en las celebraciones. Hay una corrida de toros. Es parecida a los de San Fermín pero en nuestro pueblo, los toros son más jóvenes y más pequeños. Se puede correr delante de los toros. Es un poco peligroso pero es muy emocionante. Por la noche una banda toca música tradicional en la plaza y tanto los mayores como los jóvenes se divierten bailando.

Javier

☐

c) Vivo en Ciudad de México. Una de las fiestas más importantes aquí es el Día de Muertos. Se celebra a principios de noviembre en todos los pueblos y ciudades del país. En ese día la gente va a los cementerios. Se llevan flores y comida para los muertos. También la gente se disfraza de esqueletos y preparan pan y otros comestibles especiales. No es triste, todo lo contrario, es una fiesta alegre y divertida.

Carlos

☐

[3 marks]

2 Read the texts in **1.** again. Then answer the questions.

a) What religious tradition takes place in Alicia's village in Holy Week? ....

b) What other Easter tradition does she mention? ....

c) Where does Javier usually go in August? ....

d) What does he think is dangerous but exciting? ....

e) Who can go to the evening event in the village square? ....

f) What festival does Carlos describe? ....

g) When does it take place? ....

h) Why do people go to cemeteries on this day? .... [8 marks]

3 Match the festivals to the dates.

a) **La Nochevieja**

b) **La Nochebuena**

c) **El Día de Navidad**

d) **El Día de Año Nuevo**

e) **El Día de Reyes**

i) **el primero de enero**

ii) **el seis de enero**

iii) **el veinticuatro de diciembre**

iv) **el veinticinco de diciembre**

v) **el treinta y uno de diciembre** [5 marks]

4 Match the beginnings and endings of the sentences. Then, translate the sentences into English.

a) **Asistí a la boda de**

b) **La novia llevó**

c) **Mi hermano llevó**

d) **Se casaron en**

e) **Por suerte hacía buen tiempo cuando estuvimos**

f) **Hubo una comida**

g) **Creo que gastaron**

h) **Dijeron que valía la pena porque**

i) **una casa antigua impresionante.**

ii) **un vestido blanco elegante.**

iii) **muchísimo dinero.**

iv) **solo se hace una vez en la vida.**

v) **de cuatro platos.**

vi) **un traje azul marino.**

vii) **mi hermano y su novia.**

viii) **en el jardín para las fotos.**

[16 marks]

Celebrity Culture

1 Complete the definitions with the words from the box.

Los célebres	Los influencers	Las marcas	Las redes sociales	Los seguidores

a) _____ : las personas con capacidad para influir a otros a través de la red.

b) _____ : las personas que miran los sitios de los famosos para saber lo que hacen.

c) _____ : las personas famosas.

d) _____ : las aplicaciones y los sitios en línea donde se puede comunicarse con otros.

e) _____ : los productos de una compañía, por ejemplo, de ropa o de coches.

[5 marks]

2 Read the text about Penélope Cruz. Find the Spanish for the phrases in English.

> Penélope Cruz es la actriz española más famosa del mundo. Es de un barrio de Madrid que se llama Alcobendas. De niña, hacía clases de ballet clásico durante 9 años. Después empezó a estudiar teatro y salió en su primera película a la edad de 17 años. Ha ganado muchos premios, incluyendo un Oscar y ha recibido muchas nominaciones.
>
> Penélope se casó en 2010 con el actor español Javier Bardem. Tienen dos hijos y viven entre Los Ángeles, Nueva York y Madrid. Además de ser reconocida por su talento como actriz y por su belleza, Penélope promociona la prestigiosa marca francesa de Chanel.
>
> A pesar de su vida de estrella de cine internacional, la actriz no se olvida de los menos afortunados. Trabaja en varias caridades y fundaciones benéficas para ayudar a niños y jóvenes pobres de Nepal, India y África.

a) As a child, she went to ballet classes.

_____

b) She appeared in her first film at the age of 17.

_____

c) She has won many prizes.

_____

d) She got married in 2010.

_____

e) They live between Los Angeles, New York and Madrid.

_____

f) She works for several charities.

_____

[6 marks]

3 Read the first paragraph in **2.** aloud.

[5 marks]

4 Read the text about Sergio Ramos. Find the Spanish for the sentences below.

> Sergio Ramos nació el 30 de marzo de 1986 en un pueblo en el sur de España. Empezó a jugar al fútbol cuando era muy joven y a los 6 años Sergio ya jugaba en un equipo de jóvenes. A los 9 años hizo pruebas en el Sevilla Fútbol Club y entró a entrenar como juvenil. A la edad de 17 años jugó en el primer equipo del Sevilla. Dos años después fue a jugar en el Real Madrid.
>
> Sergio conoció a su pareja, Pilar Rubio, en 2012. Tienen cuatro hijos. El 15 de junio de 2019 se casaron en la Catedral de Sevilla. ¡Salieron fotos de la boda en casi todos los medios de comunicación! Además de ser uno de los mejores jugadores del fútbol del mundo, Sergio promociona la marca Boss y tiene más de 60 millones de seguidores en las redes sociales.

a) He started to play football when he was very young.

b) When he was 9 years old he did a trial for Sevilla FC.

c) At 17, he played in the first team for Sevilla.

d) Two years later he went to play for Real Madrid.

e) Sergio met his partner, Pilar Rubio, in 2012.

f) They got married on 15 June 2019.

g) Sergio has more than 60 million followers on social media.

[7 marks]

5 Match up the beginnings and endings to complete the sentences.

a) Admiro más a los famosos que

b) Es divertido ver los videos que se ponen en la red

c) Veo los vídeos que los cocineros célebres ponen en sus sitios

d) Admiro a los modelos y los influencers que dan consejos sobre la moda y la belleza porque

e) Hay blogs y artículos que se publican en línea sobre la salud que pueden ser útiles pero

f) Me interesan los deportistas famosos porque

i) quiero saber cómo han conseguido el éxito en su deporte.

ii) quiero ser tan elegante como ellos.

iii) porque me encanta preparar platos nuevos.

iv) de animales que hacen cosas muy graciosas.

v) también hay los que dan malos consejos.

vi) usan su fama para ayudar a los demás.

[6 marks]

Travel and Tourism

 1 Read Serena's description of her family holidays.

> Durante las vacaciones de verano siempre íbamos toda la familia a la costa. Mis padres alquilaban un piso en un pueblo cerca de la playa que se llama Benicasim. Iba a la playa por la mañana con mis hermanos y nos bañábamos en el mar y jugábamos al fútbol. A veces salíamos en un pequeño barco con unos amigos. Por la tarde salía al pueblo a pasear y luego volvía al piso a cenar. Recuerdo que una vez, fuimos en autobús a la ciudad de Valencia a comer paella en un restaurante en el puerto.
>
> Para llegar a la costa, normalmente íbamos en coche pero una vez fuimos en tren y disfruté mucho de este viaje. Me gustó todo, desde la estación en Madrid hasta desayunar en el tren. Es una manera muy agradable de viajar.
>
> Este año voy a ir de vacaciones al extranjero, por primera vez. Mi padre ha comprado los billetes para ir en avión a Italia y mi madre ha organizado una vuelta en bicicleta para la familia con alojamiento en pequeños hoteles. Vamos a hacer turismo por los pueblos cerca de Roma. Este viaje me hace mucha ilusión porque van a ser unas vacaciones culturales y deportivas. Además, me encanta la comida italiana. ¡Vamos a comer bien!

Find the Spanish words and phrases in the text for the following:

a) two types of holiday accommodation

....

b) three activities at the beach

....

....

c) three cities

....

d) five types of transport

....

[13 marks]

2 Read the text in **1.** again. Which of the following statements are correct? Write the correct letters in the boxes.

A Serena and her family used to go to the coast every summer.

B They usually stayed in a hotel near the beach.

C They nearly always travelled by car.

D They once went by train and had breakfast on the way.

E Serena and her family went to Italy on holiday last year.

F They are going abroad this year.

G They are going to do a walking tour.

H Serena likes active cultural holidays.

I She loves Italian food.

[6 marks]

3 Match the sentences to the signs.

A

Restaurante Miramar

Menú del día

20 euros

Se habla inglés y francés

B

Aeropuerto con vuelos directos a Europa

C

Parque acuático

Abierto de 10.00 a 18.00 horas

D

Visitas a la catedral y al castillo:

Compra las entradas aquí

E

El tren con destino a Alicante tiene veinte minutos de retraso.

a) A mis hijos les encanta el agua. Vamos a pasar todo el día en las piscinas y en los ríos rápidos. ....

b) Hoy no hace buen tiempo para ir a la playa. Vamos a hacer turismo. ....

c) Tenemos tiempo para ir a comprar un bocadillo antes del viaje. ....

d) Tengo que ir a Alemania pero no tengo tiempo para ir en coche ni en tren. ....

e) We would like to have lunch near the beach but we don't speak Spanish. ....

[5 marks]

4 Read sentences **a)–d)** in **3.** aloud. [4 marks]

5 Match the beginnings and endings of the sentences.

a) Me gustaría hacer un viaje alrededor del mundo pero

b) Conozco el sur de Francia

c) El año que viene quiero ir a Las Islas Canarias en enero o febrero porque

d) Hicimos camping en las vacaciones de verano pero

e) Prefiero ir de vacaciones en otoño

i) hacía mal tiempo y lo pasamos fatal.

ii) pero nunca he estado en París.

iii) los vuelos son muy caros.

iv) hace buen tiempo allá en invierno.

v) porque no hace ni mucho calor ni mucho frío.

[5 marks]

Media and Technology

1 Complete the sentences with the verbs from the box.

cargar	colgar	guardar	conectar
enviar	funcionar	grabar	navegar

a) Lo bueno de la tecnología es que puedes _____ con los amigos fácilmente en el móvil o en el portátil.

b) Ahora suelo _____ mensajes a mi familia en sus cumpleaños en vez de mandar tarjetas por correo.

c) Como usamos la tecnología digital para todo, es un problema cuando el wifi deja de _____ en casa.

d) ¡Ay, qué horror! Mi amiga va a _____ unas fotos de mí disfrazada de pirata en el desfile de Carnaval.

e) Es mejor no dejar los aparatos digitales a _____ por la noche porque puede dañar la batería.

f) Mis amigos tocan música tradicional y mañana voy a _____ su nueva canción en el móvil.

g) A mi abuelo le encanta _____ por la Red para leer las noticias y para saber qué hay en la tele.

h) ¡Es un desastre! Hice los deberes en el portátil pero me olvidé de _____ el documento y lo he perdido.

[8 marks]

2 Answer the questions in Spanish.

a) ¿Quién navega más por internet en tu casa?

_____

b) ¿Para qué usas las redes sociales?

_____

c) ¿Qué tipo de fotos sueles colgar?

_____

d) ¿Te gusta escuchar música en el móvil? ¿Cuándo?

_____

e) ¿A quién envías más mensajes?

_____

f) ¿Para qué usas el correo electrónico?

_____

g) ¿Te gusta jugar a los videojuegos? ¿Qué tipo de consola tienes?

_____

h) ¿Ves la tele en casa o prefieres bajar películas y series de la Red?

_____

i) ¿Sigues a algunos influencers? ¿Por qué te interesan?

_____

[9 marks]

3 Read about two well-known Spanish influencers. Then answer the questions.

> Lola Moreno nació en Valencia en 2002. Es una influencer española muy conocida. Empezó a subir vídeos de baile cuando solo tenía 14 años. Sus vídeos han tenido tanto éxito que Lola ha colaborado con artistas famosos como Shakira y Maluma. Ahora tiene más de doce millones de seguidores.

> Ignacio Gil Conesa también es valenciano. Nació en 1990 y su nombre de usuario es "Nachter". Es conocido gracias a sus vídeos graciosos que le han convertido en estrella de TikTok y de Instagram, donde tiene unos catorce millones de seguidores.

a) When was Lola Moreno born? _____

b) Where is she from? _____

c) How did her career as an influencer start? _____

d) Which famous people has she worked with? _____

e) How many followers does she have? _____

f) What is "Nachter"? _____

g) When and where was he born? _____

h) How has he become famous? _____

i) How many followers does he have? _____

[9 marks]

4 Read the sentences. Write **P** for a positive opinion or **N** for a negative opinion.

a) Se puede conectar fácilmente con gente de todo el mundo. _____

b) Es posible cargar aplicaciones útiles e informativas. _____

c) Hay personas con malas intenciones que quieren robar información y dinero mediante las redes sociales. _____

d) Son útiles para compartir información y para saber qué pasa en tu pueblo o tu barrio. _____

e) Las redes sociales facilitan el ciberacoso porque la gente puede publicar comentarios anónimos desagradables. _____

f) Las tecnologías y las redes sociales son adictivas. _____

g) Mediante las redes sociales los pequeños negocios pueden ganar nuevos clientes. _____

h) Si solo tenemos contacto virtual, podemos perder la confianza de relacionarnos con otras personas en la vida real. _____

[8 marks]

The Environment and Where People Live

 1 Read about where Isabel and Jordi live.

Isabel

Vivo en una casa en las afueras de Málaga. Es una casa de dos plantas. En la planta baja hay una cocina comedor bastante grande y un salón pequeño. Arriba en el primer piso hay un cuarto de baño y tres habitaciones. En la mía hay dos camas porque comparto la habitación con mi hermana. Me gusta vivir aquí porque es tranquilo, hay árboles y hay espacios verdes. Además, estamos cerca de la ciudad.

Jordi

Vivo con mi familia en un piso moderno en el centro de Barcelona. Vivimos en el décimo piso y desde las ventanas se puede ver la costa por un lado y el monte de Tibidabo detrás de la ciudad por otra. Además tenemos un pequeño jardín en la terraza. Hay muchos edificios y mucho tráfico en la ciudad pero también hay parques y zonas peatonales. Para ir al instituto puedo ir a pie o en bicicleta. Me encanta vivir en la ciudad porque hay de todo: museos, cines, tiendas, cafés y restaurantes. Lo malo es que hay bastante ruido y hay contaminación del aire.

Find the words in the text for:

a) the ground floor   ....

b) a kitchen-diner   ....

c) the first floor   ....

d) a bathroom   ....

e) the bedroom   ....

f) a modern apartment   ....

g) the tenth floor   ....

h) the windows   ....

i) a small garden   ....

j) the terrace   ....

[10 marks]

2 Read the texts in **1.** again and answer the following questions.

a) Why are there two beds in Isabel's bedroom?

....

b) Why does she like where she lives? Give **three** reasons.

....

c) Does Jordi live near the coast? How do you know?

....

d) Are there places to walk near where Jordi lives? How do you know?

....

e) Does he live near his school? How do you know?

....

f) According to Jordi, what is the advantage of living in a city?

....

g) What are the disadvantages? Give **two** details.

....

[13 marks]

3 Match the requests with the most suitable homes.

A Se vende piso moderno, de cuatro habitaciones y con vistas al mar.	B Casa única y lujosa en la capital, de cuatro plantas, con jardines, piscina y cine.
C Apartamento pequeño en un barrio agradable a cinco kilómetros del centro.	D Esta casa está en un pueblo pequeño y por fuera tiene patio y jardín.

E Casa antigua con cuatro habitaciones en pleno campo para vivir en tranquilidad.

a) Me gustaría tener una casa pequeña con jardín en un sitio tranquilo. ....

b) Dos adultos buscan un piso en un pueblo o en las afueras de la ciudad. ....

c) Acabo de jubilarme y busco una casa antigua en el campo. ....

d) ¡Qué suerte! He ganado la lotería y puedo comprar la casa de mis sueños. ....

e) Busco un apartamento cerca de la playa para cinco personas. ....

[5 marks]

4 Complete the opinions about the environment using the words from the box.

apagar	recursos	contaminación	extinción	incendios	reutilizar

a) Pienso que el cambio climático es el problema más grave para el futuro del planeta porque causa desastres naturales como los .... forestales y las inundaciones.

b) Se debe reciclar todo lo posible para proteger los .... naturales del mundo.

c) Hay que reducir al mínimo el uso de petróleo y otros combustibles fósiles para reducir la .... del aire y para parar el cambio climático.

d) Se puede ayudar a proteger el medio ambiente en casa. Por ejemplo, puedes bajar la calefacción y .... las luces cuando no son necesarias.

e) Me preocupa que haya tantos animales en peligro de .... Hay que protegerlos.

f) Hay que reciclar y .... los téxtiles porque la fabricación de ropa usa grandes cantidades de agua y mucha energía.

[6 marks]

Grammar 1

Gender, Plurals and Articles

1 Complete each sentence by writing **un**, **una**, **unos** or **unas**.

a) En casa tenemos _____ gato negro y _____ peces dorados.

b) En el salón hay _____ sofá grande y _____ sillones cómodos.

c) En el patio hay _____ mesa larga y _____ sillas de madera.

d) En el pueblo hay una cafetería, _____ restaurantes y _____ parque bonito.

e) Tengo _____ hermana que vive en Francia y _____ primos que viven en Irlanda.

[10 marks]

2 Rewrite each sentence by adding **el** or **la**.

a) A mi padre le gusta escuchar radio por la mañana.

_____

b) Creo que español es un idioma importante.

_____

c) ¿Quieres ir al cine el viernes por tarde?

_____

d) En nuestro instituto uniforme es obligatorio.

_____

e) Mi cumpleaños es 4 de marzo.

_____

[5 marks]

3 Complete each sentence by writing **los** or **las**.

a) Por la ventana veo _____ árboles y _____ flores en el jardín.

b) Me lavo _____ manos antes de comer y me lavo _____ dientes despúes de comer.

c) Creo que _____ matemáticas son más difíciles que _____ idiomas.

d) Si quieres aprobar _____ exámenes debes ir a todas _____ clases.

e) Me gusta leer _____ mensajes y ver _____ fotos en el móvil.

f) Prefiero _____ series policíacas a _____ programas de telerrealidad.

g) ¿Crees que _____ chicos son más habladores que _____ chicas? [14 marks]

Adjectives, Comparatives, Superlatives and Adverbs

4 Choose the correct option in each sentence.

a) Las paredes de mi habitación son <u>azul / azules</u>.

b) Para ir a la fiesta voy a llevar un vestido <u>rojo / roja</u>.

c) Ayer compré unos zapatos <u>negro / negros</u>.

d) Nuestros vecinos tienen un perro <u>pequeño / pequeña</u> muy simpático.

e) Mi hermana mayor es <u>trabajador / trabajadora</u>.

f) La casa está cerca de una playa bonita y <u>tranquilo / tranquila</u>.

g) Hoy hace <u>bueno / buen</u> tiempo. Vamos al parque.

h) Taylor Swift es una cantante muy <u>buen / buena</u>. [8 marks]

5 Write the correct word from the box below to complete each sentence. Use each word once.

menos	como	que	mejor	peor

a) No soy tan alto _____ mi amigo.

b) Pero creo que juego _____ al fútbol que él.

c) Para mí, las matemáticas son _____ difíciles que las ciencias.

d) Este libro es aburridísimo. Es el _____ que he leído.

e) Las películas de acción son más emocionantes _____ las comedias. [5 marks]

6 Complete the table by turning the adjectives into adverbs. The first one has been done for you.

	Masculine	Feminine	Adverb
a)	lento	lenta	lentamente
b)	probable		
c)	rápido		
d)	reciente		
e)	tranquilo		
f)	fácil		

[5 marks]

7 Translate the adverbs in **6.** into English.

_____

_____

[6 marks]

Grammar 1

Interrogatives and Por v Para

1 Choose the correct word from the box below to start each question.

Por qué	Cuáles	Cómo	Cuándo
Quién	Dónde	Cuántos	Qué

a) ¿ _____ te llamas?

b) ¿ _____ vives?

c) ¿ _____ años tienes?

d) ¿ _____ hermanos tienes?

e) ¿ _____ es tu cumpleaños?

f) ¿ _____ te gusta más hacer en tu tiempo libre?

g) ¿ _____ son tus asignaturas favoritas?

h) ¿ _____ te gustan estas asignaturas?

i) ¿ _____ es tu actor o actriz preferido?

j) ¿ _____ tipo de música prefieres?　　　　　　　　　　　　　　　[10 marks]

2 Write questions in Spanish for the following answers.

a) _____

Mi mejor amigo se llama Daniel.

b) _____

Es simpático y divertido.

c) _____

Tiene 15 años.

d) _____

Vive en el mismo barrio que nosotros.

e) _____

Nos llevamos bien porque nos gustan las mismas cosas.　　　　　[5 marks]

3 Complete each sentence with **por** or **para**.

a) ¿Qué autobús tomamos _____ llegar al aeropuerto?

b) Hemos estado aquí esperando _____ dos horas.

c) Es más rápido ir _____ la autopista.

d) He comprado una camiseta _____ 20 Euros.

e) Quiero comprar un regalo _____ mis padres.

f) ¿Hay una farmacia _____ aquí?

g) ¿Cuál es el mejor sitio _____ tomar un buen café?　　　　　　[7 marks]

Present Tense, Regular and Reflexive Verbs and Negatives

4 Write the correct form of the verb in each space.

Me llamo Silvia y _____ (vivir) en España con mis padres y mis hermanos. Somos una familia bilingüe: _____ (hablar) dos idiomas en casa porque mi padre es de Australia y _____ (hablar) inglés y mi madre es de Italia y _____ (hablar) italiano. Y claro, como nosotros _____ (vivir) en España todos _____ (hablar) español.

Mi padre es ingeniero y _____ (trabajar) en una fábrica de coches. Mi madre es profesora y _____ (trabajar) en un colegio. Mis hermanos y yo _____ (estudiar) en el instituto. Ahora mis abuelos italianos _____ (vivir) en España y cuando vamos a su casa casi siempre _____ (comer) pasta.

[11 marks]

5 Choose the correct option to complete each sentence.

a) Para proteger el medio ambiente es importante <u>recicla / reciclar</u> todo lo posible.

b) En casa, <u>reciclo / reciclar</u> papel, plástico y vidrio.

c) Me molesta <u>escucha / escuchar</u> el ruido del tráfico en mi barrio.

d) A veces <u>escucho / escuchar</u> música cuando estudio.

e) Los estudiantes que <u>viven / vivir</u> cerca del insti van a clase a pie.   [5 marks]

6 Complete each sentence with the correct form of the verb in brackets.

a) Un buen amigo siempre te _____. (apoyar)

b) ¿A quién te _____ más en tu familia? (parecer)

c) Los mejores profesores nos _____ bien las clases. (explicar)

d) _____ los verbos porque no quiero suspender el examen. (repasar)

e) ¿A qué hora _____ vosotros en vuestra casa? (cenar)   [5 marks]

7 Make these sentences negative.

a) Voy al instituto a pie.

_____

b) Vivimos cerca del instituto.

_____

c) Mi hermano juega al fútbol todos los días.

_____

d) Hay un examen de español mañana.

_____

e) Me levanto temprano los fines de semana.

_____

[5 marks]

Grammar 2

Common Irregular Verbs and Present Continuous

1 Answer the questions in Spanish.

a) ¿De qué nacionalidad eres? ....

b) ¿Cuántos años tienes? ....

c) ¿Tienes hermanos? ¿O eres hijo único / hija única? ....

d) ¿Qué deportes haces en el instituto? ....

e) ¿Cómo vas al instituto? ....

f) ¿Qué tipo de regalos le das a tu madre en su cumpleaños? ....

g) ¿Qué sabes cocinar? ....

h) ¿Siempre dices la verdad a tus amigos? ....

i) ¿Puedes correr cien metros en menos de 20 segundos? ....

[9 marks]

2 Read the questions in **1.** aloud. [9 marks]

3 Write the correct form of the verbs in the present tense to complete the text.

En el futuro .... (querer) ser veterinario. Mis padres .... (pensar) que es un trabajo difícil y que hay que estudiar mucho. Pero bueno, les .... (decir) que es mi ambición. Los fines de semana y durante las vacaciones .... (soler) trabajar en una granja cuidando a los animales. Por eso, casi nunca .... (pedir) dinero a mis padres.

[5 marks]

4 Complete the conversation using the verbs in brackets in the present continuous.

Amaya:	¿Me enseñas las fotos de tus vacaciones?
Susa:	Vale, sí. Mira, esta es mi hermana. .... (comer) un helado.
Amaya:	¿Dónde está tu abuelo?
Susa:	Mi abuelo .... (dormir) debajo del árbol.
Amaya:	¿Quiénes son los chicos?
Susa:	Son mis primos, José y Jorge. .... (jugar) al fútbol.
Amaya:	¿Y tú? ¿Dónde estás?
Susa:	Pues yo estoy sentada en la cafetería al lado de la playa.
Amaya:	¿Qué .... (hacer)?
Susa:	Te .... (escribir) un mensaje a ti en el móvil. [5 marks]

Past Tenses

▶ **5** Write the correct preterite verb form in each gap to complete the sentences.

fui	vi	hice	jugué	saqué	estuve

i) Siento que yo no _____ cuando tú viniste a casa.

ii) Ayer _____ dos partidos de fútbol y me quedé muy cansado.

iii) _____ muchas fotos en la boda de mi hermana.

iv) El mes pasado _____ de vacaciones a Málaga con mi familia.

v) Anoche _____ una película buenísima en la tele.

vi) _____ un bocadillo de tortilla porque tenía mucha hambre.   [6 marks]

6 Answer the questions using the imperfect tense.

Cuándo tenías 5 años...

a) ¿qué no te gustaba comer?   _____

b) ¿con quién jugabas?   _____

c) ¿uál era tu juguete favorito?   _____

d) ¿cómo ibas al colegio?   _____

e) ¿de qué tenías miedo?   _____

f) ¿cuál era tu libro preferido?   _____

g) ¿qué dibujos animados solías ver y por qué te gustaban?   _____   [7 marks]

7 Tick the things that have happened already today at home.

Me he levantado.   ☐

Me he duchado.   ☐

He limpiado el cuarto de baño.   ☐

Todos hemos desayunado.   ☐

Mis padres han sacado el perro a pasear.   ☐

Mi hermana ha ordenado su habitación.   ☐

Mis amigos me han mandado mensajes.   ☐

[1 mark]

Grammar 2

Pronouns

1 Complete each sentence with the correct object pronoun from the box.

la	lo	los	las

a) Me encantan estas zapatillas. Voy a comprar _____.

b) Aquí hay una foto fantástica de ti. Míra _____.

c) Es un secreto, por favor no se _____ digas a nadie.

d) Mis padres me compraron un portátil y me _____ regalaron en mi cumpleaños.

e) La tarta de manzana es deliciosa. ¿Quieres probar _____? [5 marks]

2 Match the sentence halves.

a)	¿Quieres ir al cine
b)	Los bocadillos de jamón son
c)	Tu prima se parece mucho
d)	Mis tíos me han invitado a ir de vacaciones
e)	Cuando mi hermano se rompió la pierna, teníamos que hacer todo

i)	a ti.
ii)	con ellos.
iii)	conmigo mañana?
iv)	por él.
v)	para ustedes.

[5 marks]

3 Complete the conversation with the correct option in each sentence. The first one has been done for you.

a) ¿A qué hora nos/⓪s levantasteis el día que fuisteis de vacaciones?

b) Bueno, teníamos que levantar__me/nos__ a las tres para ir al aeropuerto.

c) ¿A las tres? ¡Huy! A mí no me gusta nada despertar__me/te__ tan temprano.

d) A mí tampoco. ¿Pero sabes qué pasó? Mis padres no __te/se__ despertaron.

e) ¿Y tú no __te /se__ despertaste?

f) No, pero al final mi madre __se/os__ despertó a las cuatro y nos levantamos todos con mucha prisa.

g) ¿Y llegasteis a tiempo al aeropuerto?

Sí, llegamos justo a tiempo y fuimos los últimos en sentar__nos/me__ en el avión. [6 marks]

The Future Tenses, Subjunctive and Imperative Moods

4 Match the future forms to the infinitive verbs.

a) dar	i) haré
b) hacer	ii) dará
c) hay	iii) habrá
d) ir a	iv) saldrá
e) salir	v) tendrás
f) tener	vi) vas a

[6 marks]

5 Complete the sentences with the future forms from the list in **1**.

a) ¿Qué _____ hacer este fin de semana?

b) La profesora nos _____ los resultados del examen al final de la semana.

c) ¿ _____ tiempo para hacer las compras mañana?

d) _____ más de cien invitados en la boda de mi hermana.

e) No he ordenado mi habitación pero lo _____ después de comer.

f) ¿De qué puerta _____ el avión a Madrid? [6 marks]

6 Write the sentences using the imperfect subjunctive and the conditional of the verbs in brackets. The first one has been done for you.

a) ¿Qué (hacer) tú si (ganar) la lotería? *¿Qué harías tú si ganaras la lotería?*

b) Si todo el mundo (ir) al trabajo en bicicleta, el aire (estar) menos contaminado.

_____

c) (Ser) más fácil estudiar en casa si (tener) una mesa en mi habitación.

_____

d) Si tú (vivir) un año en España, (hablar) muy bien el español.

_____

e) Si (poder) conocer a una persona famosa de la historia, creo que (elegir) a William Shakespeare.

_____ [8 marks]

7 Complete the sentences with the imperative verb forms in the box.

corráis	habla	sentaos	pon	haz

a) _____ en voz alta por favor.

b) _____ y abrid los libros.

c) No _____ en los pasillos.

d) _____ los platos y los vasos en la mesa.

e) _____ me el favor de cerrar la puerta. [5 marks]

Collins

GCSE
Spanish

H

Higher Tier Paper 1 Listening

Time allowed: 45 minutes

(including 5 minutes' reading time before the test and 2 minutes' checking time at the end of the test)

Instructions

- Download the audio material to use with this test from **www.collins.co.uk/collinsgcserevision**
- Use black ink or black ball-point pen.
- You must **not** use a dictionary.

Information

- The marks for questions are shown in brackets.
- The maximum mark for this paper is 50.

Advice

For each item, you should do the following:

- Listen carefully to the recording. Read the questions again.
- Listen again to the recording. Then answer the questions.
- You may write at any point during the test.
- In **Section A**, answer the questions in **English**. In **Section B**, which is dictation, write in **Spanish**.
- Answer all questions in the spaces provided.
- Write down all the information you are asked to give.
- You have 5 minutes to read through the question paper before the test begins. You may make notes during this time.

Name: _____

Section A   Listening comprehension

Life in Mexico

You are listening to Ignacio talk about his family and his life in Mexico.

Choose the correct answer and write the letter in each box.

Write **A** if only statement **A** is correct.

B if only statement **B** is correct.

A+B if both statements **A** and **B** are correct.

0 1 At present…

A	his brother always works hard at school.
B	he finds it hard to make friends.

[1 mark]

0 2 Last year his cousin…

A	was meant to get married.
B	worked in Spain as a musician.

[1 mark]

0 3 Next year…

A	Ignacio wants to make new friends at university.
B	he will live with his grandmother.

[1 mark]

0 4 In the future…

A	Ignacio is planning on having his own business.
B	His dad thinks happiness is more important than money.

[1 mark]

Practice Exam Paper 1: Listening

School studies

You hear Jimena and her friends talking about school subjects.

A	la informática
B	los idiomas
C	la geografía
D	el teatro
E	la educación física
F	la historia
G	el dibujo

Which subjects are they discussing?

Write the correct letter in the box.

0 5		[1 mark]

0 6		[1 mark]

0 7		[1 mark]

0 8		[1 mark]

0 9		[1 mark]

Lifestyle choices

Listen to Anya talking about her lifestyle choices.

What is Anya's opinion of each of the aspects below?

A	disappointing
B	irresponsible
C	difficult
D	annoying
E	expensive
F	important

Write the correct letter in the box.

Answer all parts of question 10.

| 1 0 · 1 | Dieting | | [1 mark] |

| 1 0 · 2 | Smoking | | [1 mark] |

| 1 0 · 3 | Doing exercise | | [1 mark] |

| 1 0 · 4 | Relaxation and meditation | | [1 mark] |

Practice Exam Paper 1: Listening

Interview with a Cuban dancer

You hear an interview with the Cuban dancer Silvio Pérez.

Answer the questions in **English**.

| 1 | 1 | Where did Silvio first start to dance?

.... [1 mark]

| 1 | 2 | How did he feel about getting into the National School of Ballet?

.... [1 mark]

| 1 | 3 | According to Silvio, what is the best part of being a ballet dancer?

.... [1 mark]

| 1 | 4 | What advice does he give about having a career in classical dance?

Give **one** detail.

.... [1 mark]

Discussion on local area

Two university students, Ana and Federico, are discussing their local area.

Complete the sentences in **English.**

Write **one** word in each space.

1 5 Federico says: In the past 10 years there has been increase in

_____, however there are now more

_____. **[2 marks]**

1 6 Ana says: Due to the increasing number of _____,

they need to build more _____. **[2 marks]**

Practice Exam Paper 1: Listening

TV programmes

Your hear this podcast where these young people are discussing TV programmes and watching TV.

Choose the correct answer and write the letter in each box.

1 7 Miguel prefers...

A	to watch TV alone.
B	to watch TV with his family.
C	not to watch TV.

[1 mark]

1 8 Alfie thinks that the quality of programmes for young people is...

A	better than it used to be.
B	gradually getting worse.
C	better at the weekend.

[1 mark]

1 9 Zara would like to see less...

A	sports programmes.
B	reality TV.
C	violence on TV.

[1 mark]

2 0 Adella thinks it's better to...

A	read and draw.
B	socialise with friends.
C	go for walks in the countryside.

[1 mark]

A gap year

Marta is talking about her gap year in Argentina.

What does she say about her experiences?

Write **P** for a positive opinion.

   N for a negative opinion.

   P+N for a positive and negative opinion.

| 2 1 | Her journey to Argentina | | [1 mark] |

| 2 2 | Her first impressions | | [1 mark] |

| 2 3 | A birthday celebration | | [1 mark] |

| 2 4 | Her flatmates | | [1 mark] |

Teachers

Kitty and Ricardo are talking about the teachers they had at school.

Answer the questions in **English**.

2 5 · 1 Why did Kitty's history teacher shout at her?

_____ **[1 mark]**

2 5 · 2 What was disappointing about Ricardo's trip to the art gallery?

_____ **[1 mark]**

2 5 · 3 What **two** items does Kitty recall her maths teacher wearing?

_____ **[1 mark]**

2 5 · 4 Why is Ricardo so grateful to his English teacher?

How did Ricardo's teacher influence his career?

_____ **[1 mark]**

Working life

Tomás is talking about his working life.

Complete the table with the correct activity mentioned and when it takes place.

A	A project with his boss
B	Stressful long days
C	A visit abroad
D	Working in a great team

Write **P** for past.

   N for now.

   F for future.

	Activity	When
2 6 · 1		
2 6 · 2		
2 6 · 3		
2 6 · 4		

[8 marks]

The environment

You are listening to a podcast about young people and the environment in Costa Rica.

Which **three** aspects are young people doing well in?

Write the letters in the boxes.

A	recycling
B	energy conservation
C	improving the local environment
D	sustainable clothing
E	reducing plastic in the sea
F	using public transport

2 7

[3 marks]

Section B   Dictation

You will hear 5 short sentences.

Listen carefully and using your knowledge of Spanish sounds, write down in **Spanish** exactly what you hear for each sentence.

You will hear each sentence **three** times: the first time as a full sentence, the second time in short sections and the third time again as a full sentence.

Use your knowledge of Spanish sound and grammar to make sure that what you have written makes sense. Check carefully that your spelling is accurate.   **[10 marks]**

Sentence 1

Sentence 2

Sentence 3

Sentence 4

Sentence 5

Collins

GCSE
Spanish

Higher Tier Paper 2 Speaking

H

Candidate's material – Role-play

Candidate's material – Reading aloud text

Candidate's material – Photo card

Time allowed: 10–12 minutes

(+ 15 minutes' supervised preparation time)

Instructions

- During the preparation time, you are required to prepare **one** Role-play card, one Reading aloud task and **one** Photo card.
- You must **not** use a dictionary, including during the preparation time.

Information

- The test will last a maximum of 12 minutes and will consist of three parts:
- **Part 1:** a Role-play card (approximately 1–1.5 minutes).
- **Part 2:** a Reading aloud text and short conversation based on the topic of the text (approximately 3–3.5 minutes).
- **Part 3:** discussion of a Photo card containing two photos (approximately 6–7 minutes).

Name: _____

Part 1: Role-play

Prepare your <u>spoken</u> answers to this Role-play.

Instructions to candidates

You are talking to your Spanish friend.

Your teacher will play the part of your friend and will speak first.

You should address your teacher as *tú*.

When you see this – ? – you will have to ask a question.

> **In order to score full marks, you must include at least one verb in your response to each task.**
>
> 1. Say what sports you do to keep healthy. (Give **two** details)
> 2. Say what you think of smoking and why. (Give **one** opinion and **one** reason)
> ? 3. Ask your friend what they have for breakfast.
> 4. Say what you do to relax. (Give **one** detail)
> 5. Give your opinion of food in the school canteen. (Give **one** opinion and **one** reason)

Practice Exam Paper 2: Speaking

Part 2: Reading aloud

When your teacher asks you, read aloud the following text **in Spanish.**

México tiene muchas fiestas bonitas e interesantes.

Un ejemplo es el Día de los Muertos que se celebra el uno y el dos de noviembre.

La gente celebra las vidas de los miembros de sus familias que ha perdido.

Creo que sería triste, pero sé que también habría buenos recuerdos.

You will then be asked four questions **in Spanish** that relate to the topic **Customs, festivals and celebrations.**

In order to score the highest marks, you must try to **answer all four questions as fully as you can.**

- ¿Cómo celebras tus cumpleaños normalmente?
- ¿A qué festival hispano te gustaría ir?
- ¿La navidad es un festival importante para ti?
- ¿Cuál es tu opinión sobre las fiestas en tu país?

Part 3: Photo card

- During your preparation time, look at the two photos. You may make as many notes as you wish on an Additional Answer Sheet and use these notes during the test.
- Your teacher will ask you to talk about the content of these photos. The recommended time is approximately **one minute**. **You must say at least one thing about each photo.**
- After you have spoken about the content of the photos, your teacher will then ask you questions related to any of the topics within the theme of **People and Lifestyle**.

Photo 1

Photo 2

Collins

GCSE
Spanish
Higher Tier Paper 3 Reading

H

Time allowed: 1 hour

Instructions

- You must **not** use a dictionary.
- Use black ink or black ball-point pen.
- Answer all questions.
- You must answer the questions in the space provided.
- In **Section A**, answer the questions in **English**.
- In **Section B**, translate the sentences into **English**.

Information

- The marks for questions are shown in brackets.
- The maximum mark for this paper is 50.

Name: _____

Section A   Reading comprehension

Spanish blogs

You read the titles of these blogs written by university students.

A	El paro juvenil hoy en día
B	El uso de drogas entre los jóvenes
C	Cocinar, ahorrar dinero y perder peso
D	Fumar y la presión de grupo
E	La protección de los bosques
F	Alquilar un piso – cada vez más caro

Which headline matches each description?

Write the correct letter in each box.

| 0 1 | Nutrition | | [1 mark] |

| 0 2 | Improving the environment | | [1 mark] |

| 0 3 | Housing issues | | [1 mark] |

| 0 4 | Unemployment | | [1 mark] |

Customs and Traditions

You see this article about a Spanish festival.

Los Carnavales de Tenerife es el segundo carnaval* más grande del mundo, después del de Río de Janeiro. Se celebra entre febrero y marzo y es el festival más popular de las Islas Canarias.

Mucha gente viene del extranjero para disfrutar de las procesiones con disfraces espectaculares, caballos, y bailes tradicionales, y no hay que perder el momento más bonito: la selección de la Reina del Carnaval. Son unos días muy animados y llenos de risa.

El ayuntamiento recomienda usar la red de transporte público por una falta de aparcamiento. La policía advierte que hay que tener cuidado con los objetos personales, sobre todo los teléfonos móviles, debido al aumento de delitos en los últimos años.

*el carnaval – carnival

Complete these sentences. Write the letter for the correct option in each box.

0 5 Los Carnavales de Tenerife…

A	is the biggest festival in Spain and the Canaries.
B	attracts many tourists from Río de Janeiro.
C	is getting more and more popular each year.

[1 mark]

0 6 The highlight of the festivities is...

A	the horse parade.
B	the beautiful costumes.
C	the crowning of the Carnival Queen.

[1 mark]

0 7 The local council is...

A	putting on a bus service.
B	concerned about traffic and congestion.
C	going to provide new parking areas.

[1 mark]

0 8 The local police warn that...

A	criminal gangs used to target this festival.
B	there has been an increase in crime.
C	mobile phones may not get a good network reception.

[1 mark]

School problems

Read Taqwa's email to her maths teacher.

Hola Señor Blanes,

Le escribo porque estoy muy preocupada porque encuentro las clases demasiado complicadas. Me cuesta mucho concentrarme en clase y tengo miedo de no aprobar mi examen al final del mes que viene.

¿Qué me recomienda hacer para mejorar mi nivel? ¿Hay un sitio web que puedo usar para practicar lo que aprendimos en clase? El libro que usamos me parece muy difícil de seguir.

Mis padres son muy estrictos y han dicho que si no saco buenas notas, no puedo ir a un concierto de música con mi prima al final del curso y tendría que estudiar durante el verano.

Muchas gracias

Taqwa

Complete these sentences. Write the letter for the correct option in each box.

0 9 Taqwa is worried about...

A	the pressure the teacher is putting on her.
B	the noise in the class.
C	the difficulty of the lessons.

[1 mark]

1 0 She has an exam…

A	next week.
B	next month.
C	at the end of the year.

[1 mark]

1 1 She is keen to…

A	attend extra lessons at school.
B	find a better text book.
C	consolidate her learning online.

[1 mark]

1 2 Taqwa's parents…

A	are putting pressure on her.
B	will pay for extra lessons in the holidays.
C	are taking her to a music concert.

[1 mark]

Practice Exam Paper 3: Reading

A National Park in Peru

You see a website about the Huascarán National Park in Peru.

El Parque Nacional de Huascarán es un lugar bonito situado en las montañas peruanas. Tiene la cordillera* tropical más alta del mundo y el año pasado el número de visitantes aumentó. Es un sitio ideal para los que les gusta hacer deportes al aire libre y actualmente están construyendo más espacios para las bicicletas.

El parque prohibió la caza* hace unos años y a causa de eso, hoy en día se puede ver especies de animales increíbles. En los próximos cinco años, habrá aún más proyectos para proteger la naturaleza en el parque.

*la cordillera – mountain range

*la caza – hunting

What does the article say about these aspects?

Write **P** for something that happened **in the past**.

    N for something that is happening **now**.

    F for something that is going to happen **in the future**.

Write the correct letter in each box.

1	3	An increase in the number of visitors		[1 mark]

1	4	Building of cycle paths		[1 mark]

1	5	The prohibition of hunting		[1 mark]

1	6	Conservation projects		[1 mark]

Future Plans

Read these comments from some Spanish students.

Xavier

Después de terminar mis exámenes tengo la intención de pasar un año en el extranjero, pero no sé si tengo suficiente dinero para hacerlo este año, así que tendré que encontrar un trabajo a tiempo parcial en el otoño.

Marcos

En cinco años quiero tener mi propia empresa como mi padre. No quiero trabajar para un jefe porque no tendría libertad.

Maya

Aunque ganar bien es importante, lo que más me interesa es ayudar a los demás, así que tengo ganas de trabajar con las víctimas de la violencia.

Kahlo

Estoy bajo presión para ir a la universidad y estudiar matemáticas, pero preferiría ser escritor y acabo de ganar un premio por una historia.

Maribel

No puedo imaginar que sería feliz trabajando en un ordenador en casa como hace mucha gente hoy en día. Dicho esto, tener que coger el autobús al trabajo cada día causaría estrés.

Juliana

Cuando termine mis estudios en el instituto, pienso buscar un aprendizaje en una peluquería porque en el futuro quiero tener mi propio negocio. Sin embargo, sé que tendré que trabajar bastante antes de realizar este sueño.

Answer the following questions in **English**.

| 1 | 7 | What does Maribel say about the idea of working from home?

.... [1 mark]

| 1 | 8 | What will Xavier do in the autumn?

.... [1 mark]

| 1 | 9 | What is the most important thing for Maya?

.... [1 mark]

| 2 | 0 | How do we know that Kahlo is a good writer?

.... [1 mark]

| 2 | 1 | What does Marcos' father do for work?

.... [1 mark]

| 2 | 2 | What is Juliana's dream for the future?

.... [1 mark]

Free-time activities

Read Zara's social media post.

> Empecé a tocar el piano a los siete años pero lo dejé dos años más tarde, porque era demasiado difícil. Ahora llevo cinco años tocando la guitarra. Anoche toqué en un concierto con una orquesta local, ¡fue un gran éxito!
>
> Lo que más me gusta de tocar un instrumento es poder expresarme a través de la música. La desventaja es que tengo que ser muy trabajadora ya que hay que practicar cada día. Es verdad que pueder ser molesto porque tendré exámenes muy pronto.
>
> En el futuro mi sueño es ser miembro de una orquesta profesional, será muy <u>exigente</u> lograrlo, pero estoy dispuesta a trabajar duro.

What does the article say about these aspects?

Write **P** for something that happened **in the past**.

    N for something that is happening **now**.

    F for something that is going to happen **in the future**.

Write the correct letter in each box.

| 2 3 | Learning the piano | | [1 mark] |

| 2 4 | Playing the guitar | | [1 mark] |

| 2 5 | A successful performance | | [1 mark] |

| 2 6 | Taking exams | | [1 mark] |

| 2 7 | Read the last sentence again. Which is the best translation for **exigente**?

A	enjoyable
B	expensive
C	demanding

[1 mark]

My Town

Read Parsa's blog about his town.

Vivo en un pueblo pequeño, cerca de Córdoba. He visto muchos cambios en los últimos años. Antes las calles estaban llenas de basura y había muchos edificios vacíos. Mi pueblo me parecía muy sucio y feo. Afortunadamente el ayuntamiento ha invertido* mucho dinero en los últimos años y ha creado espacios verdes con árboles y flores. Hay grupos de vecinos que trabajan como voluntarios para limpiar los barrios locales. Los cambios no eran sencillos pero como consecuencia mucha gente quiere vivir aquí hoy.

***invertir** – to invest

Answer the question in **English**.

2 8   What was Parsa's town like in the past? Give **two** details.

    1. ....

    2. ....

                                                   [1 mark]

2 9   What impression of the town did this give? Give **two** details.

.... **[1 mark]**

3 0   Who invested money in his town?

.... **[1 mark]**

3 1   Who set up a voluntary cleanup service?

.... **[1 mark]**

3 2   What is the consequence of this improvement?

.... **[1 mark]**

Health Concerns

Read Adria's text to her aunt and her aunt's response. Choose the correct answer.

¡Hola tía!

Lo estoy pasando muy mal en este momento, así que no puedo dormir y cuando voy al insti estoy cansada. Hace unos días un chico en mi clase escribió unos mensajes en las redes sociales diciendo que debería perder peso si quiero encontrar novio. Estoy muy triste aunque sé que es verdad que necesito comer más sano y hacer más ejercicio. Lo he intentado, pero es tan difícil.

Options   Exit

Hola Adria,

¡Me siento enojada que un chico esté mandándote mensajes así! Primero, hay que decirlo a tu profe y segundo, la mejor manera de perder peso es ir a pie en vez de en coche. Estar de régimen no vale la pena. ¡Llámame cuando puedas y no te preocupes! Un abrazo.

Options   Exit

Complete these sentences. Write the letter for the correct option in each box.

3 3 Adria can't sleep because…

A	she is worried about finding a boyfriend.
B	she has exam stress.
C	she is the victim of cyber bullying.

[1 mark]

3 4 She is…

A	aware of her issue with weight.
B	in denial of her weight issue.
C	refuses to change the way she looks.

[1 mark]

3 5 Her aunt feels…

A	angry.
B	sad.
C	disappointed.

[1 mark]

3 6 Her aunt recommends…

A	going on a diet.
B	doing varied exercise.
C	walking as much as possible.

[1 mark]

Practice Exam Paper 3: Reading

Young people and the environment

Read the results of this survey carried out in a school in Mexico.

- **89 % de los alumnos considera la destrucción del medio ambiente el problema más grande del mundo**
- **71 % intenta andar al colegio o ir en autobús**
- **83 % recicla en casa**
- **La mitad de los encuestados* nunca trae su propia bolsa al supermercado**
- **Solo 25 % apaga la luz al salir de una habitación**
- **32 % es miembro de un grupo medioambiental**

***los encuestados** – the people surveyed

Complete the sentences in **English**.

An example has been done for you.

Example: 89% think that the destruction of the environment *is the biggest world problem.*

3 7   71% try to ....

[1 mark]

3 8   50% never ....

[1 mark]

3 9   A quarter ....

[1 mark]

4 0   Nearly one third ....

[1 mark]

Section B Translation into **English**

4 1 Translate these sentences into **English**.

Mañana mis padres van a viajar al extranjero en tren.

[2 marks]

Acabo de ganar un concurso de baile, ¡fue emocionante!

[2 marks]

Tuve que pasar horas estudiando anoche.

[2 marks]

En invierno me gusta levantarme muy pronto, aunque hace frío.

[2 marks]

Hace dos semanas mi primo aprobó su examen de informática.

[2 marks]

END OF QUESTIONS

Collins

GCSE
Spanish

H

Higher Tier Paper 4 Writing

Time allowed: 1 hour 15 minutes

Instructions

- Use black ink or black ball-point pen.
- You must answer **three** questions.
- In **Section A**, you must answer Question 1.
- In **Section B**, you must answer **either** Question 2.1 **or** Question 2.2. You must only answer **one** of these questions.
- In **Section C**, you must answer **either** Question 3.1 **or** Question 3.2. You must only answer **one** of these questions.
- Answer all questions in Spanish.
- Answer the questions in the spaces provided.

Information

- The marks for questions are shown in brackets.
- The maximum mark for this paper is 50.
- You must **not** use a dictionary during this test.
- In order to score the highest marks for Question 2.1 / Question 2.2, you must write something about each bullet point.
- In order to score the highest marks in Question 3.1 / Question 3.2, you must write something about both bullet points.

Name: ....

Section A Translation into **Spanish**

0 1 Translate the following sentences into Spanish.   **[10 marks]**

I did my science homework last night.

I am going to travel to Spain with my grandparents.

I like to eat fish three times a week because it's healthy.

I used to go to the gym but now I don't have time.

I have to wear the correct uniform.

Practice Exam Paper 4: Writing

Section B   Answer **either** Question 2.1 **or** Question 2.2

You must only answer **one** of these questions.

Either Question 2.1

0 2 · 1 You are emailing your Peruvian friend about school.

Write approximately **90** words in **Spanish.**

You must write something about each bullet point.

Mention:

- your opinion of your teachers
- activities you did at school this week
- your plans for after your exams.   **[15 marks]**

Or Question 2.2

0 2 . 2 You are preparing a leaflet on your local area to give to your Spanish exchange partner.

Write approximately **90** words in **Spanish**.

You must write something about each bullet point.

Mention:

- things you can see and visit in your local area
- a description of what you did in your local area last weekend
- what changes there will be in your local area in the future.   **[15 marks]**

Practice Exam Paper 4: Writing

Section C Answer **either** Question 3.1 **or** Question 3.2

You must only answer **one** of these questions.

Either Question 3.1

| 0 | 3 | · | 1 | You are writing a post for a Spanish website about customs and celebrations.

Write approximately **150** words in **Spanish.**

You must write something about both bullet points.

Mention:

- details of a festival from a Spanish-speaking country
- a description of a memorable birthday celebration.   **[25 marks]**

Or Question 3.1

0 3 . 2 You are writing about lifestyle choices for your school magazine.

Write approximately **150** words in **Spanish.**

You must write something about both bullet points.

Mention:

- your opinion of smoking, alcohol and drugs
- how you will change your lifestyle in future to be healthier. **[25 marks]**

END OF QUESTIONS

Notes

Answers

Pages 148–149: Identity and Relationships with Others

1. a) slim [1], patient [1], hard-working [1]
   b) 15 [1]
   c) Elisa [1]
   d) his father [1]
   e) sporty [1]
   f) Any three from: they are retired, they live nearby, they look after José Luis and his siblings sometimes, they're kind and always proud of their grandchildren [3]

2. a) v) [1]
   b) ii) [1]
   c) iii) [1]
   d) i) [1]
   e) iv) [1]

3. In order: hermanos; llevamos; pelo; ojos; gemelas; llamo; comprensiva; tía; tío; bien [10]

4. a) is an only child [1]
   b) some cousins [1]
   c) look alike [1]
   d) like twins [1]
   e) understanding and sensitive [1]
   f) a musician [1]

5. a) C [1]
   b) A [1]
   c) B [1]

Pages 150–151: Healthy Living and Lifestyle

1. a) B [1]
   b) A [1]
   c) B [1]
   d) A [1]

2. a) 10 [1]
   b) 8 [1]
   c) 7 [1]
   d) 6 [1]
   e) 5 [1]
   f) 2 [1]
   g) 4 [1]
   h) 1 [1]
   i) 3 [1]
   j) 9 [1]

3. Read sentences aloud then listen to sentences to check. **(1 mark for each sentence read correctly)**

4. a) los dientes [1]
   b) la pierna [1]
   c) el estómago [1]
   d) cabeza [1]
   e) los ojos [1]
   f) los pies [1]

5. a) i) [1]
   b) iii) [1]
   c) v) [1]
   d) ii) [1]
   e) vi) [1]
   f) vii) [1]
   g) iv) [1]

Pages 152–153: Education and Work

1. In order: tecnología; ciencias; difíciles; idiomas; comercio; emocionante [6]

2. a) She likes, science [1], IT [1], technology [1] and languages [1].
   b) Maths [1] because he finds it difficult [1].
   c) Languages [1]
   d) She doesn't find them interesting. [1]
   e) Oriol's favourite subject is drama. [1] He says it's exciting. [1]

3. [11]

4. a) v) [1]
   b) iv) [1]
   c) i) [1]
   d) ii) [1]
   e) iii) [1]

Page 154–155: Free-time Activities

1. a) Tomás [1]
   b) Omar [1]
   c) Sonia [1]
   d) Tomás [1]
   e) Sonia [1]
   f) Tomás [1]
   g) Sonia [1]
   h) Omar [1]
   i) Omar [1]
   j) Tomás [1]

2. a) ii) [1]
   b) vii) [1]
   c) iv) [1]
   d) viii) [1]
   e) i) [1]
   f) iii) [1]
   g) vi) [1]
   h) v) [1]

3. a) C [1]
    b) D [1]
    c) B [1]
    d) A [1]
    e) F [1]
    f) E [1]

4. a) plays football or goes swimming [1]
    b) listening to music and reading [1]
    c) cartoons [1]
    d) because he's not interested in game shows, soap operas or reality TV / he finds the adverts annoying [1]
    e) because he can choose the ones he likes [1]
    f) to celebrate his sister's birthday [1]
    g) his sister [1]
    h) by going to a music festival with his friends [1]

Pages 156–157: Customs, Festivals and Celebrations

1. a) B [1]
    b) C [1]
    c) A [1]

2. a) a religious parade through the village [1]
    b) a group of singers who go from house to house to sing traditional songs that are amusing and joyful [1]
    c) to his grandparents' village [1]
    d) running through the streets in front of the bulls [1]
    e) everyone (both old and young people) [1]
    f) Day of the Dead [1]
    g) at the beginning of November [1]
    h) to remember their family members that have died [1]

3. a) v) [1]
    b) iii) [1]
    c) iv) [1]
    d) i) [1]
    e) ii) [1]

4. a) vii) I attended the wedding of my brother and his girlfriend. [2]
    b) ii) The bride wore an elegant, white dress. [2]
    c) vi) My brother wore a navy blue suit. [2]
    d) i) They got married in a beautiful, old house. [2]
    e) viii) Luckily the weather was nice when we were in the garden for the photos. [2]
    f) v) There was a four-course meal. [2]
    g) iii) I think they spent a lot of money. [2]
    h) iv) They said it was worth it because you only do it once in a lifetime. [2]

Pages 158–159: Celebrity Culture

1. a) Los influencers [1]
    b) Los seguidores [1]
    c) Los célebres [1]
    d) Las redes sociales [1]
    e) Las marcas [1]

2. a) De niña, hacía clases de ballet. [1]
    b) Salió en su primera película a la edad de 17 años. [1]
    c) Ha ganado muchos premios. [1]
    d) Se casó en 2010. [1]
    e) Viven entre Los Ángeles, Nueva York y Madrid. [1]
    f) Trabaja en varias caridades. [1]

3. Read sentences aloud then listen to sentences to check. **(1 mark for each sentence read correctly)**

4. a) Empezó a jugar al fútbol cuando era muy joven. [1]
    b) A los 9 años hizo pruebas en el Sevilla Fútbol Club. [1]
    c) A la edad de 17 años jugó en el primer equipo del Sevilla. [1]
    d) Dos años después fue a jugar en el Real Madrid. [1]
    e) Sergio conoció a su pareja, Pilar Rubio, en 2012. [1]
    f) El 15 de junio de 2019 se casaron. [1]
    g) (Sergio) tiene más de 60 millones de seguidores en las redes sociales. [1]

5. a) vi) [1]
    b) iv) [1]
    c) iii) [1]
    d) ii) [1]
    e) v) [1]
    f) i) [1]

Pages 160–161: Travel and Tourism

1. a) un piso [1], pequeños hoteles [1]
    b) nos bañábamos en el mar [1], jugábamos al fútbol [1], salíamos en barco [1]
    c) Valencia [1], Madrid [1], Roma [1]
    d) en autobús [1], en coche [1], en tren [1], en avión [1], en bicicleta [1]

2. A, C, D, F, H, I (in any order) [6]

3. a) C [1]
    b) D [1]
    c) E [1]
    d) B [1]
    e) A [1]

4. Read sentences aloud then listen to sentences to check. **(1 mark for each sentence read correctly)**

5. a) iii) [1]
    b) ii) [1]
    c) iv) [1]
    d) i) [1]
    e) v) [1]

Pages 162–163: Media and Technology

1. a) conectar [1]
    b) enviar [1]
    c) funcionar [1]
    d) colgar [1]
    e) cargar [1]
    f) grabar [1]
    g) navegar [1]
    h) guardar [1]

2. Student's own answers. **(1 mark for each sentence)**

3. a) 2002 [1]
    b) Valencia [1]
    c) She started posting dance videos (when she was 14). [1]
    d) Shakira and Maluma [1]
    e) Over 12 million [1]
    f) Ignacio Gil Conesa's username / handle [1]
    g) In Valencia in 1990 [1]
    h) Through his funny videos (on TikTok and Instagram) [1]
    i) About 14 million [1]

4. a) P   [1]
    b) P   [1]
    c) N   [1]
    d) P   [1]
    e) N   [1]
    f) N   [1]
    g) P   [1]
    h) N   [1]

Pages 164–165: The Environment and Where People Live

1. a) la planta baja   [1]
    b) una cocina comedor   [1]
    c) el primer piso   [1]
    d) un cuarto de baño   [1]
    e) la habitación   [1]
    f) un piso moderno   [1]
    g) el décimo piso   [1]
    h) las ventanas   [1]
    i) un jardín pequeño   [1]
    j) la terraza   [1]

2. a) Because she shares her bedroom with her sister.   [1]
    b) Yes. It's quiet [1], there are trees and green areas [1] and it's near the city [1].
    c) Yes [1], because he says he can see the coast from his apartment [1].
    d) Yes [1], there are parks and pedestrianised areas [1].
    e) Yes [1], he can walk or cycle to school [1]
    f) There are so many places to go [1] (such as museums, cinemas, shops, cafés and restaurants).
    g) It's noisy [1] and there is air pollution [1].

3. a) D   [1]
    b) C   [1]
    c) E   [1]
    d) B   [1]
    e) A   [1]

4. a) incendios   [1]
    b) recursos   [1]
    c) contaminación   [1]
    d) apagar   [1]
    e) extinción   [1]
    f) reutilizar   [1]

Pages 166–167: Grammar 1

Gender, Plurals and Articles

1. a) un [1], unos [1]
    b) un [1], unos [1]
    c) una [1], unas [1]
    d) unos [1], un [1]
    e) una [1], unos [1]

2. a) A mi padre le gusta escuchar **la** radio por la mañana.   [1]
    b) Creo que **el** español es un idioma importante.   [1]
    c) ¿Quieres ir al cine el viernes por **la** tarde?   [1]
    d) En nuestro instituto **el** uniforme es obligatorio.   [1]
    e) Mi cumpleaños es **el** 4 de marzo.   [1]

3. a) Por la ventana veo **los** [1] árboles y **las** [1] flores en el jardín.
    b) Me lavo **las** [1] manos antes de comer y me lavo **los** [1] dientes después de comer.
    c) Creo que **las** [1] matemáticas son más difíciles que **los** [1] idiomas.
    d) Si quieres aprobar **los** [1] exámenes, debes ir a todas **las** [1] clases.

    e) Me gusta leer **los** [1] mensajes y ver **las** [1] fotos en el móvil.
    f) Prefiero **las** [1] series policíacas a **los** [1] programas de telerrealidad.
    g) ¿Crees que **los** [1] chicos son más habladores que **las** [1] chicas?

Adjectives, Comparatives, Superlatives and Adverbs

4. a) Las paredes de mi habitación son **azules**.   [1]
    b) Para ir a la fiesta voy a llevar un vestido **rojo**.   [1]
    c) Ayer compré unos zapatos **negros**.   [1]
    d) Nuestros vecinos tienen un perro **pequeño** muy simpático.   [1]
    e) Mi hermana mayor es **trabajadora**.   [1]
    f) La casa está cerca de una playa bonita y **tranquila**. [1]
    g) Hoy hace **buen** tiempo. Vamos al parque.   [1]
    h) Taylor Swift es una cantante muy **buena**.   [1]

5. a) No soy tan alto **como** mi amigo.   [1]
    b) Pero creo que juego **mejor** al fútbol que él.   [1]
    c) Para mí, las matemáticas son **menos** difíciles que las ciencias.   [1]
    d) Este libro es aburridísimo. Es el **peor** que he leído. [1]
    e) Las películas de acción son más emocionantes **que** las comedias.   [1]

6. b) (probable) probablemente   [1]
    c) (rápida) rápidamente   [1]
    d) (reciente) recientemente   [1]
    e) (tranquila) tranquilamente   [1]
    f) (fácil) fácilmente   [1]

7. a) slowly   [1]
    b) probably   [1]
    c) quickly   [1]
    d) recently   [1]
    e) quietly   [1]
    f) easily   [1]

Pages 168–169: Grammar 1

Interrogatives and Por v Para

1. a) ¿**Cómo** te llamas?   [1]
    b) ¿**Dónde** vives?   [1]
    c) ¿**Cuántos** años tienes?   [1]
    d) ¿**Cuántos** hermanos tienes?   [1]
    e) ¿**Cuándo** es tu cumpleaños?   [1]
    f) ¿**Qué** te gusta más hacer en tu tiempo libre?   [1]
    g) ¿**Cuáles** son tus asignaturas favoritas?   [1]
    h) ¿**Por qué** te gustan estas asignaturas?   [1]
    i) ¿**Quién** es tu actor o actriz preferido?   [1]
    j) ¿**Qué** tipo de música prefieres?   [1]

2. a) ¿Cómo se llama tu mejor amigo?   [1]
    b) ¿Cómo es?   [1]
    c) ¿Cuántos años tiene?   [1]
    d) ¿Dónde vive?   [1]
    e) ¿Por qué sois amigos? / ¿Por qué os lleváis bien? [1]

3. a) ¿Qué autobús tomamos **para** llegar al aeropuerto?   [1]
    b) Hemos estado aquí esperando **por** dos horas.   [1]
    c) Es más rápido ir **por** la autopista.   [1]
    d) He comprado una camiseta **por** 20 euros.   [1]
    e) Quiero comprar un regalo **para** mis padres.   [1]
    f) ¿Hay una farmacia **por** aquí?   [1]
    g) ¿Cuál es el mejor sitio **para** tomar un buen café? [1]

Present Tense, Regular and Reflexive Verbs and Negatives

4. vivo **[1]**; hablamos **[1]**; habla **[1]**; habla **[1]**; vivimos **[1]**; hablamos **[1]**

trabaja **[1]**; trabaja **[1]**; estudiamos **[1]**; viven **[1]**; comemos **[1]**

5. a) Para proteger el medio ambiente es importante **reciclar** todo lo posible. **[1]**

   b) En casa, **reciclo** papel, plástico y vidrio. **[1]**
   c) Me molesta **escuchar** el ruido del tráfico en mi barrio. **[1]**
   d) A veces **escucho** música cuando estudio. **[1]**
   e) Los estudiantes que **viven** cerca del insti van a clase a pie. **[1]**

6. a) Un buen amigo siempre te **apoya**. **[1]**
   b) ¿A quién te **pareces** más en tu familia? **[1]**
   c) Los mejores profesores nos **explican** bien las clases. **[1]**
   d) **Repaso** los verbos porque no quiero suspender el examen. **[1]**
   e) ¿A qué hora **cenáis** en vuestra casa? **[1]**

7. a) **No** voy al instituto a pie. **[1]**
   b) **No** vivimos cerca del instituto. **[1]**
   c) Mi hermano **no** juega al fútbol todos los días. **[1]**
   d) **No** hay un examen de español mañana. **[1]**
   e) **No** me levanto temprano los fines de semana. **[1]**

Pages 170–171: Grammar 2

Common Irregular Verbs and Present Continuous

1. Example answers (student's own answers):
   a) **Soy inglés / inglesa / escocés / escocesa, etc.** **[1]**
   b) **Tengo 15 años.** **[1]**
   c) **Sí, tengo dos hermanos. / No tengo hermanos. Soy hijo único. / Soy hija única.** **[1]**
   d) **Hago gimnasia y juego al fútbol.** **[1]**
   e) **Voy al instituto en autobús.** **[1]**
   f) **Doy ropa, libros y flores a mi madre en su cumpleaños.** **[1]**
   g) **Sé cocinar una tortilla.** **[1]**
   h) **Sí, siempre digo la verdad a mis amigos.** **[1]**
   i) **No, no puedo correr cien metros en menos de 20 segundos.** **[1]**

2. Read sentences aloud then listen to sentences to check. **(1 mark for each sentence read correctly)**

3. quiero **[1]**; piensan **[1]**; digo **[1]**; suelo **[1]**; pido **[1]**

4. Está comiendo **[1]**; está durmiendo **[1]**; Están jugando **[1]**; estás haciendo **[1]**; estoy escribiendo **[1]**

Past Tenses

5. i) Siento que yo no **estuve** cuando tú viniste a casa. **[1]**
   ii) Ayer **jugué** dos partidos de fútbol y me quedé muy cansado. **[1]**
   iii) **Saqué** muchas fotos en la boda de mi hermana. **[1]**
   iv) El mes pasado **fui** de vacaciones a Málaga con mi familia. **[1]**
   v) Anoche **vi** una película buenísima en la tele. **[1]**
   vi) **Hice** un bocadillo de tortilla porque tenía mucha hambre. **[1]**

6. Example answers (student's own answers.)
   Cuando tenía 5 años...
   no me gustaba comer verduras. **[1]**
   jugaba con mi hermano. **[1]**
   mi juguete favorito era un oso de peluche. **[1]**
   iba al colegio a pie. **[1]**
   tenía miedo de los perros. **[1]**
   mi libro favorito era *The Gruffalo*. **[1]**
   solía ver *Bluey* y me gustaba porque era divertido. **[1]**

7. Student's own answers. **(1 mark for completing activity)**

Pages 172–173: Grammar 2

Pronouns

1. a) Me encantan estas zapatillas. Voy a **comprarlas**. **[1]**
   b) Aquí hay una foto fantástica de ti. **Mírala**. **[1]**
   c) Es un secreto, por favor no se **lo** digas a nadie. **[1]**
   d) Mis padres me compraron un portátil y me **lo** regalaron en mi cumpleaños. **[1]**
   e) La tarta de manzana es deliciosa. ¿Quieres **probarla**? **[1]**

2. a) iii) **[1]**
   b) v) **[1]**
   c) i) **[1]**
   d) ii) **[1]**
   e) iv) **[1]**

3. a) ¿A qué hora **os** levantasteis el día que fuisteis de vacaciones?
   b) Bueno, teníamos que **levantarnos** a las tres para ir al aeropuerto. **[1]**
   c) ¿A las tres? ¡Huy! A mí no me gusta nada **despertarme** tan temprano. **[1]**
   d) A mí tampoco. ¿Pero sabes qué pasó? Mis padres no **se** despertaron. **[1]**
   e) ¿Y tú no **te** despertaste? **[1]**
   f) No, pero al final mi madre **se** despertó a las cuatro y nos levantamos todos con mucha prisa. **[1]** ¿Y llegasteis a tiempo al aeropuerto?
   g) Sí, llegamos justo a tiempo y fuimos los últimos en **sentarnos** en el avión. **[1]**

The Future Tenses, Subjunctive and Imperative Moods

4. a) ii) **[1]**
   b) i) **[1]**
   c) iii) **[1]**
   d) vi) **[1]**
   e) iv) **[1]**
   f) v) **[1]**

5. a) vas a **[1]**
   b) dará **[1]**
   c) Tendrás **[1]**
   d) Habrá **[1]**
   e) haré **[1]**
   f) saldrá **[1]**

6. a) ¿Qué harías tú si ganaras la lotería?
   b) Si todo el mundo **fuera** al trabajo en bicicleta, el aire **estaría** menos contaminado. **[2]**
   c) **Sería** más fácil estudiar en casa si **tuviera** una mesa en mi habitación. **[2]**
   d) Si tú **vivieras** un año en España, **hablarías** muy bien el español. **[2]**

e) Si **pudiera** conocer a una persona famosa de la historia, creo que **elegiría** a William Shakespeare. [2]

7. a) Habla [1]
   b) Sentaos [1]
   c) corráis [1]
   d) Pon [1]
   e) Haz [1]

Pages 174–185
Higher Tier Paper 1: Listening – Mark Scheme

Section A Listening comprehension

01 A [1]; 02 A+B [1]; 03 B [1]; 04 B [1]; 05 G [1]; 06 F [1]; 07 B [1]; 08 E [1]; 09 C [1]; 10.1 C [1]; 10.2 E [1]; 10.3 A [1]; 10.4 F [1]

11 Family parties / social events (must include 'family') [1]

12 Surprised [1]

13 Having the opportunity to / he can express himself through dance or ballet / by dancing [1]

14 Believe in yourself OR know you will come across / encounter (significant) obstacles / difficulties [1]

15 roadworks / building works [1]; green areas / parks [1]

16 homeless people / people who live on the street [1]; affordable / cheap / budget etc. housing / accommodation (must include adjective) [1]

17 A [1]; 18 C [1]; 19 C [1]; 20 B [1]; 21 P+N [1]; 22 N [1]; 23 P+N [1]; 24 P [1]

25.1 She arrived late to class. [1]

25.2 He wasn't able to stay longer (at the art gallery). [1]

25.3 (All) pink clothes and large / enormous / huge glasses [1]

25.4 He inspired him to become a journalist. [1]

26.1 A [1]; F [1]

26.2 C [1]; P [1]

26.3 D [1]; N [1]

26.4 B [1]; F [1]

27 F E C (in any order) [3]

Section B Dictation

The dictation is assessed for:
Communication of meaning [5 marks]
Spelling and grammatical accuracy [5 marks]
No marks will be lost for missing out just one accent unless it changes the meaning of the word.

Pages 186–189

Higher Tier Paper 2: Speaking – Mark Scheme

Part 1: Role-play

Teacher script and sample answers:

1. Teacher: ¿Qué deportes haces para estar en forma?
   Student: *Juego al... hago / practico + sport, en el polideportivo / campo de fútbol / estadio el fin de semana / después del colegio / dos veces a la semana / me encanta / me gusta porque es...*
2. Teacher: ¿Qué opinas de fumar?
   Student: *Creo que / pienso que / opino que es horrible / repugnante / asqueroso / caro / un desperdicio de dinero / adictivo / tonto*
3. Teacher: Respond appropriately to the question.
   Student: *¿Qué desayunas? / ¿Qué tomas de desayuno? / ¿Qué sueles desayunar?*
4. Teacher: ¿Qué haces para relajar te?
   Student: *Para relajar me, leo / escucho música / hago meditación / juego deportes / veo la tele / juego a los videojuegos*
5. Teacher: Háblame de la comida en la cantina.
   Student: *Creo que / pienso que / opino que (no) es variada / sana / deliciosa / sabrosa / fresca / malsana / grasa*

Part 2: Reading aloud

Sample answers:

- *Normalmente, hago una fiesta / voy al cine con mis amigos / lo celebro con mi familia.*
- *Me gustaría ir en Semana Santa a Sevilla para ver los desfiles / a los Carnavales de Tenerife por el ambiente en la calle / al Día de los muertos para ver los disfraces.*
- *Sí, me encanta la Navidad porque la pasamos en familia / la comida es muy buena / me dan muchos regalos.*
- *En mi país, no hay tantas fiestas en la calle / hay muchos festivales de música que me encantan / celebramos las fiestas en casa con familia o amigos.*

Part 3: Photo card

Sample answers:

Photo 1: Students could begin their answer with a construction such as *veo / hay / se puede ver* and then go onto say *estudiantes / alumnos / gente / jóvenes en una biblioteca / en un colegio / una universidad*. They could also give physical descriptions of the people, for example: *el chico es alto / la chica tiene el pelo largo* etc. They could say what they are doing *están estudiando / hablando / leyendo / estudian / hablan / leen*. They could then give more details of the scene *la gente parece contenta / seria, la biblioteca parece tranquila* etc.

Photo 2: Students could begin their answer with a construction such as *Veo / hay / se puede ver* and then go onto say *un chico / un estudiante / un hombre / un joven* and then say the activity *trabajando / sirviendo en un café / restaurante* or *el chico trabaja / sirve.* They could also give physical descriptions of the young person, *tiene el pelo... es alto / delgado*. They could then give more details of the scene *el café es moderno / animado / está lleno*, and then the activity of people in the scene, *los clientes están bebiendo / comiendo....* And finally how the people are *el chico parece estresado / contento / ocupado, la gente parece relajada / satisfecha.*

Teacher script:
Theme: **People and Lifestyle**
The candidate is given a card containing two photos from the same topic and makes notes on them in the preparation period.

You ask the candidate to talk about the photos. At Higher tier, the recommended time is approximately **one and a half minutes.** The candidate must say at least one thing about each photo.

You then have an unprepared conversation which is recommended to last between **four and a half to five and a half minutes.**

Candidates may use any notes they have made during the preparation time. You begin by asking the candidate to tell you about the photos.

- Háblame de las fotos.

When the candidate has finished talking about the photos for approximately one and half minutes, you have a conversation within the theme **People and Lifestyle**. This can include any or all of the prescribed topics:

- Identity and relationships with others
- Healthy living and lifestyle
- Education and Work

At Higher tier, Part 3 of the test is recommended to last in total **between six and seven minutes**. This includes the description of the photos and the unprepared conversation.

Pages 190–205

Higher Tier Paper 3: Reading – Mark Scheme

Section A Reading comprehension

01 C [1]; 02 E [1]; 03 F [1]; 04 A [1]; 05 A [1]; 06 C [1];
07 B [1]; 08 B [1]; 09 C [1]; 10 B [1]; 11 C [1]; 12 A [1];
13 P [1]; 14 N [1]; 15 P [1]; 16 F [1]
17 She wouldn't be happy / she can't imagine she would be happy. [1]
18 Find / get / look for a part-time job (must include 'part-time') [1]
19 Helping others [1]
20 He has just won a prize / award (for his story). [1]
21 He has his own business. [1]
22 To have her own hairdressing business [1]
23 P [1]; 24 N [1]; 25 P [1]; 26 F [1]; 27 C [1]
28 Streets are full of rubbish, (lots of) empty buildings [1 mark: both elements needed]
29 ugly and dirty [1 mark: both elements needed]
30 council / town hall / city council [1]
31 neighbours [1]
32 (many) people want to live in the town (today) [1]
33 C [1]
34 A [1]; 35 A [1]; 36 C [1]
37 71% try to walk (to school) or take the bus [1]
38 50% never take their own bag to the supermarket [1]
39 A quarter of those surveyed turn / switch off the light when leaving a room [1]
40 Nearly one third are members of an environmental club [1]

Section B Translation into English

41 Tomorrow my parents are going to travel abroad by train. [2]
I have just won a dance competition / contest. It was exciting! [2]
I had to spend hours studying last night. [2]
In winter I like to get up very early in the morning although it is cold. [2]
Two weeks ago my cousin passed his ICT / computing exam. [2]

Pages 206–211

Higher Tier Paper 4: Writing – Mark Scheme

Section A Translation into Spanish

01 Hice mis deberes de ciencias anoche. (Time can be at start or end) [2]
Voy a viajar a España con mis abuelos. (accept viajaré) [2]
Me gusta comer pescado tres veces a la semana porque es sano (accept saludable) [2]
Iba al gimnasio pero ahora no tengo (el) tiempo [2]
Tengo que llevar el uniforme correcto (accept hay que) [2]

Section B

02.1 and 02.2

This section is marked out of **15**.
You will be awarded up to 10 marks for your **content**.
To achieve the best marks, you will need to:

- cover all three bullet points (no need for equal coverage)
- have clear communication
- regularly develop your ideas with a lot of relevant information.

You will be awarded up to 5 marks for your language and accuracy.
To achieve the best mark you should include:

- A good variety of vocabulary.
- Regular attempts at complexity of language and structure.
- References to all three time frames (past, present and future) which are mainly successful.
- Only minor errors (but some major errors may occur in more complex structures).

Section C

03.1 and 03.2

This section is marked out of **25**.
You will be awarded up to **15** marks for **content**.
To achieve the best mark you must have:

- A lot of information relevant to the task.
- Regular successful development of ideas and descriptions.
- Clear communication.

You will be awarded up to **5** marks for **Range and use of language**.
To achieve the best mark you must have:

- A very good variety of appropriate vocabulary and grammatical structures.
- Regular complex language which is often successful.

You will be awarded up to **5** marks for **accuracy**.
To achieve the best mark you must have:

- A response which is usually accurate, with only occasional errors.
- Correct verbs and tenses.

Collins

GCSE
SPANISH

Higher Tier Paper 1 Listening Transcript

Section A		Listening comprehension

01   **M1**   Mi hermano menor siempre pasa mucho tiempo estudiando y saca muy buenas notas en las ciencias. Afortunadamente, tiene un buen grupo de amigos que son iguales que él.

02   **M1**   Hace un año, mi primo Fernando que iba a casarse, empezó a pelearse con su novia y ya no están juntos. El decidió ir a Barcelona para trabajar como cantante en un bar.

03   **M1**   Iré a la Universidad de Monterrey, pero está lejos de mi casa, así que tendré que vivir con mi abuela. Creo que será una buena oportunidad para mí.

04   **M1**   Antes quería tener mi propio negocio y ser rico, pero mi padre me dijo que la felicidad es más importante. Al final, me puse de acuerdo con él.

05   **F1**   Es una asignatura muy artística y puedes expresarte. Me encanta que me influyan mis pintores favoritos.

06   **M1**   Lo malo es que el profe es bastante estricto y a veces hay que trabajar en silencio, dicho eso, aprender sobre eventos importantes del pasado es muy interesante.

07   **F2**   Encuentro difícil recordar todas las nuevas palabras pero cuando voy al extranjero me siento feliz cuando comunico con la gente.

08   **F3**   Sé que es importante estar en forma pero odio correr bajo la lluvia.

09	M2	Aprender sobre el cambio climático y desastres naturales me encanta, pero recordar los nombres de ríos y montañas puede ser difícil.
10	F1	Algunas de mis amigas están siempre de régimen, pero para mí sería imposible no poder comer las cosas que más me gustan. La gente que fuma, no solo gasta mucho dinero sino también corre el riesgo de enfermedades serias. Decidí ir al gimnasio para conocer a más gente, sin embargo, fue una experiencia decepcionante ya que la mayoría de las personas no te habla. Llevo mucho tiempo haciendo meditación. Al principio pensé que sería difícil concentrarme, pero me acostumbré y es una parte clave de mi vida.
11	F1	¿Dónde empezaste a bailar?
	M1	Cuando era niño bailaba sin parar en las fiestas familiares, me encantaba la música salsa y bailar me hizo sentir feliz.
12	F1	¿Por qué decidiste hacer ballet?
	M1	Mi tía tenía una escuela de baile y cada sábado iba a clases ahí, y aprobé los exámenes para la Escuela Nacional de Ballet a los catorce años, algo que me sorprendió mucho.
13	F1	¿Cuál es el mejor aspecto de tu trabajo?
	M1	Hay muchos, por ejemplo, bailar en teatros famosos del mundo y conocer a nueva gente, dicho eso, lo mejor es tener la oportunidad de expresarme a través de bailar.
14	F1	Qué consejos darías a alguien que quiere hacer una carrera en el baile?
	M1	Pues, tener un gran talento no es suficiente, necesitas creer en ti mismo y reconocer que encontrarás grandes dificultades en tu carrera.
15	M1	En los últimos 10 años ha habido un aumento en las obras por todo el pueblo, dicho eso, ahora se pueden ver más espacios verdes, pero todavía necesitamos más árboles.
16	F1	Es muy preocupante ver que haya cada vez más personas que viven en la calle y por eso es importante que construyan más alojamiento económico.
17	M1	Después de estar todo el día en el trabajo no hay nada mejor que pasar el tiempo solo viendo mis emisiones favoritas.

18	M2	No suelo pasar mucho tiempo viendo la tele entre semana, ya que la calidad de programas es peor que el fin de semana.
19	F1	Lo que no me gusta nada es ver escenas con gente que mata a otras personas. Yo necesito sentirme tranquila cuando estoy viendo la tele.
20	F2	Me fastidia que la gente hoy en día pase demasiado tiempo enfrente de pantallas, mucho mejor sería pasar el tiempo con otros cara a cara.
21	F1	El vuelo fue muy cómodo y me encantó ver películas durante todo el viaje, en cambio la llegada al aeropuerto fue un desastre ya que tuve que hacer cola durante más de una hora.
22	F1	Los primeros días fueron difíciles porque poca gente hablaba inglés en el pueblo donde vivía y me sentía muy sola.
23	F1	Celebré mi cumpleaños en un restaurante con un grupo de profesores del instituto donde trabajaba. Fue una noche increíble con música, un pastel, y regalos, lo único malo fue que perdí mi cámara en el camino a casa.
24	F1	Tuve mucho en común con Elena, la chica argentina con quien compartía un piso. Pasábamos horas juntas riéndonos y cocinado platos típicos. ¡Qué suerte tenía!
25	F1	Recuerdo que mi profe de historia siempre me gritaba porque llegaba solo dos minutos tarde a clase.
	M1	Pues me gustó mucho mi profesora de arte y me encantó la excursión al Museo del Prado donde vimos pinturas de artistas famosos. Lo único malo fue que no pudimos quedarnos más tiempo.
	F1	La profesora que más recuerdo fue mi profe de matemáticas porque siempre se vestía de una manera extraña con la ropa toda rosa y gafas enormes.
	M1	Nunca olvidaré a mi profe de inglés y me ha influido mucho. Es a causa de él que hoy soy periodista.

26   **M1**   Dentro de dos semanas tendré que participar en un proyecto con mi jefe, es una cosa que me llevará mucho tiempo. Hace tres meses tuve la oportunidad de ir a Sudamérica. Desafortunadamente llovía todo el tiempo. Soy muy afortunado porque mi equipo es un grupo de personas super simpáticas y graciosas. Sé que pronto voy a tener que trabajar días más largos porque me van a promover el mes que viene.

27   **F1**   Costa Rica es un país que ha hecho mucho en cuanto al medio ambiente. Hoy en día se puede ver un aumento en el número de jóvenes que toman el bus o van a pie en vez de usar el coche. Todavía queda mucho que hacer en cuanto a comprar ropa, ya que la gente joven piensa en la moda primero y los efectos en el medio ambiente en segundo lugar. Los colegios informan a los alumnos sobre el peligro de plástico en el mar; como consecuencia el nivel de plástico en los mares es menos que en otros países. Hay una campaña nacional para limpiar las playas y cada fin de semana se pueden ver adolescentes cogiendo basura en las playas y parques. Recordar apagar el ordenador y la luz al salir de un cuarto aún parece ser algo difícil para la gente joven.

Section B   Dictation

Sentence 1   **F1**   A veces / llevo zapatos / rojos.

Sentence 2   **M1**   Hay demasiados / niños / en el café.

Sentence 3   **F2**   Me apetece / comer / una manzana.

Sentence 4   **M2**   Jugué / al baloncesto / ayer.

Sentence 5   **M2**   La gente / suele ser / abierta.

END OF TEST

Notes